Additional Praise for

Get Acquired for Millions

"Get Acquired for Millions is the comprehensive roadmap to maximize the payoff of all your hard work and makes sure you get a fair reward along the way. This book is a must-read. Tap into Linda's experience and insights to get the most out of your business, now and when you decide to exit. This may be the most important business book you read in your career."

Mark S. A. Smith, Author and Business Growth Strategist, BijaCo.com

"Linda Rose is the definitive source on buying, selling, and aggregating a Technology Service Provider business. If you have a Channel Partner business and want the highest value for your investment, Get Acquired for Millions is a must read for you."

Mike Gillis, Owner/Principal RSM US LLP

"Linda Rose delivers a comprehensive and well written book that will put more money in your pocket. Her actionable advice, specific examples, and valuable resources will assist any TSP Owner considering selling their business. Get Acquired for Millions reminds us that selling a business is not just about financials; it's about your future and the future of your employees."

Bob Cohen, Channel Partner Growth Advisor, Vescynt Consulting

"Technology entrepreneurs who've spent 10+ years building their business with loving care and have no idea what it takes to sell their baby. I wish I read this book before selling my first business. . . I would have about $10 million more in my bank account."

Mike Dickerson, CEO, ClickDimensions

GET ACQUIRED
—*for*—
MILLIONS

Anini Press

Anini Press ™
1084 North El Camino Real, Ste B-501
Encinitas, CA 92024

Email: engage@aninipress.com
Phone: 858 794-9401

ISBN: 978-1-7332082-0-8 (paperback)
ISBN: 978-1-7332082-1-5 (ebook)
ISBN: 978-1-7332082-2-2 (hard cover)

Ordering Information:
Special discounts are available on quantity purchases by corporations, associations, and others. For details, email our team at engage@aninipress.com or call 858 794-9401.

GET ACQUIRED

—for—

MILLIONS

A Roadmap for Technology Service Providers to Maximize Company Value

LINDA ROSE

Contents

To my fellow technology partner entrepreneurs who have
the courage, focus, and dedication to make your dreams a reality.

To Glen, the half of me who has made me whole for more than 30 years.

To my son Matt, you will always be my proudest accomplishment.

Thank you all for allowing me to be part of such an amazing journey.

INTRODUCTION

ABOUT THE AUTHOR

Linda Rose has spent over 25 years as an entrepreneur. She understands intimately the joy and freedom, and more often the trials and tribulations, of founding and growing successful technology and professional services companies. She has started and bootstrapped four companies; acquiring one and selling three over a 17-year period. In this book, she shares not only her successes, but also, and equally important, the mistakes she made along the way as she sold to a shareholder, a strategic buyer, and a private equity firm. In writing about her journey of building and selling companies, she gives readers an inside perspective of what owners can expect during each of those processes. To give you relevant financial examples, she draws upon her years of experience not only as a CEO but also as an accountant and tax CPA. She gives readers an insight into how buyers view the changing landscape of IT businesses and technology service firms, and how owners can increase the value of their companies as they prepare themselves to capitalize on their years of hard work.

When Linda is not out exploring trails in the wilderness, kayaking on the open waters, or tending to her gardens, she speaks to and advises owners on how best to plan and build company value so that one day they too can *be acquired for millions*. She is a wife of 29 years and a mother of one son. She calls the Pacific her backyard—triangulating between her homes in Southern California, Oregon and Hawaii.

DISCLAIMER

The advice and tips in this book have been created from the author's own experiences and her observations of good practice, and they are there for you to use in any way you think fit in the context of your own business. Neither the author nor the publisher makes any representations or warranties regarding the contents or the materials provided in this book and exclude all representations, conditions, and warranties, express or implied.

Neither the author nor publisher shall be liable in contract, tort (including negligence), or otherwise for indirect, special, incidental, punitive, or consequential losses or damages or loss of profits, revenue, goodwill, or any financial loss whatsoever, regardless of whether any such loss or damage would arrive in the ordinary course of events or otherwise.

Neither the author nor the publisher assumes any responsibility for errors, inaccuracies, or omissions. Any perceived slights of people or organizations are unintentional.

This publication is not intended for use as a source of security, technical, legal, accounting, financial, or other professional advice. If advice concerning these matters is needed, seek the services of a qualified professional, as the information in this book is not a substitute for professional counsel.

Neither the author nor the publisher accepts any responsibility or liability for your use of the content presented herein. Conversely, neither the publisher nor the author will lay claim to any profits you may make based on the suggestions contained in this book.

Some suggestions made in this book concerning business practices may have inadvertently introduced practices deemed unlawful in certain states, municipalities, or countries. You should be aware of the various laws governing your business practices in your particular industry and location.

While the websites referenced were personally reviewed by the author, there are no guarantees as to their accuracy or security; therefore, make sure you are comfortable with your computer security settings and computer practices before accessing these sites.

So, now that we have gotten all that out of the way, let's get started...

HE LEFT MONEY ON THE TABLE –
A NOT UNCOMMON STORY

It was 11 p.m. and Robert was going over the final settlement statement for the last time. He now knew the actual number, down to the penny, that would show up in his bank account tomorrow. In a way it was anticlimactic and thrilling at the same time. He knew from the day he had signed the Letter of Intent, that at some point, after the never-ending due diligence and contract refinements, the number—an abstract representation of his efforts and the work of his staff—would eventually show up in his bank account. Tomorrow, after 22 years, someone else would own his company and he would be a multi-millionaire.

Tomorrow, he would be sharing the news with the rest of the team—his key managers were already aware of the transaction, but the other members of his team were essentially in the dark. The new owners weren't going to arrive until all the documents had been signed and the agreed amounts had hit his account. But they wanted to hit the ground running so there would only be the morning hours to assemble the team and let them know that he appreciated all of their hard work and effort and that now he was no longer their leader.

He had rehearsed what he was going to say for days, but he also knew that the announcement wasn't going to come as a complete surprise to everyone. Robert had made it clear over the years that he had intentions of selling the company at some point. Since the sale of his consulting division four years earlier, Robert had been working diligently with an exit strategy always at the top of his mind. Regardless, all of his team would be surprised that he would be leaving in only a month. Due to his company's high percentage of monthly recurring revenue, the new owners were comfortable with his immediate exit and were willing to offer 100 percent upfront cash—a seller's dream. Thankfully, the lesson he had learned from his previous disposition of the consulting division gave him the confidence and insight he needed to make this last company sale such a success.

FOUR YEARS EARLIER

Robert had received his first serious inquiry about selling his consulting division at a bar—after a long day at a technical conference. A good number of tequila shots had already been downed by all, so he listened with a smile on his face as the partner of a competing organization expressed an interest in buying his consulting practice. This was the part of the business that provided all the implementations for the manufacturing solution that his company supported. The competing firm was expanding rapidly but needed a location in Northern California to complete their lock on the state. They had a great reputation in the industry and a culture that would match well with his own. It would be a perfect place for his consulting team to land and the timing couldn't have been better.

Robert had built a "moderately successful" consulting business most-ly due to his love of technology, his ability to sell, and a solid grip on his company's financials. Equally important, he felt like he had control over his own life and could take the time to coach his son's football team each year. His business wasn't something that had grown spectacularly, but it was a very solid business and it had grown at least 15 to 20 percent each year—a cash cow if you ran it right. He had been able to send his kids to college without any financial stress, and he had managed to sock away enough money to buy a condo in Lake Tahoe—the favorite family retreat.

While he had enjoyed strong revenue and profits over the past decade, things had started to change. His primary software vendor had altered its structures and also its margins, as the competitive market matured, thus putting a constant downward pressure on pricing. As a consequence, the revenue from the products he had been selling had dropped dramatically so the margin he was making from selling the manufacturing application wasn't bringing in the money it had once brought in. At his level of business, that wasn't fatal. Still, while his ratio of sales to consulting had historically been 50/50 (sales to service), it was now more like 30/70. And the margins from *service* weren't nearly as good as those from software, given that the cost of keeping top-notch, seasoned consultants continued to escalate each year.

Then there were the summers—when he would have liked to relax and enjoy some time off. But they were always somewhat difficult months as both consultants and customers deserted their desks for the beach and the mountains. Revenue during those months was always "off" and it was always a source of worry. Usually, it wasn't until the fourth quarter that he knew for sure how the year would end up.

He knew his customers, while happy with his service, could be lured away by cheaper technical support rates or lower per-hour consulting rates from local competitors. Other than his team of experienced professionals, he had nothing sticky to ensure that he would be able to keep a grip on his hard-earned customers.

Nevertheless, he had managed to increase revenue every year, even as he was concerned about the reduction in margins from his main software vendor coupled with a downward pressure on the price of the products he was selling.

He knew that even though his revenue might increase year over year, his gross profit margin was on a decline. He needed to make a change and to focus his attention on building the cloud side of his business, something that he had started a few years back.

In 2010, after weathering a crazy recession, Robert had slowly begun selling his applications on a monthly subscription basis. His prospects wanted ways to save cash, but they still needed to implement new solutions. Since the manufacturing solution he was supporting wasn't cloud enabled yet, he turned to an established public cloud that he could trust and then began hosting his solutions there. At the time, it was a blue ocean; no one else was offering the same service. His customer adds were slow, but he was starting to see his monthly recurring revenue building and his margins increasing.

Thankfully, a competing firm reached out with an offer to buy his consulting division in order to expand geographically. Within a few months, Robert sold the consulting division for a reasonable price, but for far less than what he had hoped for. Let's face it, he was inexperienced! Although it was not an ideal offer, he took comfort in the fact that he could now focus his attention 100 percent on his cloud business, which was gaining more and more traction.

OLDER, WISER, MUCH BETTER PREPARED...

Yes, looking back, he had learned a lot. Selling his consulting division had taught him painful lessons. The buyer had a critical eye and looked at various things differently than Robert did. This reduced Robert's sale price due to the lack of a number of key factors: No recurring revenue, no penetration into a specific vertical, and no defined sales process, or a sales team, to execute it. He learned about business value drivers. He learned about the things that he had done as a founder-owner-manager that actually *hurt* the value of his business—in particular, his tendencies to play the hero as a rainmaker and to be the technical problem solver.

Several years back, Robert had tried unsuccessfully to find a book, or even a good magazine article, that was written specifically for technology professionals—that would clue him in on the steps he needed to take to sell his company. Then thankfully, Robert had the good fortune of having to perform emergency IT services for a local software industry analyst—getting the analyst out of a serious jam when his on-premises network was compromised. Eventually, they formed a close friendship and remained in contact over the years, talking about industry trends and about deals in the marketplace. Then Robert asked him if he would agree to be his "coach" as he prepared his company for sale. The analyst agreed.

As an industry analyst, he was well versed with SaaS metrics and he knew what buyers valued in cloud service companies. He explained to Robert how customers now preferred OpEx over CapEx, a switch that clearly had been fueled by the earlier recession, where financing for software was almost impossible to secure and cash in the bank was more important than ever.

Customers were looking for predictable monthly fees that they could budget for annually and scale as needed, but they also wanted the ability to exit quickly if the solution didn't meet their needs. Rewards without risk. As the stocks of publicly traded SaaS companies (even unprofitable ones) soared, the philosophy of recurring revenue became a mantra for every private equity firm, the type of buyer Robert wanted to someday attract. For them, the more recurring revenue you had, the more they were willing to pay.

Robert took his coach's advice and began to focus his attention on several major value drivers. The first two were recurring revenue and customer retention rates—two factors that buyers would ask to see. Robert made sure that all contracts clearly stated the monthly fees as well as the fixed installation fee. Gone were the days of project-based time and material installations. While he increased his contracts from one to two years, he also gave his customers the ability to terminate quickly in the first 90 days with no termination fees—thus removing for them the risk factor of making a bad decision. This small change increased his win rate dramatically. And he provided a financially-backed service level agreement for 24/7/365 support with a two-hour response guarantee. Of course, there was an upcharge for this, but his customers valued this service and he rarely had a customer terminate.

He also focused on customer satisfaction. Early on, his coach advised him to make sure he kept his churn rate to less than 7 percent, which would allow him to increase his monthly recurring revenue number much quicker. At the end of each year, his marketing team would send out a press release announcing the high customer retention rate and he made a point of displaying this on the home page of his website for every future customer and potential buyer to see.

Robert then focused on making sure that every customer on-boarding experience and every service call was *exceptional*. His management team was alerted if a case was not reviewed within the stated amount of time or if the case volume reached a certain threshold. A new self-service customer portal was also in the works so that customers would know 24/7 how their case was progressing. Basically, Robert was creating a well-oiled-machine, free of issues related to employee vacations, sick time, and departures—all items which, in the past, had affected his revenue in the consulting division. Robert now knew that if he kept revenue growth numbers over 20 percent each year, employee and customer retention stable, customer satisfaction high, and EBITDA trending up for three years, it would allow him to exit his company within a year of a sale.

Finally, there was his "niche." He knew that he needed to set himself apart from his competition and thereby not become a commodity—even in the early cloud days. Robert had worked hard with his marketing team to position the company as a leader in cloud regulatory manufacturing applications. He then added to his management team a chief compliance officer who could not only work with the teams to create internal policies and procedures that would appeal to companies who had certain regulatory requirements but who could also speak the language of the auditors who would be asking regulatory questions. Once Robert was viewed as an expert in this area, he no longer had to compete with similar companies offering cloud services for less money. He could sell less but maintain a higher gross profit margin, which allowed him to minimize the headcount and dramatically increase his revenue per employee.

This time, Robert was not going to get dinged on his sales price because of the lack of depth in his management team. He made sure that all critical functions were handled by competent managers so that no key function of the company was performed by *him*.

The four years of working with his coach had made a significant difference, and the sale of his cloud business was different in almost every way. The years of work had been about getting everything right in the organization so that if the perfect buyer appeared, Robert could sell, and then he could walk out the door without having to go through a long extended earn-out. So, for most of his team, what was going to come as a real surprise was Robert's immediate exit.

TIME TO SELL AND EXIT

Robert knew he had built a strong company so he wanted more than just one offer; he wanted a few so he could pick the best one. And this time Robert was going to engage the help of an M&A advisor/business broker so he could look beyond the normal list of buyers in his immediate space and possibly attract someone else who might be interested in his company. He viewed the broker's commission or success fee as a small price to pay for introducing him to an ideal buyer.

Robert's decision to hire an M&A advisor turned out to be a good one. While he was focused on increasing his monthly recurring revenue, his advisor, along with his coach, created a plan to prepare him for the process. He began by uploading many of the items needed for due diligence to a virtual data room, while his advisor carefully and efficiently created the necessary marketing materials that they needed to send to prospective buyers. Within 45 days of the start of the marketing phase, Robert had received responses from over 20 qualified potential buyers.

Over the next 30 days, a final buyer had been identified and the LOI had been signed, and then life went into overdrive. The buyer, unlike in Robert's previous sale, was a Private Equity Group. They were accustomed to a 60-day close routine, and they had an experienced due diligence team waiting in the wings.

The combined phase of due diligence and contract negotiations took less than 90 days, but those 90 days were a physical, mental, and emotional drain for Robert. The buyers were very skilled at purchasing companies with a strong customer base, little churn, and a strong recurring revenue stream —and Robert's company was a perfect fit.

So, there was Robert sitting at this desk for the last time as he put the final touches on the settlement statement. As he worked with his CFO on the final payroll accrual, the realization hit him that tomorrow would be his final paycheck. The plan that he had begun to execute 48 months before had come to fruition, and Robert would not have to work ever again if he didn't want to. He had just been *acquired for millions*.

WHY I WROTE THIS BOOK

"The channel is aging and 40 percent of channel owners plan on retiring by 2024."

- Jay McBain, Principal Analyst - Channels, Partnerships & Alliances, Forrester Research

If your curiosity has taken you this far, there's a very good chance you are a technology service provider entrepreneur/business owner—or someone in a similar business sector. Maybe you are just wondering what the value of your business is today or there's an even better chance that, at some point, you have wondered about the pros and cons, and the ins and outs, of selling your business.

If that's you, I get it! And I've been there! Most of all, I have learned how easy it is to lose out on the value you have built through years of concentrated effort. That has happened to me and I have learned a lot of costly lessons. In this book, I want to share with you those lessons and what I learned from my experiences of selling multiple companies.

Maybe you love your business, maybe you are tired of it and can't wait to move on, or maybe you are waiting for that "perfect time" in the market so you can sell. Regardless, there are things that you need to learn and steps that you need to take NOW.

I am sure you wouldn't let an employee steal money from you, right? And you would be upset if a customer decided to only pay 70 percent of their invoice amount, right? So, why do so many owners end up accepting less than the potential worth of their business?

It boils down almost entirely to a lack of *knowledge*. Those who have that knowledge have taken the right steps to make sure their company is sold at the best price. And now so can *you*.

LESSONS, LESSONS, AND MORE LESSONS

My 25 plus years as a technology business owner and entrepreneur were focused on growing my companies. It wasn't until I turned 50 that I gave much thought to the details of when or how I might go about selling my company, or what it might feel like to be...well, dare I say it...RETIRED. Up until that point, the sale of my business was simply an event that would mark the end of a (hopefully) profitable career. I also tended to view my exit as a *choice* and *not* as a necessity—no illness, no ugly divorces, no splits with partners, no mismanagement of finances, no major economic downturns forcing me to sell—so I could do it on my own time and at my own pace. I was just waiting for the time to feel "right."

Until that time, I would continue to focus on creating value for my customers and providing a wonderful workplace for my employees, while increasing my geographic reach—all the while stashing as much money as I could into my 401(k) plan. While all that was great, never once did I think about what preparing my company for a sale would actually mean, or how "preparing" my company could increase its value. Like many other business owners, I was working for many years "in" my business and not "on" it, selling most of our services myself and managing a pretty flat org chart.

Even though, from a profitability perspective, I was "ready," and when it came time to actually begin the "sale" process, I found myself rather unprepared. And statistically, so will most of the 40 percent of the channel owners mentioned above. Even though I had sold two companies before, it still felt like new territory. Up to this point, I had only read press releases about other channel owners selling and most of the time I had no idea of the amount they had sold their company for, unless they were close friends or I could pry it out of them over a round of cocktails. But even then, the details were slim, mostly due to the signing of nondisclosure agreements.

So, there I was, ready to sell, but I had no one to turn to for help with valuations, and no one to talk to who had already had experience selling a cloud service company of my size or industry specialty. Fortunately, I did have someone to call on who intimately understood the industry and the financial metrics. He sat with me for an hour as I took copious notes on what metrics I needed to have ready (sales, profits, recurring revenue, and customer retention) to show my company in its best light. Even after two previous company sales, I realized I needed to look at this *final* exit through the eyes of a buyer and not those of the seller. I also knew it would take me three years to get my company ready for this important event.

As I read the quote above (*The channel is aging and 40 percent of channel owners plan on retiring by 2024*), I realized that I was not alone in this process. There are over 500,000 technology service providers internationally, which means that at least 200,000 will contemplate selling in the next several years. Many of these owners, whom I have sat with at conferences and industry groups, will not know how to step through this critical, and potentially "one-time," process to exit their business.

While there are a number of well-written books published on mergers and acquisitions (M&As), they tend to be big and overly technical, geared toward larger companies in manufacturing or retail industries, and written by brokers or attorneys. I also found that many were long-winded and used overly complex examples—which made my eyes glaze over, even though I'm a numbers person. In short, they didn't speak to our industry or our business size.

Like myself, most business owners don't have the time to wade through a large fine print book on the subject. There is no one book for technology providers to understand what specifically they can work on so as to measurably increase the value of their company. While there are a number of business consultants and brokers who can assist in creating additional value for your business (for a fee), not everyone will have the desire to engage external help, especially if you have a three-year or even longer plan—as I had. And there is certainly no guide readily available to tell you *what not to do*.

In this book, I will share with you my own experiences of selling three services/technology companies to *three completely different buyer types*. Each one of these "buyer profiles" is unique in how they value and approach the purchase of a company. In addition to my own transactions, I have interviewed dozens of sellers, buyers, and brokers to collect advice, tips, and tactics for a successful sales transaction.

Since many of these interviews were confidential, I have summarized their experiences through our main character "Robert," who you will encounter throughout this book. He will help you to identify some of the challenges and confusing options ahead of you.

It was also through these extensive interviews that I formulated the eight company value maximizers and the Value Maximizer Assessment™ discussed in Part II. I will share with you my checklists, sample offers, tools, due diligence lists, spreadsheets, and tips, all of which are downloadable and ready to use.

Whether you are someone who may be considering a lifestyle change, someone who is looking to cash out and start a new venture, or simply someone who wants to exit now while the market is still hot, this book is for you. I wrote this book for all business owners so they can benefit and become more knowledgeable and strategic in how to *Get Acquired...for Millions*.

Who should read this book

"Build a business today as if you will own it forever but could sell it tomorrow."

– Bo Burlingham,
Finish Big: How Great Entrepreneurs Exit Their Companies on Top

This book is for anyone who considers themselves to be a technology service provider, an IT business, or more specifically, a channel partner. A channel partner sells either to other partners in their specific vendor-driven channel, or direct to the end customer whether B2B or B2C, or a combination of all of the above. The solution they sell is usually built upon a larger vendor solution that drives its success through their channel partners via sales margins. Many Microsoft, Salesforce, Sage, Citrix, SAP, Oracle, and NetSuite owners consider themselves channel partners, but it is certainly not limited to this group. If you are not tied specifically to a software vendor but consider yourself one of the following—independent software vendor (ISV), value-added reseller (VAR), managed service provider (MSP), infrastructure as a service or platform as a services (IaaS/PaaS), or you have been historically known as a "hoster" or custom developer, then we are of the same community and this book was written with *you* in mind. From this point on, we will refer to you as a Technology Service Provider or **TSP.**

So, is this book confined to this group? No, definitely not. The examples will revolve around these types of companies, but the concepts can be applied across multiple types of businesses and the value maximizers mentioned are relevant in many industries.

Finally, this book is written for two types of owners: Those who plan on selling in the next five years and those that have made the decision to sell now and need to know what to do next. If your plan is to **sell in the next five years,** congratulations! —you are a planner and you will have time not only to assess your current strengths but also to implement the eight value maximizers to their fullest.

If you plan on **selling within the next 12 months,** then understanding your current strengths, determining your best fit with a buyer type, and preparing yourself for the sale via checklists and tools will be hugely helpful, as will gaining an understanding of what is important to buyers so you can market your company successfully.

Regardless of your timing, there is no time like the present to focus on the *value maximizers* discussed in this book. The technology service provider and IT markets are hot, and if a buyer presents herself or himself tomorrow, you will want to be in the position to earn the greatest valuation for your company. So, this book is for you, too!

This book will help you to answer the following questions:

1. When is the right time to sell?
2. What is my company worth?
3. How long does it take to sell?
4. Who will find the most value in my company?
5. Where do I find someone who wants to buy my company?
6. How do brokers work and what do they charge?
7. Can I sell the company myself?
8. What do I need to prepare in advance?
9. What should I do if someone approaches me with an offer?
10. What can I do now to increase my company value?

Most technology entrepreneurs start a company and spend years of their life building it with the goal of creating significant wealth through a successful sale. For most entrepreneurs, this will be their *only* sale, and it is something for which they will have little or no experience. Even in the current seller's market, it's important to understand what motivates buyers and to know the likely pitfalls inside and out before heading into the sales process. After reading this book, you will be more educated and more competent in selecting advisors, buyers, timelines, and deal transaction structures.

How to get the most out of this book

This book is organized into three parts. Each section can be read independently and does *not* require that you read the part before it. You as the reader will get the greatest value by first taking the Value Maximizer Assessment™, which will: 1) give you an estimate of the potential value of your company, 2) highlight your strengths and weaknesses, and 3) highlight where you can increase the value of your company.

After reviewing the results of your assessment, you will be able to focus on those areas that can create the most value in the shortest amount of time, while also planning how to exceed in other more complex areas in the future.

The assessment can be found at https://rosebizinc.com/ValueMax. The assessment is free, and it is 100 percent confidential. The results will be emailed to you immediately upon your completion of the assessment. We definitely recommend that you take the assessment prior to beginning Part II.

Part I – Driving from a Desire to a Deal

No one sells a company without first having some idea of what their company is worth. First you need to determine your category, which will give you a starting point in determining company value. But, will that company valuation number be enough? You might want to determine your personal retirement goals to see if your company sale will meet those needs. How are most deals structured? How long will it take for you to see the entire proceeds of the sale? You also need to consider the timing of a sale. Will you need to stay after the sale, and for how long? Knowing these answers will be key in defining your own timeline for a successful sale.

Part II – Eight Value Maximizers

Understanding the various buyer types, and what they look for when acquiring either a platform or add-on company, will help you market your company. Buyers focus not only on *quantitative* aspects such as topline revenue, gross profit, year-over-year growth, and earnings before interest, taxes, depreciation, and amortization (EBITDA), but also on *qualitative* factors. In this section, we will focus on eight factors relevant to achieving a higher sales price/valuation.

The Value Maximizer Assessment Tool™ will take the pulse of where you are in the following key metrics:

1. Financial fitness
2. Revenue readiness
3. Management muscle
4. Value propositions/verticalization
5. Customer satisfaction/retention
6. Sustainable success
7. Sales and marketing strength
8. Intellectual property presence

Regardless of whether you are planning to sell in one, three, or five years, this book will give you actionable steps that you can take *immediately*. Some can be implemented in a short period of time, others will take more time and effort.

Part III – Advisors, Advice, and Resources

The successful sale of a business typically involves advisors, and usually three: An M&A advisor, an attorney, and a CPA. This section will help you determine which type of advisor or advisors you need and how that will help with the success of your transaction. Specifically, we will look at an advisor agreement with regard to the specific language and the different types of fees charged by advisors.

We will also cover how to handle a buyer's request for an office visit and when to disclose to your employees the pending transaction—always touchy subjects.

Success is sometimes measured in "what not to do." The list of 100 tips, traps, and tactics herein is a compilation of responses from interviews with multiple TSP business owners. In this list, you will find out what they learned and what they would have done differently in the sales of their companies.

Do you want to put yourself in the shoes of the buyer? Then you will like the bonus chapter written by Revenue Rocket, namely "*What Are Buyers Thinking?*" This chapter is written from a buyer's perspective and it reviews the four pillars of a successful acquisition as well as the general rules for a well-planned, post-merger integration.

Finally, the Resources section will give you samples of various standard agreements that you may encounter in the process of selling; many will be downloadable from the author's website (https://rosebizinc.com/book-resources) as checklists and helpful forms.

While no amount of resources will completely prepare you to be acquired, this book will provide a more direct path to help you get there and to help you increase your company's value.

PART I:
DRIVING FROM A DESIRE TO A DEAL

This initial section covers the general fundamentals of a deal. But before you engage in an opportunity, it is important to understand what your ultimate financial goals are, and whether the sale of your company will result in you achieving those goals.

In addition, we will cover these important areas: How much your company is worth today, the different types of buyers, the timeline of a sales transaction, and how an offer is structured. These will help you determine **your personal exit timeline**.

Are you ready to sell? Or to be acquired?

In the end, all businesses are either sold, given away, or liquidated. If liquidating, or handing your business to your children, is not an option and you want to successfully sell or be acquired, let's start planning *now*. The earlier you start the process, the better, stronger, and more resilient a company you will create, which means you will achieve a higher valuation. Unfortunately, most owners don't think about or start this process *soon* enough because they haven't planned on selling. Instead, they are busy working in the business and building their empire, and they are completely focused on increasing sales and the bottom line. While those are important, they are ultimately *not* what drives maximum value.

Yes, many businesses have sold for high values with no positive cash flow, but those are becoming increasingly rare. Increasing sales year over year is also important, but is it *recurring revenue* that is increasing or is it revenue that must be earned over and over each month? In Part II of this book, we will discuss how recurring revenue can improve EBITDA multiples by up to 200 percent!

Preparing your company for a sale in advance of an unexpected offer, or as a result of your own decision to sell, can potentially *double* the value of your company. The majority of business owners whom I interviewed didn't plan on selling when they did, but an offer came out of the blue that was appealing and after some negotiation between the parties a deal was struck. Did they sell their company for its highest value? Maybe, but probably not. If not, why did they sell? Was it because they became so emotionally involved in the deal? And since they didn't have another buyer to counter with another offer, did they just continue with the only one they had? And did they continue even if the offer had decreased since the initial Letter of Intent (LOI) was provided prior to the due diligence process?

Receiving a formal LOI is such an exciting event! And many sellers have already cashed the check in their mind, so the idea of turning back or declining a somewhat low offer can become incredibly difficult, especially if multiple partners are involved. You may find yourself moving forward with the deal at an emotional level because your mindset has already been altered. However, in this case, sellers are often unhappy in the end; they feel like they have left money on the table.

To have a successful business exit, the first key is to identify the factors that led you to decide to sell. Why now? And what is the monetary outcome you are looking to achieve? And over what period of time? If you decide to use a business broker, these are usually the first questions they ask. And "why now?" will certainly be one of the first questions a buyer will ask. So be prepared with an answer. It should be honest, sincere, and thoughtful. Savvy buyers will be able to see through your answer if it is not.

The second key to having a successful business exit is to know what you will do *after* you sell the company. For some, cashing in on years of hard work and *staying* in the company is what they envision. They land a nice chunk of cash in the bank and then they work with the new owners for a potential second liquidity event. Other sellers know that they want to move onto another business or industry, or perhaps they have a passion to start something new and different. Still others know that they are done with working and they want to spend their days playing golf and spending time with family. The point is, it is important to know *in advance* what you want to do AFTER the sale.

Not having a clear idea of those "keys" in advance can create endless mind games, consternation, and possible regret—if it doesn't cause you to back out of the deal altogether.

Almost every broker has a story about how a deal fell apart the night before the close—because the owner didn't know what they would do *after* they sold their company. It sounds crazy, but it's not. Many CEOs have their entire identity wrapped up in their business, especially if they are the founder. It is who they are and what they have become, and it is what gets them up in the morning. That doesn't mean they don't care about their family and friends, but the success of their company and what they have built is what validates their existence at some level. Once the business is sold, what's next?

Who are they? This is a very common situation. It is always better to be *moving towards* something new and exciting in the future, rather than just celebrating the past.

As you think about when you might want to sell, be sure you can answer the following questions. And then share those answers with your business partners and significant family members so everyone is clear on the future goals.

1. Why do you want to sell?
2. How much do you need in the bank to meet your retirement goals, and is this sale the means to that end?
3. What is the minimum cash price you will accept, not including any earn-outs?
4. If you are required to stay, will you be able to work for someone else after being your own boss?
5. If not, who can take your place so you can exit sooner?
6. What will you do after the sale if you will not be remaining in the company?
7. How quickly can you transition into your new life?

WHY SELL NOW?

There is clear evidence that transactions in the technology sector are still *on the rise*. The information technology sector is the second largest industry for growth in merger & acquisition (M&A) deals with a compounded annual growth rate (CAGR) of 8.1 percent, and it shows no signs of letting up as of the publishing of this book. Meanwhile, vendors like Microsoft, NetSuite, Salesforce, and Sage are all looking to increase their install base, and they are rewarding their larger partners who show increased selling capacity and verticalization while creating their own intellectual property.

There are numerous articles you can point to that cite the following as reasons why *now* might be a good time to sell your business:

1.   *A ton of private money sitting on the sidelines.* Private equity managers
     are sitting on a record $963.3 billion of dry powder[13]—as they call
     money that they've raised but have yet to invest. The size of that pile,
     and the fact that it keeps rising, is making everyone antsy. A little dry
     powder is great if managers are holding out for better deals. But a lot
     makes private equity (PE) firms look at deals that they may never have
     looked at in the past. This is great for sellers, as PE firms are looking
     at smaller deals (i.e., $5M in revenue and/or $1M in net profit). This
     historically has not been the case.

2.   *Keeping pace with specialized skills.* Specialized areas of expertise in the
     consulting sector are evolving at a record pace, in part based upon
     customer demands and the constant pace of technology. For example,
     it is hard to find one single company that can manage infrastructure,
     implement an ERP or CRM system, assist in the deployment of a
     business analytics package, and start mining data for AI (artificial in-
     telligence). It is just too much for one company to do, but customers
     would prefer to work with *one* organization—that can handle their
     email and ecommerce site and also build a data warehouse in the
     cloud. In short, technology companies have to *buy* human capital to
     keep up with customer demands.

3.   *Access to debt is cheap.* Cash is cheap, and buyers who may or may not
     have cash are no longer restricted by the lack of it to find companies
     to purchase. However, at this writing, interest rates are rising in North
     America while Europe looks to hold rates at historically low levels for
     at least another year. Looking forward to the medium- to long-term
     interest rates across the globe will almost certainly be higher, mean-
     ing companies—especially ones hoping to finance an acquisition —are
     incentivized to act now on planned deals to save on the future rising
     interest costs.

4.   *The US economy is growing.* With unemployment rates at an all-time
     low of 4 percent, the stock market still on the rise, and the cut in
     corporate income tax rates, these are good times for sellers. For now.
     Of course, we all know that this can change overnight.

All this great news also means that buyers are seeing a greater number of companies willing to sell. This creates an interesting market situation in which both the supply and demand are growing together. This means buyers targeting growth through acquisition can be more selective relative to opportunities. What does this mean for the seller? There is still a good appetite and money to spend, but it also means there is more competition out there. However, by deploying many of the value maximizers we discuss in this book—well-structured financials, emphasis on recurring revenue, and a strong management team—owners can prepare for their highest valuation possible. Now that we understand why the present time is a good time to *sell* in the tech sector, let's then discuss how to identify when is a good time to *exit* the business.

WHEN TO SELL

There comes a point in your life when you know it's time to do something different. Beyond any physical issues, owners generally reach a conclusion that it is time to exit for either emotional and/or economic reasons. The typical business owner, however, never truly announces that they are ready to sell. What you hear instead is that they will sell in the next three to five years. It's a long enough period that one doesn't need to be anxious and a short enough period that something will probably happen. Usually when owners make this kind of statement, the thought of exiting is already weighing on their mind. Many owners decide it is time to sell when they see one or more of the following:

Emotional Reasons

- You've reached your own glass ceiling – You have taken the company to a certain revenue threshold and anything beyond that is not appealing anymore.
- It is time to "un-partner" with your other owners – The ride has been good but it is time to let someone else take the reins and let them run the show.

- You want to transition to a new career or start the next stage of your life, whether that is starting another company or truly retiring and enjoying hobbies you haven't had time for.
- It is just no longer fun.

Economic Reasons

- Double digit YOY growth has stalled and you see a downward trend
- Gross profit margins have stalled or are starting to decline by 1 or 2 percent
- Declining EBITDA (earnings before interest, taxes, depreciation and amortization) numbers due to increased labor or other costs
- Margin erosions by your largest vendors
- You see "events" unfold that make your future questionable (i.e., products you are selling are becoming obsolete, your code is becoming obsolete, new educational requirements will make it impractical to stay current)

When you know it's "time," the next decision is how you want to make your exit.

It's important to have a plan so as to time the sale appropriately. Too many business owners wait too long, and they lose more value than they would have if they had developed an exit plan and sold earlier. Without a plan, and if you ignore the obvious signs that it is time to sell your company, you can work for years for basically no pay, meaning that the decline in the value of your company is more than your annual salary.

Many owners lose sight of this because they don't realize that even though revenue may be increasing, the overall value of the company is declining. While no one can perfectly time the sale of a business, I see too many business owners make the mistake of waiting too long before they sell and thus lose more value than what they were paying themselves in salary. Don't wait for your growth to fall below double digits before trying to sell.

You know it is time...but?

More than one deal has failed at the eleventh hour, not because all the terms and deal points weren't finally negotiated and representations and warranties weren't disclosed, but because the seller didn't know what they would do next with their life. Retirement is NOT appealing to everyone. As I interviewed many sellers as part of this book, I heard this concern pop up more than once. Those who had a clear plan after the sale of their business were happy, those who didn't struggled. I admit, I also struggled with this as I went through the sale process.

Most owners, especially founders, struggle with an identity outside of their work. The longer you've owned your business, the more likely your personal identity and self-worth will become defined by your status as the owner. If you feel a deep connection to your business and a large part of your day-to-day satisfaction is derived from your ties to your business, you will find the decision to sell more difficult. And, the longer you have had your company the harder this may be.

If you are struggling with what you will do in retirement, and all your friends and much of your social life is wrapped around your business in one way or another, you will need to sort this out in advance or your life post-sale will be unfulfilling. The sooner you can sort this out, the happier and easier you will approach the sale of your company.

If you know you will struggle with this, I highly recommend two resources to help. The first is an assessment called PREScore™ which will calculate your readiness to exit your company on a *personal level*. It is an eight-minute online questionnaire and like the Value Maximizer™ assessment, it is confidential and arrives in your inbox after you take it. You can take the assessment here: https://rosebizinc.com/PersonalScore.

Second, I recommend you read the book, *Finish Big: How Great Entrepreneurs Exit Their Companies on Top* by Bo Burlingham. The author interviewed dozens of entrepreneurs across a range of industries and identified eight key factors that determine whether owners are happy after leaving their businesses. He explores in detail the emotional challenges that owners face in selling their businesses. Owning a business is about more than selling goods and services. It's about making choices that shape your entire life, both professional and personal. In the end your business is a thing, not a person. While it may have been heavily influenced by you, it is not you!

WHAT IS YOUR EXIT NUMBER?

Depending upon where you are in your business life, this may be your first company sale, your one and only sale, or your last company sale. Whichever the case, it is important to understand the ultimate target that you are striving for financially. Otherwise, how will you know if it will be enough? Knowing your "magic number" ahead of time will allow you to back into what you need as *your* share of your company's sales proceeds in order to line up with your exit plan.

A surprisingly large number of business owners haven't really thought about that "magic number"—the value that would get them to a particular retirement lifestyle, or perhaps fund some other "adventure" —and so they aren't able to make clear choices and move in the optimal direction.

Again, Robert found help in getting to the "magic number" by working with a financial planner who had the expertise necessary to change vague goals and ideas into facts and figures.

I am always amazed at how an owner can have a good handle on their business finances and yet not know how much they will need to sell their company for in order to reach their retirement goals. That of course is dependent on your "magic number," the number that will allow you to live a fulfilling lifestyle without ever having to work again. Since very few owners truly know what their "magic number" is, it means they also don't know how much money they need to sell their company for.

You should, of course, enlist the help of a financial planner to determine what your actual long-term financial goals and requirements are, but for simplicity's sake, we can calculate a quick "magic number." For now, we are just going to focus on the number you would need in order to maintain the same lifestyle you have today for the rest of your life without having to work again.

In our example, you can adjust your salary up or down to meet your future needs. Here's a quick example:

Robert's current salary is $125,000 per year before taxes, also the amount he spends each year. Take this number and multiply it by 25. Many financial planners will tell you to multiply your annual income by 15, or even 20. But today, with such low returns on safe investments, that's not realistic. Since these are going to be his more conservative years, we will use a 4 percent return on his investments as a more conservative assumption. Ten times your income assumes a 10 percent return. Twenty times your income assumes a 5 percent return. If you want to be ultra conservative, 25 times represents a 4 percent return.

If we take $125,000 and multiply that by 25, Robert will need $3,125,000 **after taxes** in the bank to meet his annual goals at his current spend rate. Or another way to look at this is by taking $3.125M x .04, which gets us to his $125,000 gross annually. (You will pay your taxes out of this gross amount, like you do today; therefore, we don't need to consider taxes in our calculation.)

We will also assume Robert doesn't have any other savings in the bank, but if he does, he can subtract that amount from the proceeds he needs for the sale of his company. If he already has $100,000 in other savings, he then would need ($3,125,000 − 100,000) $3,025,000 **after tax.** Keep in mind that if that savings is a 401(k) or other pre-tax account, he will have to pay taxes on it when he withdraws the funds.

Since most technology companies don't have inventory or a considerable amount of fixed assets, most of the gain (in the US) will likely be capital gains. (See the discussion later regarding differences in stock sale vs. asset sale.) Based upon the capital gain, federal tax rate and state tax rate, and the potential for alternative minimum tax, you may need to sell your company for anywhere between $4M and $4.5M to achieve the $3.025M after tax. Again, getting the right tax advice is critical to knowing the proceeds you will need on a sale.

I have purposely not addressed social security here because the number you may or may not receive will depend on your age and how much you have paid in over your working life. If you are fortunate enough to receive social security benefits, consider it a gift each month and use it towards travel, additional long-term care, or a cost of living increase, but keep it out of this calculation for simplicity.

There are a few items that will reduce your net proceeds, such as broker fees (assuming you use one), legal and accounting fees, and any employee bonuses. If you have other shareholders, they will need to figure into the calculation based upon their ownership percentages. Also, any debt on the balance sheet will most likely need to be paid in full as part of the transaction and will therefore reduce the "take-home" amounts, assuming you don't have excess cash in the company to pay these off. On the flip side, if you have excess working capital, you can withdraw that prior to the transaction via either a distribution, dividend, salary, or other form of compensation, and that will reduce the amount you need from the sales proceeds.

Finally, we have assumed the "take-home" number is the amount you are guaranteed in cash. If your deal contains either an earn-out, which 90 percent of all deals typically have, or future earn-outs on the sale of the business down the road, be extremely conservative on what those future earn-outs may be when you calculate your magic number. Remember, those may not be achieved at the expected value, or at all. Here is an example, pulling everything we discussed together:

Net Proceeds for Sale

Sale Proceeds: *		$ 4,375,000
Broker Commissions:	5%	(218,750)
Legal/Accounting Fees:		(60,000)
Employee Bonuses:		(200,000)
Net Cash Proceeds:		**$ 3,896,250**
Federal Capital Gain Rate:	20%	(779,250)
Net cash after tax (assumes no state or other taxes)		**$ 3,117,000**

* After all debt paydown and working capital requirements

Fig.1.1

Please note in the calculation above that we assumed *no* state income tax or alternative minimum tax. Unless you live in a state where there is none, you can expect anywhere from 5 to 13 percent extra in taxes. Don't assume that all states adhere to the federal capital gain rates, and furthermore, it is rare to escape alternative minimum tax on extensive capital gains. Again, it is so important to consult a tax advisor to get a better handle on a proforma sale number.

Understanding your "magic number" is key to help determine what the sales price of your company needs to be after tax. You cannot reach your financial dreams unless you know how much it will take to get there. And once you do know it, it becomes a beacon of light in the fog.

ROBERT INSIGHT

After reviewing his expenses, Robert realized there were several personal expenses that appeared in his financial statements that he would now have to pay for personally. Items like cell phone, car expenses, gas, and personal health and disability insurance would now need to be paid out of his personal funds. Robert had also used his company credit cards to pay for as many business services as possible, so he could reap the points from the cards for personal travel and gifts. After careful review of his personal expenses and perks, he realized he was receiving another $2,500 a month in personal benefits that he would no longer receive once he sold the company. He added ($2,500 x 12) $30,000 to his current annual salary to calculate his "magic number" going forward.

WHAT IS YOUR COMPANY WORTH?

Not all TSPs are created equal, and no two are alike, no matter how similar they seem. Different partner types are valued and acquired for different reasons. Understanding the type of partner you are today, why a buyer might be interested in you, and what you could potentially sell your company for in today's market are key to determining your next move.

Companies are acquired for a number of reasons, of which some are not always obvious to the casual outside viewer. Most acquisitions happen to increase growth quickly, as organic growth can take a while. Here are the top reasons buyers acquire companies:

1. Geographic expansion – both nationally and internationally
2. Customer acquisition – to cross-sell, upsell other products
3. Vertical expansion – buy instead of build a vertical solution or customer base
4. Accretive value – creating a larger company, which creates greater value
5. Remove a competitor

A buyer may have multiple reasons, not just one, for making an acquisition. For example, a private equity group (PEG) may acquire a company to expand the customer base where they can cross-sell the products of another company that are complementary, or an MSP is acquired along with a CRM partner to upsell and cross-sell the services of each company. Finally, an existing ISV may find that providing professional services directly to its end customers may be more profitable and provide stronger long-term customer retention and growth, so they acquire a consulting practice that sells and consults on a complementary product.

In preparation to sell, many partners explore independent valuation companies to receive a formal valuation. This has it merits and will help you determine if you are ready to sell (mostly from a financial standpoint). But generic valuations often provide little value in terms of what you can assume you will be acquired for. If you are going to take the "formal" valuation path, find a firm that specializes in this industry. For a formal business valuation prepared for a merger or acquisition, tax purposes, estate planning, or litigation, IT Valuations (https://www.itvaluations.com/valuations) is a great resource. IT Valuations provides Certified Business Valuations and Calculations of Value specifically for the IT Services and Technology industry, and it is certified by the National Association of Certified Valuators and Analysts.

For those who don't want to spend the time or money for a formal plan, there are three online generic solutions (some require speaking briefly to an advisor) that will help you determine the range of your value. They are fun to take and give you some insights as to what you need to do to grow your business. Here are a few generic valuation assessments you might look at. All have advisors associated with them, but they will give you the results without you having to pay a fee or signing up for a formal program.

- Value Builder System: https://valuebuildersystem.com. You can take this one immediately online.
- Core Values: http://www.corevalueforadvisors.com/. You will need to find an advisor.
- BizEquity: https://www.bizequity.com/smb.

Below is a sample graph generated by BizEquity. It shows the three value types with an explanation of each, and a graph of your company value over a given time period:

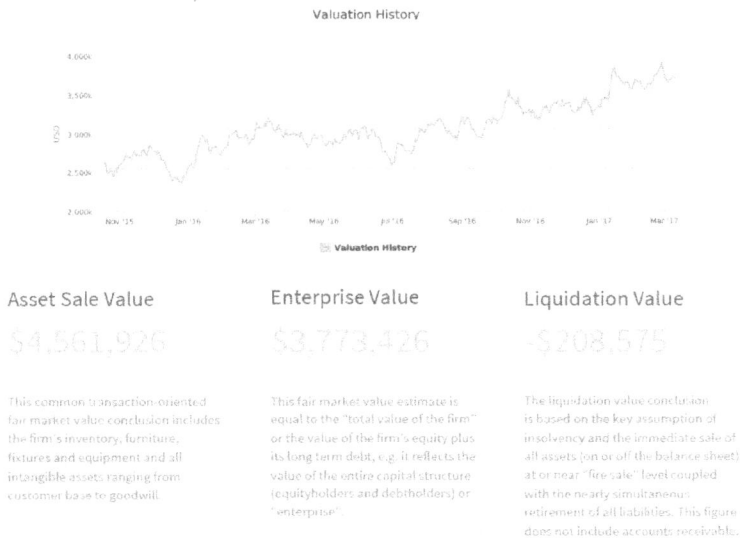

Valuation History

Asset Sale Value

$4,561,926

This common transaction-oriented fair market value conclusion includes the firm's inventory, furniture, fixtures and equipment and all intangible assets ranging from customer base to goodwill.

Enterprise Value

$3,773,426

This fair market value estimate is equal to the "total value of the firm" or the value of the firm's equity plus its long term debt, e.g. it reflects the value of the entire capital structure (equityholders and debtholders) or "enterprise".

Liquidation Value

-$208,575

The liquidation value conclusion is based on the key assumption of insolvency and the immediate sale of all assets (on or off the balance sheet) at or near "fire sale" level coupled with the nearly simultaneous retirement of all liabilities. This figure does not include accounts receivable.

Fig.1.2

(Source: BizEquity Business Valuation Report – 2018. Numbers are based on sample data entered and are not representative of any particular partner category.)

While all three are worthwhile in different ways, BizEquity is probably the best for assessing your true "generic industry" value and will probably most resemble a formal valuation done by a certified professional. The Value Builder System and CoreValue System are great for owners of smaller companies (sub $3M) who want guidance on how to grow their business over time with the assistance of an advisor who will help you focus on your organizational weakness and capitalize on your strengths. Both programs operate using independent advisors who have been trained in the program, so ideally you want to find one that understands the technology industry.

THE VALUE MAXIMIZER ASSESSMENT™

None of the assessments mentioned above, other than a formal business valuation by IT Valuations, address the technology space specifically and the different types of service providers or the potential value each brings to a buyer—either financial or strategic. Therefore, we created our own **free** tool, The Value Maximizer Assessment.

The Value Maximizer Assessment is a tool for business owners to assess their current company value and highlight areas where additional value can potentially be gained. This assessment is unique to technology service providers as it determines value and value gaps by combining your business type (VAR, MSP, ISV, CSP, or Custom Developer) with your revenue, profit margins, and year-over-year growth statistics with additional qualitative values.

The tool works hand-in-hand with this book and follows the eight value drivers discussed in Part II. The data you enter in your assessment is paired with the "8 Value Drivers," which is a proprietary weighting model designed to look at not only your quantitative data but also your qualitative data, based upon the value assigned to each metric by actual recent buyers of companies like yours. The EBITDA baseline values are updated in the assessment as additional market data becomes available, so it always has the latest comparables for companies similar to yours.

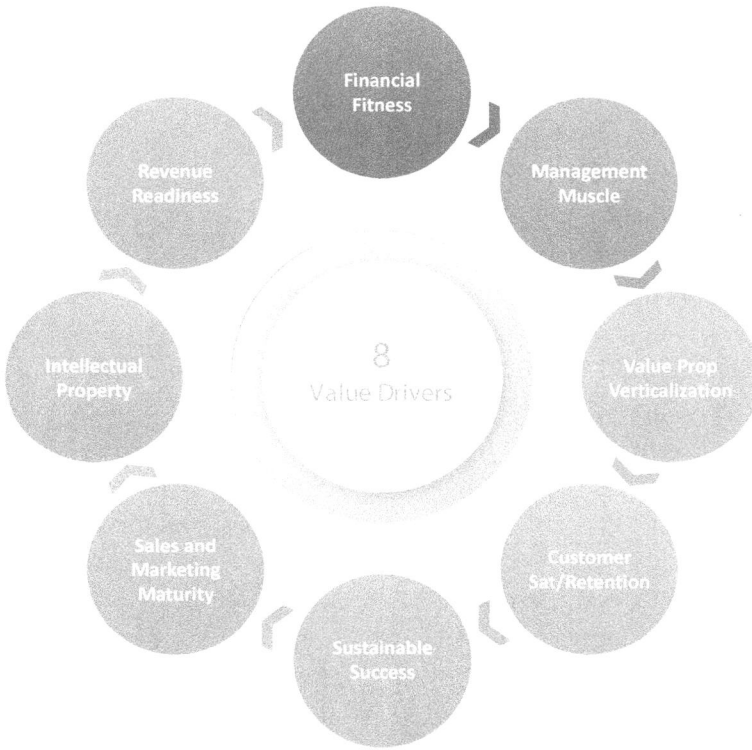

Fig.1.3

In addition to your overall potential business value, you are given a monetary VALUE GAP by category. The VALUE GAP represents the difference between the highest value associated with that section and how you scored against those metrics. The VALUE GAP represents areas where your performance can be increased.

Red flags and cautionary signs are presented if your response would be a concern for a buyer. If presented with either a red or cautionary sign, start by improving these areas first for greatest gains. With this information, we believe that you will have a starting point from which to increase the value of your company over time. If you haven't already taken the free confidential assessment, go to https://rosebizinc.com/ValueMax.

It is very important for you to remember that company valuation is not based on an exact science. Rather, there are some key metrics, which we will discuss later, that PE firms can and do use when determining the price they are willing to pay for your company.

REVENUE MULTIPLES VS. EBITDA

Before we discuss what your company is actually worth, let's get a few definitions out of the way. Often you hear people use the terms *revenue multiples* vs. *EBITDA*. The M&A community usually uses revenue multiples to describe deals for fast growth and early stage startup companies. Companies with negative profits cannot use a multiple of EBITDA because they have no profits, so instead they use revenue multiples. Revenue multiples are more useful when comparing companies that have different levels of profits but similar business characteristics (i.e., products, customer base, margins). This also allows someone to express what the company sold for without truly disclosing their EBITDA multiple (in case you are below an industry standard), so it is used quite often.

EBITDA multiples are more commonly used to value profitable cash flow positive companies. They are generally more telling and accurate because most TSPs share the same level of gross profit margins and typically spend the same amount on sales, marketing, and general and admin expenses.

That said, the *terms* of a deal are significantly more important than the multiples a company sold for. I tell partners not to compare themselves with a deal they may have just heard about, as no two businesses are alike, and no two offers are alike. It really comes down to how the terms are structured. Also, factors like recurring revenue, customer retention, and unique value proposition all play into the purchase price, as well as the type of buyer—financial or strategic—which we will discuss later in this section.

The different flavors of technology service providers

Technology service providers (TSPs) come in all different sizes and flavors, and it would be nearly impossible to list all the variations and combinations that you might find in this ecosystem. We will take a simplistic view and categorize technology service providers into one of five categories. Each category has a distinct role as well as a distinct value to the buyer. As we note in the chart below, they also have different EBITDA multiples. For partners who have the time, and the appetite for change, migration from one type to another could ultimately increase the value of your company, although it may cause a temporary drop to the bottom line. Depending on where you are in your lifecycle, this could be a very viable and profitable option. Here are the five categories of technology service providers that we have categorized for this book:

1. Value added reseller (VAR) – A VAR resells hardware, software, and networking products, and then typically provides services to implement and use the products, as well as ongoing technical support. Most hardware resellers have moved into the MSP category, so for this discussion we will classify VARs as those companies that sell mostly software. A VAR could also be considered a systems integrator (SI) if it sells multiple products to create a unified IT solution. Conversely, a SI could act as a VAR, reselling products to customers as part of a systems integration project. *Accenture* is a good example of a firm that could technically be viewed as both an SI and a VAR. VARs, however, tend to focus on SMBs (small and midsize businesses) and small IT systems, while SIs tend to be involved with larger enterprise customers that span multiple locations and multiple countries. Most SIs are in the $100M+ revenue category and are beyond the multiples we will present in this book.

Value added resellers typically implement and support a couple of main software vendors' products. They typically have a large on-premise customer base that consumes a perpetual license renewed on an annual basis. Margins for software can have a wide range but have been declining over time as software vendors migrate to cloud solutions where margins are considerably less. VARs source their products either directly from the vendor, or through distributors if the vendors they work with use a two-tier distribution model.

Most VARs still perform work on a project basis, but many have transitioned to fixed-fee engagements to increase margins. Support packages are also common and are sold either on an annual or call pack basis. Historically, VARs have had very little recurring revenue, other than annual software renewals and support contracts. It is the group most in jeopardy of declining valuations, unless a niche vertical is developed, or unless a packaged solution consisting of multiple products that can be sold in volume with low costs and relatively high margins is part of their offering. Most VARs have transitioned to a cloud-based deployment, allowing them to expand outside their geographical area. Typically, VARs average $200K to $225K in revenue per employee but incur high labor costs for technical consultants. More recently, VARs have chosen to become managed service providers (MSPs). As product margins decline and competition among solution providers intensifies, VARs have looked to managed services as a source of recurring revenue and improved profitability. A VAR may become a pure-play MSP or add managed services as a line of business to complement its VAR operation.

> **Buyer appeal:** strong customer base, geographic location, billable consultants.
>
> **Buyer concerns:** low gross profit margin, time and material (by the hour work), little recurring revenue.
>
> **Path to higher value:** multiple vendor products, more cloud products, supporting high margin complementary ISV solutions, prepackaging solutions for volume sales.
>
> **The Big Play:** acquire MSP or smaller ISV to upsell/cross-sell.

2. Managed service provider (MSP) – An MSP typically manages and assumes responsibility for providing a defined set of IT services to its client base. Microsoft Exchange, Citrix hosted desktop, and remote backup services are just a few of the typical services being provided. This definition has evolved over time as most MSPs used to sell a significant amount of hardware residing on premises with the customer. While this is still prevalent, and break-fix contracts are still very much in play, most MSPs are transitioning completely to a cloud-focused business, which allows for greater automation, less experienced employees, and higher volumes. More support with fewer employees allows for higher gross profit margins to be realized as this partner transitions to the cloud. Like the VAR, however, it is dependent on vendor margins and higher labor rates. This partner has more control over their margins but really needs to manage labor costs tightly as the industry is somewhat commoditized, and if you charge too much, your customer will move to the next MSP. This group has also experienced commoditization with a downward trend on monthly fees per user, as larger MSPs consolidate and drive down monthly fees. Some MSPs are finding verticals, such as legal and healthcare, in which to distinguish themselves, and those companies are able to drive higher valuations. MSPs, like VARs, are more valuable once revenue is north of $25M. The last couple of years we have seen a lot of MSPs combining to form a larger organization for accretive value. The average revenue per employee is around $175K–$190K.

> **Buyer appeal:** large customer base, economies of scale.
>
> **Buyer concerns:** no vertical focus, commoditization of services, break-fix contracts for on-premise hardware.
>
> **Path to higher value:** multiple cloud offerings, higher subscription billing percent.
>
> **The Big Play:** purchasing smaller players to gain accretive value.

3. Cloud Service Provider (CSP) – CSP is now a catch-all for what was formerly referred to as a hoster, infrastructure as a service (IaaS), and platform as a service (PaaS) partners.[10] These partners offer some form of cloud computing to their customers, either in their own private datacenter, a co-located data center, or from one of the big three providers: Amazon Web Services (AWS), Microsoft, and Google.

In the IaaS model, the cloud service provider, delivers infrastructure components that would otherwise exist in an on-premise data center. These components could consist of servers, storage, and networking, as well as a virtualization layer. While historically this has been deployed using private clouds, most of the new business is moving to the public cloud due to stronger security levels, increased bandwidth, the refresh rate on servers, and patching of systems and hardware. PaaS providers will add more of the application stack, such as operating systems, databases and middleware, or the software that "glues together separate, often complex, and already existing programs to the underlying infrastructure."[11] These partners have a higher long-term stickiness with the customer as they are truly the extended IT department for patching together multiple disparate applications in a cloud environment.

In general, these partners make their offerings available as an on-demand, self-provisioning purchase, or they provide a one-time setup of the applications being managed in the cloud. Customers then pay for the cloud-based services on a subscription basis either monthly, quarterly, or annually, usually in advance with a true-up at the end of the billing cycle to account for additional services added or removed. These services can also include a subscription for software such as Microsoft Office, an ERP or CRM system, along with other ISV solutions; and the result is combined into one monthly fee. The value add is providing a service level agreement on the applications that may not be included by a public or private cloud provider.

Some cloud service providers have differentiated themselves by tailoring their offerings to a vertical market's requirements. Their cloud-based services might seek to deliver industry-specific functionality or help users meet certain regulatory requirements. For instance, some cloud providers specialize in the security and regulatory requirements around Sarbanes-Oxley, HIPAA, and FDA, all of which have special audit and documentation needs. This added level of security and documentation allows them to set themselves apart and therefore upcharge significantly for their monthly services.

The benefit of this category is that fewer people are needed to serve up the applications in the cloud, given the range of monitoring tools that flag issues well in advance; plus, this group does not support any on-premises hardware. Technical support volume is typically lower so support can be staffed with lower cost employees. The emphasis is on keeping margins high and labor costs low. Each employee, on average, can support more customers, and even with 24/7 support, the revenue per employee ranges from $350K to $450K if there is a strong infrastructure of control and provisioning. Partners in this category can easily achieve 95 percent in recurring revenue, while maintaining a high gross profit margin. One key component to success in this category is maintaining a low churn rate—less than 10 percent annually. The second key is creating either a vertical or functional niche that will allow monthly rates to remain high. The healthcare, life science, and legal industries are other prime candidates for services provided by these partners. Partners not specializing are becoming commoditized as end customers are bypassing them and going directly to the public or private cloud providers for generic services.

As a point of clarification, only partners who are responsible for maintenance and uptime of the applications or servers in the cloud, and where the company offers a service level agreement (SLA) to the end customer, are included in this category. I am refraining from using CSP in the header in the chart below as it is loosely used in the Microsoft community for anyone selling a cloud product provided by Microsoft on Azure. These partners, while offering cloud solutions, typically are not required to maintain or patch the applications and hence do not fall into the true definition of a CSP. So, as not to confuse anyone, I am going to stay away from this catch-all title.

Partners that sell and consult on cloud applications supported by the vendor (meaning application patching and uptime), such as Salesforce, NetSuite, Microsoft Dynamics, Sage Intacct, or other similar software, are considered VARs with cloud services for the purposes of the valuation chart.

> **Buyer appeal:** large customer base, support of more than one public cloud, strong recurring revenue.
>
> **Buyer concerns:** horizontal play, no vertical differentiator, downward trend on GPM in public clouds.
>
> **Path to higher value:** move from private data centers to multiple public cloud offerings.
>
> **The Big Play:** consolidation, buy your competitor.

4. Custom developer – The custom application developer typically designs a specific software application for a specific user or group of users within an organization. The software or specific entire application is designed to address their needs precisely, as opposed to the more traditional and widespread off-the-shelf software. Successful partners typically start with a scoping engagement, which leads into a build project. Once the project is delivered, the developer typically sells additional maintenance or ongoing support services. While this type of partner doesn't necessarily create recurring revenue in the traditional way, they can create a significant amount of repeat revenue from either the same customer or customers in a particular industry. Typically, costs are lower to have the application supported by the developer rather than the client's IT staff. While this group of partners hasn't received extensive love from large vendors in the past, they currently consume vast amounts of cloud services with the big three public cloud providers mentioned above. Either those services are self-consumed or billed back to the customer as the application is delivered to the end user.

This partner type has a great appeal to a strategic buyer who is looking for application developers to round out their offering. There is less of an appeal to financial buyers as they don't truly understand custom developed applications and they are more comfortable with recurring revenue over repeat revenue. However, a partner that produces considerable cash flow will appeal to even a less risk-tolerant financial buyer. Both buyer types will look carefully at the customer retention rate as well as the gross profit margins. Many custom developers, as they become larger, morph into system integrators as well, as they continue to touch the same systems (i.e., ERP/CRM and e-commerce) over and over again, and therefore become experts in implementing and connecting multiple applications.

> **Buyer appeal:** talent, specific industry solutions.
>
> **Buyer concerns:** repeat revenue is not recurring revenue; smaller organizations rely on "key" developers.
>
> **Path to higher value:** industry specific solutions that can be reused on the next project.

The big play: creating IP that turns into a SaaS product.

5. Independent software vendors (ISVs) – An ISV makes and sells software products that run on one or more computer's hardware, either physical or virtual. This category differs from the custom developer (albeit that is most likely where their roots originated). They provide a standard packaged solution with updates on a semiannual or annual basis. While most ISVs have started as perpetual on-premise licenses, many have begun the transition to the cloud or at least to subscription pricing that can be deployed either on premises or in the cloud. Historical on-premises partners with a strong customer base can find it challenging to move their customers to a subscription basis. The transition to recurring revenue can be slow and arduous. Annual enhancement or maintenance renewals are usually solid and can represent 30 to 40 percent of the annual revenue. ISVs are seeing a downward pressure on the monthly subscription prices for their products, especially if they are connected or rely on a larger vendor solution as their backbone. If the major vendor decides to reduce the price of the product, the ISV may find themselves representing a larger cost of the overall solution, which typically wasn't the issue in the past with on-premises perpetual licenses. ISVs now try to create smaller, more manageable applications that can easily be consumed by the buyer and can lead to add-on applications for additional features and functionality.

Partners that have created only cloud solutions and provide the entire SaaS solution to their customers are able to achieve the high recurring revenue percentages. Hence the large swath of 50 percentage points in the amount of recurring revenue in the chart below. Software as a service (SaaS) is a software distribution model in which a third-party provider hosts applications and makes them available to customers in the cloud. Online marketplaces such as AppSource by Microsoft and AppExchange by Salesforce can provide ISVs with the perfect online marketplace to showcase their solutions.

Margins and gross profit in this category are the highest (cloud or on premises). This partner can have the highest amount of recurring revenue if deploying a cloud solution. ISVs typically garner the highest gross profit margins, especially as the application matures. As you can see from the chart below, these are the highest valued companies.

Buyer appeal: strong recurring revenue and gross profit margin potential.

Buyer concerns: long transition to the cloud if application is available on premise, horizontal solution.

Path to higher value: industry specific solutions, subscription pricing.

The big play: OEM deal or creating your own partner channel.

VALUES AND APPEAL BY SERVICE PROVIDER TYPE

		Category Description	VAR Value Added Reseller	MSP Managed Service Provider	Hoster, IaaS, PaaS	Custom Developer	ISV --> SaaS Independent Software Vendor
		% of Recur/Rev:	10% - 20%	40% - 60%	85%+	40%- 60%	45% - 95%
		GP Margins:	25% - 40%	35% - 45%	40% - 55%	50% - 60%	65%+
		Valuation Appeal:	Depends on buyer: geography, expanded customer base	Moderate - the larger the more attractive	Higher - if multiple cloud offerings	Higher – if consistent repeat revenue	Highest - if a SaaS offering
		EBITDA Multiples:					
Revenue		Under $10M	3 - 5	5 - 8	5 - 7	6 - 8	6 - 10
		Over $10M	5 - 8	6 - 9	6 - 8	7 - 9	8 - 12
		Over $25M	7 - 9	7 - 10	7 - 10	10 - 12	10 - 15
		Buyer Focus:	Geography and human capital	Gross profit and Strong EBITDA	Gross profit, YOY growth and churn	Vertical specialty and string repeat revenue	Vertical specialty and YOY growth

Multiples in all categories can increase with sustainable EBITDA > 15%+ and revenue growth of 25% - 30%+ YOY

Fig.1.4

The chart above reflects the current percentages of recurring revenue, gross profit margins, and valuation appeals based upon various benchmarking studies of TSPs worldwide. These are not numbers published by specific large vendors directly or via third party research firms. The EBITDA multiples are based upon closed deals and the input of several brokers that represented the sale and purchase of partner organizations from 2016 to 2018. View this chart like you would a balance sheet—this was a point in time during 2019. These numbers can change overnight based on the current economic climate. The

EBITDA multiples broken down by revenue category are also an important distinction. If your organization spans multiple categories, you can certainly calculate your value using a ratio of percentages from multiple categories.

While the numbers above can certainly be used as a guide, and I caution **ONLY** as a guide, there are a number of items to consider before determining the value of your company. Factors that can negatively affect these numbers are as follows:

- Declining revenue YOY
- Declining EBITDA YOY
- Single or low digit EBITDA
- High churn rate – rate at which customers leave your company
- Lack of cloud-based applications
- Narrow geographic focus
- Lack of vertical focus
- One customer representing more than 20 percent of your revenue

Use this chart as your guide, not your bible!

If you cannot simply categorize revenue as one type and have revenue that spans across multiple categories—say more than 30 percent—then another approach to valuations is a method created by Service Leadership, Inc. (www.service-leadership.com.) This group works extensively with a wide variety of IT firms of various sizes and business models. As part of this service, the organization benchmarks the financial performance of solution provider companies worldwide and has visibility into the sale value of the companies they consult, including the two data points listed below. They suggest that you find the approximate value of your company in each, and then average the result. The upside of this approach is: if you have revenue that crosses multiple lines of business, you would just multiply that line of revenue by the category below that most closely represents it.

Let's review this below in more detail...

The first chart represents the value in terms of **revenue multiples**. First find the line(s) that most closely approximates your line(s) of revenue. For example, let's say you have a $2M business, of which 50 percent is project services and 50 percent is managed services. In our example, we will also assume that this business generated 10 percent EBITDA in 2018. You would multiply each by the values in the 2018 column. Therefore, $1M for project service is about 0.64 of revenue or $640K, and $1M of managed services is approximately worth 1.4x revenue or $1.4M, for a total of $2.4M in value.

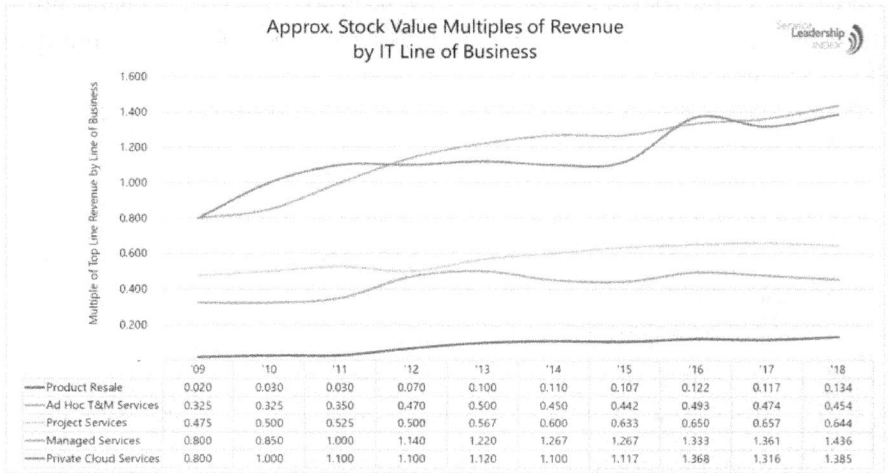

	'09	'10	'11	'12	'13	'14	'15	'16	'17	'18
Product Resale	0.020	0.030	0.030	0.070	0.100	0.110	0.107	0.122	0.117	0.134
Ad Hoc T&M Services	0.325	0.325	0.350	0.470	0.500	0.450	0.442	0.493	0.474	0.454
Project Services	0.475	0.500	0.525	0.500	0.567	0.600	0.633	0.650	0.657	0.644
Managed Services	0.800	0.850	1.000	1.140	1.220	1.267	1.267	1.333	1.361	1.436
Private Cloud Services	0.800	1.000	1.100	1.100	1.120	1.100	1.117	1.368	1.316	1.385

Fig.1.5

In this second chart, we are looking at values based upon **EBITDA multiples.** Again, find the line(s) that most closely approximates your business and multiply it by the EBITDA value, this time based upon the percent of EBITDA you earn. Again, in our example we assumed a 10 percent EBITDA or $200,000 above. Here we just multiply this number by 7.28 for a value of $1,456,000.

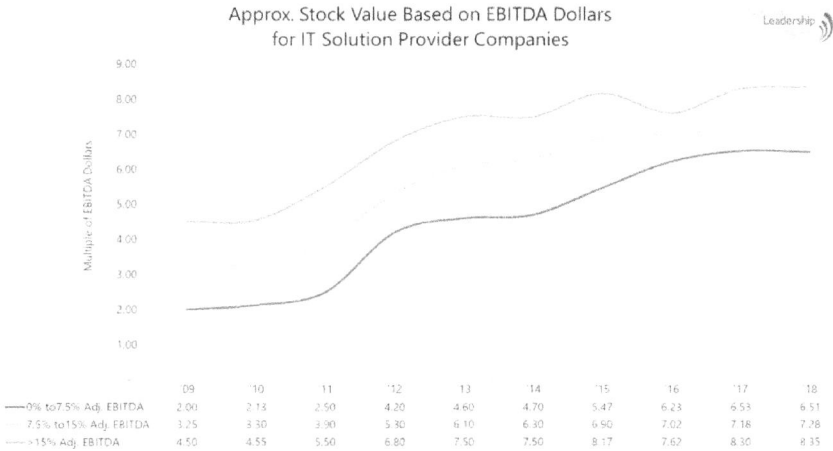

Approx. Stock Value Based on EBITDA Dollars for IT Solution Provider Companies

Leadership

	09	10	11	12	13	14	15	16	17	18
0% to7.5% Adj. EBITDA	2.00	2.13	2.50	4.20	4.60	4.70	5.47	6.23	6.53	6.51
7.5% to15% Adj. EBITDA	3.25	3.30	3.90	5.30	6.10	6.30	6.90	7.02	7.18	7.28
>15% Adj. EBITDA	4.50	4.55	5.50	6.80	7.50	7.50	8.17	7.62	8.30	8.35

Fig.1.6

Let's now average the value from the two charts: ($2,040,000 + $1,456,000 = $3,496,000/2 = $1,748,000). That same example using the value and appeal chart (Fig 1.5) would yield you a high value of about $1,600,000. So, you can see that the result can vary significantly depending on the revenue of the company, the EBITDA, and the type of business. The most important point to keep in mind with all of these charts is that revenue and EBITDA multiples are *comparative benchmarks*. They are not *valuations*. In the end, you are worth what someone is willing to pay for you. No benchmark will change that.

SIZE MATTERS

As indicated above, as the revenue of your company increases so will your value, assuming your EBITDA stays in line with that growth.

I have been in more than one conversation where a partner sat in on a broker webinar, heard an EBITDA number based upon a case study presented, and then assumed he could sell his company on that multiple. The case study featured a company with revenue in excess of $30M. This partner was generating $4M in revenue. You cannot use the same multiple.

Multiples increase as the revenue and EBITDA of a company increase. Of course, there are exceptions to this rule as well, but an investment in a $6M company with $1M in EBITDA is generally riskier than investing in a $12M company with $2M in EBITDA. While the percentages are the same, the value of the larger company in terms of multiples is clearly higher.

Valuation: Key Concepts

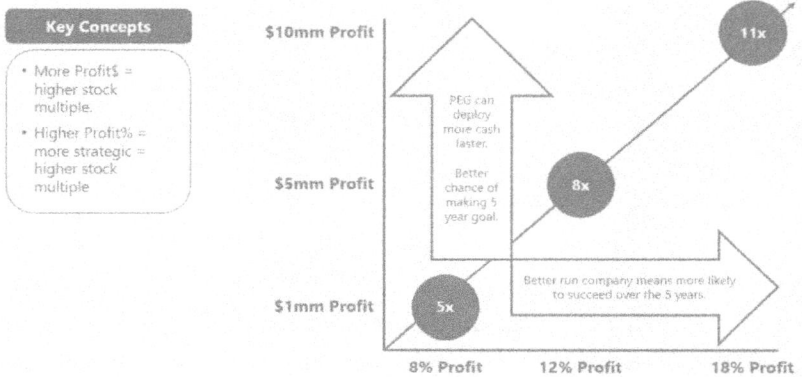

Key Concepts
• More Profit$ = higher stock multiple.
• Higher Profit% = more strategic = higher stock multiple

$10mm Profit — 11x

PEG can deploy more cash faster.

$5mm Profit — 8x

Better chance of making 5 year goal.

Better run company means more likely to succeed over the 5 years.

$1mm Profit — 5x

8% Profit   12% Profit   18% Profit

Fig.1.7
Source: www.service-leadership.com

TERMS MATTER

While EBITDA multiples are certainly guides—as we will see shortly, they are not the entire picture. For example, the same company may receive two different offers. Just because one company received a higher multiple, it doesn't necessarily mean the offer is better. It is really about the terms that surround the offer. Let's see how this plays out in an example below:

Company A receives two offers: One for 5X EBITDA and one for 6x EBITDA. The offer for 5X EBITDA consists of $4M upfront in cash and $1M in the form of an interest-bearing note over two years. The second offer is for 6x EBITDA, which consists of 50 percent upfront in cash and the remaining

50 percent tied to an earn-out that will be paid at the end of the second year. The actual proceeds of the offer are listed below: In this case, the 5x offer was actually a better deal in the long run by about $5K, tax consequences aside. The average earn-out achieved in deals tracked by a large international M&A firm, Equiteq, per their 2016 Buyers Research Report, is 77 percent; but due to variables out of their control, only 71 percent of the earn-out is achieved. Applying a 71 percent earn-out calculation, it is almost a breakeven between the two offers. If a lower earn-out percentage was achieved, the 6x deal would be even less advantageous. Of course, if more than 71 percent is achieved you may be ahead of the game.

	Sales Price Example		
Adjusted EBITDA at Close:	*1,000,000*		
Multiple of EBITDA:	**5x**		**6x**
Sales Price:	$ 5,000,000	$	6,000,000
Terms:			
Cash:	4,000,000		3,000,000
Note (Paid over 24 months with 5% interest):	1,052,913		-
Earn-out (over 24 months):			3,000,000
Average earnout-out achieved: 71%			2,130,000
Cash at close invest with 4% return:	326,400		244,800
Total Proceeds after 24 months:	$ 5,379,313	$	5,374,800

Fig.1.8

My point is: While an offer with a higher EBITDA multiple may seem better, it is not always more profitable in the end. If all other variables, such as culture or organizational fit, anticipated profitability of the combined organizations, and future noncompete are not major concerns, be sure to work through the entire deal with your accountant and attorney to assess your comfort level of risk and to determine the least, best, and most likely scenarios for total payout.

WHAT IS YOUR EXIT TIMELINE – 1, 3, OR 5 YEARS?

Those businesses that carefully plan for their ultimate exit will be the most attractive in a crowded marketplace. Those that do not give careful attention to their exit plans may find themselves holding a fire sale for their companies, or worse, simply folding up the tent and going home.

To sell a business in the coming years, owners must be able to determine what would make their businesses attractive to prospective buyers and then begin their planning process with that in mind. Owners must also focus on growing the key drivers of their business and invest in sales, marketing, and business infrastructure if necessary.

The **BOTTOM LINE** for business owners planning on listing their businesses soon (within two years): it is vital that the process begin **NOW!**

"I am not interested in selling, but if a good offer showed up at my door, I would consider it." Ever hear that line? I know I have, and I am probably guilty of saying it myself. Sadly, for most companies that "offer" never materializes because no plan is put in place to create an exit.

CEOs who have an exit in mind have tended to respond to the question "when do you plan to exit?" with a number like "five years." Five years is common because it is a safe answer. Five years is a long enough period of time to continue to make substantial strides on revenue and profitability while moving the company strategically into a vertical or strong recurring revenue model. Five years is sufficient time to build a stronger management team, create a sustainable customer base, and build out a cloud practice with high gross profit margins.

Five years is also a safe response to ward off concerns from shareholders or employees who otherwise might be concerned about their careers. But, five years is still a short enough time for the notion that "one day" you would entertain an offer from a prospective buyer. Unfortunately for some, five years is always five years, not four, or not even three. Even after two more years pass, the answer is still *five* years. Sound familiar?

Understanding and being clear about your exit timeline will help align your personal and professional priorities. First, as we discussed earlier in the book, it will require you to be clear about your own exit goals, both financially and mentally. Secondly, by completing your Value Maximizer Assessment, you will be able to prioritize those areas of your business where you could create additional value quickly. It will also help you determine if extending a year or two to address your priority areas will be worth the additional value. Working toward an exit will align all shareholders as to the goals of the company over a given period of time and not leave everyone on the "eternal" five-year plan. A well-planned timeline can help you articulate to your buyers with clarity your financial and future career goals. Finally, and maybe most importantly, it may prevent you from keeping your company beyond its point of greatest value.

Being realistic about your own personal and professional goals is key to determining which plan will be realistic for you and your shareholders. Many owners choose to monetize their years of hard work through a sale but then continue to work side-by-side with the new owners, not only to achieve the earn-out, but because they find the new environment rewarding to their personal growth. Some owners, however, know enough about their own personality or their post-sale goals to know that they will not make great employees long term within the acquired company. Knowing which camp you fall in, or think you fall in (as you may change your mind after a deal is done), is key to determining your own timeline.

When determining your timeline, ask yourself these questions:

1. Will your share of the cash proceeds at sale achieve your magic number?
2. Is there a point where the company's YOY growth will potentially top out?
3. Are there external forces in the market that will make your products or services less desirable?
4. How quickly might your market share erode due to competition, or other external factors?
5. What are your strengths and weaknesses based on the Value Maximizer Assessment? How quickly can they be elevated?
6. Where are your partners/shareholders in their lifecycle and personal goals?

THE 5-YEAR PLAN

Let's say that five years is truly your goal, meaning the day you want to exit. Working backwards from the day you want to exit, or no longer work at the company, here is what this might look like:

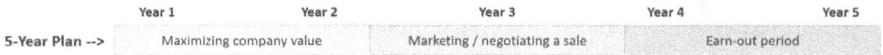

	Year 1	Year 2	Year 3	Year 4	Year 5
5-Year Plan -->	Maximizing company value		Marketing / negotiating a sale	Earn-out period	

A typical earn-out where the owners will need to remain with the company is currently averaging two years. If you sell to a PEG, they may want you to stay longer while they build value in the new company to sell three or five years later. Between researching and selecting a broker, engaging a buyer, and working through the negotiation and contracts of a sale, that requires another year of time. This then leaves you two solid years to work on maximizing your company's value. If you don't have a large percentage of recurring revenue today, or are still very horizontally focused, two years may not be a sufficient amount of time to maximize your company value.

THE 3-YEAR PLAN:

For those companies who are well established in a vertical and have a large amount of recurring revenue, a three-year plan is very feasible. I would begin by interviewing the "Big 3" as discussed in Part III of this book to begin assembling your external advisors. Most sellers, from the date of signing with an advisor/broker to finalizing a deal, will take six to eight months before finalizing a transaction. This gives you four months to interview and assemble your external team. These same four months should be used to prepare the documents that will be needed in the due diligence process as discussed in Part III. As a practical matter, many of the documents you will need for due diligence can be, and should be, part of your normal recordkeeping process; and if they are well organized as you go about your normal record retention, they will help alleviate a massive document search and retrieval process at due diligence time.

If you are looking for a three-year exit, then timing may look more like this:

	Year 1	Year 2	Year 3
3-Year Plan -->	Marketing / negotiating a sale	Earn-out period	

An alternate plan might look like this: if you already have greater than 40 percent recurring revenue, you could reduce the earn-out period, and still give yourself time to work on improvements to the company that don't require as much time but still provide value to a prospective buyer.

	Year 1	Year 2	Year 3
3-Year Plan -->	Maximizing company value	Marketing/negotiating a sale	Earn-out period

THE 1-YEAR PLAN:

If you are on the one-year exit plan, you must be prepared to begin the sales process immediately and hope that you are not required to remain with the purchasing entity, or at a minimum remain for a few short months as you hand over the reins to your management team or other shareholders who will remain as part of the transaction. While an all-cash offer with no earn-out is still rare, it is increasingly becoming a reality for companies with high recurring revenue, high customer retention rates, and a strong management team.

	Year 1
1-Year Plan -->	Marketing / negotiating a sale / walking out the door

Fig.1.9

Finally, the one-year timeline for marketing and negotiating a sale assumes you are working with a broker. If you plan on marketing your company on your own, be prepared for this to take longer than a year. Even with a strong management team in place to offload your normal workload, marketing your own company is an incredibly time-consuming project. Unless you can manage multiple offers and play them off of each other, not only for company value but for timing, then there is less of a sense of urgency on behalf of the buyer and the process usually drags on. It is not uncommon for a sale to drag on longer than one year. Unfortunately, the longer the process drags on, the less likely it will close. Should the initial LOI not close, it means you are back to square one with a minimum three- to nine-month time loss. Therefore, if you plan to be marketing and attracting buyers independent of a broker, be conservative and add another year to your timeline.

Once you have completed your Value Maximizer Assessment, you will be able to determine on a scale from 0 to 100 how well you score in the eight assessment areas. The graph below depicts the time and effort required to increase your score in each of the eight areas. Intellectual property is the value that takes the longest amount of time and it is the most difficult to master, while financial fitness and customer satisfaction and retention can provide fairly immediate results once work begins in these areas.

Companies that score well on their Value Maximizer Assessment, in the areas above the horizontal midpoint axis, can achieve maximum value in as little as one to three years. If those areas are weak, then you should assess the total value gap and see how that aligns with your magic number, your revenue growth, and the continuing market share for your products and services. This will then help you determine the optimal timeline for your company.

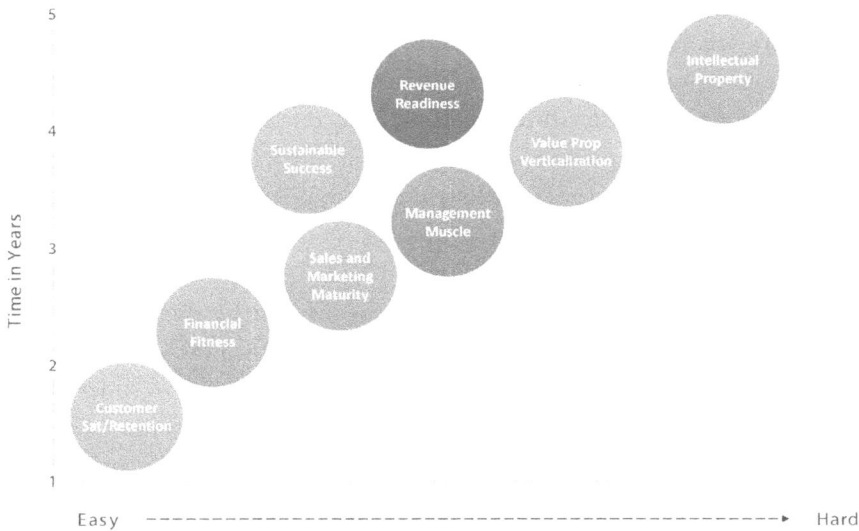

Fig.1.10

Once you have determined your viable timeline, the question most owners ask is: What if an offer is presented to the company *prior* to the completion of your timeline? Then what do you do? This question becomes much easier to answer once you know your "magic" number—how long you want to continue to work, and how you score using the Value Driver Assessment Tool. If you feel the offer achieves these objectives, and you are sure there is not a larger value gap than can easily be eliminated with small changes, then it may be worth pursuing.

WHO WILL BUY YOUR COMPANY?

Once you mentally decide to sell your business, the question of who will buy it quickly follows.

Who will buy you largely depends on how much revenue you generate. Smaller companies with less than $5M in revenue and/or $1M in EBITDA are typically acquired by strategic buyers. Companies larger than this start to attract the interest of private equity groups. Most transactions in the technology industry are completed by strategic buyers and not private equity firms. The vast majority of these transactions do not involve a broker, as the strategic buyer approaches the seller directly. Many are completed quietly with only insiders aware of the pending transaction. Most of these transactions are not even publicly announced (only publicly traded companies are required to announce acquisitions that are material), so it is hard to gather exact numbers; but over the last few years, it seems more transactions have occurred this way.

The question of who will buy your company can be divided into five distinct buyer categories. These buyers are segregated into two distinct buyer classes: Strategic and financial buyers. The first four—strategic buyers—are those most likely to acquire companies under the $5M in revenue. The last group —PEGs, as mentioned above—are typically interested only in larger companies. More on this in the next chapter. Each category, along with the level of risk, timeline for completion, and payout components, are listed below:

Buyer Type	Strategic Buyers				Financial Buyer
	Partners/Shareholder/ Key Employees	Direct Competitor	Complimentary Partner	Customer or Vendor	Private Equity Firm
Risk the deal will fail:	Low	Medium- High	Low to Medium	Low to Medium	Low
Timeline:	1- 3 months	4 - 6 months	5 - 7 months	4 - 6 months	4 - 8 months
Payout:	Cash + Note	Cash + Note + Earn - out	Cash + Note + Earn - out	Cash + Earn - out + equity (sometimes)	Cash + Earn-out + Equity in NewCo.

Fig.1.11

PARTNERS/SHAREHOLDERS/KEY EMPLOYEES

Typically, these people have been with the company for a while and have helped grow the company alongside you. You may have already granted them stock through a stock option plan or other mechanism, or you may have just granted them shares over time for their sweat equity at no additional cost. In the case of nonemployee other shareholders or partners, they already legally own part of the company and may have plans to continue, even though you as the majority owner may want to exit. Being upfront with your shareholders regarding your personal plans is important. While announcing you want to exit (in the future) may create a bit of anxiety, communicating and careful planning can help you achieve a positive outcome. Don't wait until you are exhausted or about to retire before you announce your exit plan to your shareholders. This will negatively impact your sale price. Of course, that is in a perfect world, and sometimes life events (illness, divorce, death) or escalating shareholder or partner disagreements don't allow for a well-planned exit.

Regardless of the situation, it is common courtesy to give your shareholders the right of first offer to make you an offer to purchase your interest. Even if you are selling to someone you know, you still want to retain your own counsel, accountant, and someone you can all agree on who will give you an independent valuation for your company. In addition, you might also consider hiring an M&A coach who can walk you through some of the common issues and be a good sounding board during the process. Be careful not to use the same attorney you used as your outside company attorney. It will be hard for this person to be independent, and they must get consent from all other shareholders to represent you personally. It is best to find a different attorney.

> **Risk of failure:** Low—assuming a reasonable price and terms can be agreed upon quickly. Everyone involved already understands what they will be acquiring.

> **Timeline:** Usually these transactions can be completed in three months or less. Most of this is creating and reviewing legal documents. All parties know the business and little due diligence, if any, is needed.

> **Payout:** cash + note (typically three-year payout on the note).

DIRECT COMPETITOR

Selling to a competitor can be a tricky situation but can also be a very viable buyer for your company. Most transactions in the past two years have been larger partners buying smaller partners to increase their geographic footprint, extend an existing vertical, or add a complementary product. Many have been competing head-to-head for years. Others learn about one another via conferences, user groups, or advisory councils.

Ideally, if you are selling to a competitor, it is not someone in your immediate geographic area, product line, or niche. Should the deal not happen, even though both parties have hopefully signed an NDA, it exposes your customer base, your intellectual property, and your most valued employees to your competition.

Where things can go off the rails a little is when your most immediate staunch competitor (same product/same geography) finds out that you are up for sale. Once they learn of it, the employees (who might not be aware of the NDA) will immediately share this news with your customers, vendors, employees, social media, and anyone else who would be interested, thereby weakening your position in the sales process. Before you take that risk, you need to determine if the buyer is legitimate, or if they are just fishing around to get information. If you do decide to move forward, upon signing an NDA, immediately ask for their financials, or proof that they have the wherewithal to make a purchase. You never want your revenue to be more than 30 to 40 percent of theirs; otherwise, it may be difficult for them to undertake the transaction and remain profitable. Be cautious and don't provide too much information early on. If they are unwilling to answer questions on timing and deal structure, then it's not a good sign.

Does that mean selling to a competitor is not an option? Absolutely not.

Selling to a competitor has some great upsides, especially if they are new to the geographic area and offer an opportunity for your team to grow and offer more services to your existing customer base. For example, a CPA firm acquiring an ERP partner in the same geography.

> **Risk of failure:** Medium to high. Agreement on purchase price can be difficult and due diligence lengthy, as everyone

has a business to run. And since there are no other offers, there is nothing driving the close of the deal other than dates you both have agreed upon, which almost always slip.

Timeline: usually these transactions can be completed in four to six months or less—all parties know the business, but due diligence can take time.

Payout: usually consists of cash + note and a small earn-out with upside for performance goals.

ROBERT INSIGHT:

The firm that made an offer on his consulting practice was, without a doubt, a direct competitor but didn't have an office in his part of the state. Robert was confident that a deal was going to go through, but just in case, he wanted to protect his employees and protect his customer base during the due diligence process. Even though the nondisclosure agreement was specific with regard to the data being shared between the companies, he wanted to take extra steps. While it is customary to provide a list of the revenue generated by customers over the last three years and a complete list of employees' tenure, compensation and title, Robert had his accounting department create an alias for each customer and each employee (but something his team would recognize) before sharing the data with the potential buyers. Should the deal then not happen, Robert wouldn't have to worry about sensitive data ending up in the wrong hands.

COMPLEMENTARY SERVICE PROVIDER

A complementary partner can be described in two ways. The first refers to two partners with the same major vendor who have complementary applications. For example, a Microsoft CRM and a Microsoft ERP partner—same major vendor. Large software vendors who sell multiple applications can make it difficult for one organization to provide all the services. Microsoft, for example, with the new "One Commercial Partner" concept, almost necessitates the need for a larger partner organization to service the customer under this new model, as it includes not only Office, but ERP, CRM, Business Intelligence, Azure, and Artificial Intelligence. Most partner organizations are not large enough to support the entire Microsoft stack of products; therefore, creating stronger, "formal" arrangements via purchase is becoming more common.

The second refers to two partners with different complementary vendors. For example, an SAP ERP partner and a Business Intelligence partner. These are different vendors for each of the products but with complementary solutions. This example is especially popular with large CPA firms that provide consulting services across multiple products. They have been very active as buyers by acquiring partners with complementary products to sell to their existing customer base.

Partner conferences or vendor-sponsored trainings are a good place to begin these conversations, and while some don't go anywhere, many end up in a closed transaction nine to 12 months later.

> **Risk of failure:** Low to medium—both parties realize that coming together makes sense but both have a business to run. So, unless the acquiring firm has an acquisition team, these deals can take time and often don't move past the initial discussion stage. Failure rates are lower with PEGs as they have a dedicated team to find, analyze and close transactions. More on this below.

> **Timeline:** While both parties understand the other's business in general, each has different expectations on profit margins and agreements with vendors. Deals can get done in five to seven months, but a strong emphasis on the post-acquisition outcome needs to be considered.

> **Payout:** cash + note + earn-out.

CUSTOMER OR VENDOR

Both customers and vendors are potential buyers. The most common scenario is the software vendor acquiring a professional services firm or a large software vendor purchasing a custom application that integrates well into their solution. With custom applications, the vendor typically purchases the IP and the key developers to maintain and support the application and leaves behind the professional services team if one exists.

Apple, Salesforce, and Microsoft are all vendors with a strong acquisition appetite.

Microsoft, on average, acquires 10 companies per year.[14]

Apple, on average, acquires eight to 10 companies per year.[15]

Salesforce, on average, acquires four to six companies per year.[16]

However, Accenture, a large Systems integrator (SI), has been on a roll, aiming to diversify its offerings and expand operating markets. The company closed 37 acquisition deals worth approximately $1.7 billion in fiscal 2017. Also, over the last three fiscal years, Accenture has invested approximately $3.4 billion in acquiring nearly 70 companies, including start-ups.[18]

However, these companies typically are not targeting smaller, i.e., less than $20M companies, unless they have a potential disruptive technology or can significantly and rapidly be accretive to their earnings.

Risk of failure: Medium to low—most larger vendors have teams who focus solely on identifying and closing transactions. Once an LOI is issued, barring any showstoppers during due diligence, these transactions have a high close rate.

Timeline: Length can vary based on the size and complexity of the transaction, with legal documentation being rather arduous. It is hard to quote an average, but most deals are done within six months of issuing a Letter of Intent.

Payout: usually consists of cash + earn-out + stock or options.

PRIVATE EQUITY GROUP (PEG)

Over the last few years, private equity groups have become an increasingly large buyer in the lower midmarket technology space. These investors are looking for a place other than Wall Street to invest their money. The technology industry is hot, and more and more private equity money continues to show up in the TSP deals. While PEGs historically invested only in larger companies, this has not been the case with technology providers. PEGs now show interest in companies with only $5M in revenue and/or $1M in EBITDA.

PEGs selectively look for high-growth companies with unique value propositions. Their goal is to buy low and sell high. They buy low with the expectation of increasing the value of their portfolio companies over time (typically three to seven years), and then sell their companies at a much higher price. Anything smaller than $5M in revenue and/or $1M EBITDA is usually not worth it to them. The time and effort for due diligence and preparing and negotiating legal documents don't produce sufficient rewards. PEGs want to hear about companies greater than $20M, but there are exceptions. Especially if the platform company (the initial company) is looking for a follow-on acquisition in the same area, then a $5M company may just be the right add-on investment. This is when PEGs start acting more like strategic buyers. More on this later.

Historically, PEGs have paid less for companies than a strategic buyer would, but to stay competitive, they have increased their offerings, which are many times higher (usually in the form of the earn-out) than with strategic buyers.

It is important to understand that there are basically two types of PEGs: Those with committed funds and those with "search" or "dry" funds. A committed or dedicated equity fund is one where the investors have actually invested capital into the fund. A search or dry fund is where a fund manager goes out looking for opportunities, then comes back to the investors, often larger private equity firms, to obtain the capital for the acquisition; meaning the capital is not yet sitting in the fund to make the acquisition.

Search funds usually are launched by entrepreneurs. Surprisingly, though, these entrepreneurs often have limited experience in the sector in which they hope to invest. Their goal is to get stellar managers into a situation where, in conjunction with the investors, they can achieve success.

The important thing to understand here is that they don't have the money and it is possible that they won't.

Knowing the difference between the two can seriously change the outcome of the equity you will have to invest into the newly formed company, so be sure to understand which type of PEG you are dealing with. I am not saying that speaking to a PEG with a dry fund is a bad idea. On the contrary, they can be just as lucrative and the earn-out achievable. The best question to ask to determine which type they are, is to ask them directly who their investors are and whether the fund is already in place. If so, how much is in the fund and over what period of time will this fund need to be invested? A good place to start is the PEG's website. If there are no companies listed in their portfolio, this may be a sign that it is a dry fund.

Finally, there is one last type of PEG. I call this the true "private" type, formally known as a "family office," truly one family's or one person's money. These investors do regularly offer 100 percent cash up front and no equity in a new company. These *family offices* are not interested in selling their portfolio companies in three to seven years; instead, they want to maintain and grow their companies. The buyers are very strategic and specific in the types of companies they look to purchase. They, in many respects, are the ideal buyer for someone who wishes to exit immediately with cash in hand.

Many TSPs receive unsolicited emails from PEGs asking if they are interested in selling. While it is always fun to take a call to learn more, this is not the way to get the best offer. If one PEG is interested, many others are likely to be as well.

> **Risk of failure:** Low—PEGs usually have a formula. If the LOI is signed, they are full steam ahead with their due diligence

and legal team. Again, barring any showstoppers during due diligence, these transactions have a high close rate.

Timeline: Length can vary depending on the size and complexity of the transaction. The contract can be lengthy. Most deals are completed within four months of signing the LOI.

Payout: Cash + earn-out + equity in new company. Earn-out period is one to two years. Return on equity investment is three to seven years depending on the age of the fund.

ROBERT INSIGHT:

After understanding more about each of the buyer types, Robert decided that he might be able to garner a higher price for his company if he looked outside his normal network of competitors and complementary partners. Robert reviewed many press releases about how private equity firms were entering more and more into the technology services space and at lower revenue points. The low interest rates for a number of years had created a large supply of private money that was looking for a good home. Traditionally, PEGs offered a lower price for companies than strategic buyers, but that tide was starting to turn as more and more PEGs were trying to purchase technology firms. This was not a buyer he knew, so Robert decided he would use an M&A advisor to help him seek out these buyers.

UNDERSTANDING THE STRATEGIC VS. THE FINANCIAL BUYER

Understanding the objectives and goals of these two separate buyer types is key to achieving optimal success in your own exit strategy. Research shows that each buyer type will value qualities like strength of management team, intellectual property, and revenue composition differently. Therefore, depending on your strengths as an organization, understanding these differences will help determine which buyer may provide better terms. Generally, these two buyers compensate owners differently, with financial buyers providing more long-term upside, and strategic buyers providing stronger certainty to the final outcome via cash and a note payable for the majority of the sales price.

While you may decide that one type of buyers is more aligned with your personal exit goals, including both in your bidding process with a broker to assist you is advantageous, as we will see below. And while you may have an obvious buyer in mind, your broker will often introduce buyers you've never heard of.

STRATEGIC BUYERS OR TRADE BUYERS

In the M&A world, it is often said that strategic or trade buyers pay higher valuations than financial buyers. Is it because they are less savvy or simply an irrational buyer? No, neither and actually quite the contrary. Strategic buyers have a much better understanding of the companies they purchase, as well as the synergistic value the acquisition will achieve. Because they are either a competitor or have a very thorough understanding for the products you sell and the customers you serve, they typically know where to look to find the unpolished gems. They also know how to increase value by upselling and cross-selling between your customer base and theirs.

A strategic buyer is usually a larger company already in your industry: A competitor, a vendor, or someone who has a complementary business and is looking for an add-on company to increase its customer base, geographic reach, or services. A strategic buyer can also be a customer. They are most concerned with how the acquisition fits with their company's goals. They are evaluating your business based on what it can be with them operating it. While the financial condition of your company is important, it is not the primary motivator for the acquisition. They are evaluating how much more of their products and services they can sell if they add your company to the mix. A strategic buyer looks to accomplish the following:

- Reduce competition.
- Increase presence in a geographic market.
- Add to or increase a current vertical focus or niche.
- Acquire strategic or complementary IP.
- Acquire experienced employees.
- Eliminate redundant positions, facilities, or costs.

Strategic buyers typically pay more, especially if involved in a competitive situation with a financial buyer. That's not to say they will begin with a low-ball offer, but a competitive bidding situation will get them to increase their offer. On the whole, they are more savvy than a financial buyer because of their similar industry experience.

For the most part, strategic buyers are motivated by different factors than financial buyers. They have less of a need for a management team, marketing team, or administrative team since they have their own personnel to fill those positions. They come with their own infrastructure, so they don't need yours. And they usually have a robust set of policies and procedures around their selling and marketing process. If you feel you are light in any of these areas but have a strong customer list that fills a geographic or vertical void, a strategic buyer is a great fit.

Financial buyer

A financial buyer is primarily interested in the return on their investment and usually little else. Typically, a PEG will evaluate your business based on how profitable you are and how reliable that profit stream is. They are interested in cash flow. They may merge the target acquisition with similar companies, thereby creating economies of scale, or keep the company as a separately running entity. It really depends on what will work best for their company.

Financial buyers are investors, not company operators, and therefore they look for companies that have a solid management team that will stay intact until they can sell for a profit. Attributes such as the percentage of recurring revenue and customer retention rates are high on their list. The goals of the financial buyer are as follows:

- Maintaining a high customer satisfaction rate or low churn rate.
- Internal rate of return between 20 and 30 percent.
- Increase cash flow by growing revenue or cutting cost.
- Economies of scale by combining companies.
- Investment that can be sold within three to seven years for a considerable profit.

They play the buy-low, sell-high game and look for a five-year return on investment at a minimum. They are under pressure to hit a target return percentage on the money under management, which limits what they can pay for a company. Because they are driven by Internal Rate of Return (IRR) and return targets, the amount they are willing to pay will be predominately based on an EBITDA multiple, forecasted performance, and the IRR that they need to hit. They will use this to calculate the purchase price. So, while they may pay less due to their constraints as noted above, their outcome in a deal is more certain.

In addition to the IRR that financial buyers must achieve, they also can't always create economies of scale like strategic buyers do. Unless they are purchasing multiple companies with similar client needs, they cannot benefit from the operational synergies that frequently result from strategic deals. This operational synergy generally results from cost reduction of redundant personnel and infrastructure or cross-market revenue growth.

Unlike strategic buyers, price is a very important consideration as it ultimately affects the return on their investment. If they can't buy you for the price they want, they will find another target company, often times in a different industry. Financial return is their ultimate objective, and the industry they invest in is secondary, so they can be more selective.

Financial buyers typically purchase the assets of the company which then they use to create a new company. The seller then will have an equity investment in this *new* company to keep them committed. This can lead to a nice return on investment or a second sale, assuming the team ensures that the company remains well run and profitable. It is almost always a good idea to include financial buyers in your target buyers list. First, having this kind of buyer helps with deal discipline and pacing. Because they purchase many companies, as many as a dozen in one year, they have a process that is well paced. As a result, financial buyers tend to have an excellent handle on the structure and timing of a deal. They know what a standard transaction looks like, exactly what the next steps are, and how long they should take. They know how a normal NDA looks, when to submit one, what needs to be in a data room for confidential information (they have their own), and how to structure an LOI. And because they are usually under pressure to put capital to use within a tight timeframe, having these PEGs on your buyer list will keep the process on track and moving forward. It will also keep your strategic buyers moving along if they know a financial buyer is in the picture.

Finally, not only does including financial buyers help with deal discipline, it helps provide deal certainty—because those buyers will always be there at a price, which gives you a bit of a safety net if your deal with a strategic buyer falls through.

Strategic vs. Financial Overview

Buyer Category	Strategic	Financial
Looks like:	Competitors, vendors, customers	PEG, high wealth Individuals
Reason for acquisition:	Extend geography, customer base, eliminate competition, cross sell	Need to spend fund to achieve returns quickly, cross sell*
Purchase price:	Higher	Lower
Willingness to negotiate price:	Higher	Lower
Deal structure: **	Cash + Note + Earn - out	Cash + Equity + Earn – out
Deal certainty:	Lower	Higher
Speed of deal closure:	Slower	Faster

Fig.1.12

* Financial buyers can sometimes appear as strategic buyers, especially if buying a platform company and then acquiring additional companies to round out services and cross-sell to customers.

** In both cases, an all-cash offer is achievable based on the strength of not only quantitative but also qualitative metrics.

QUANTITATIVE VS. QUALITATIVE METRICS

When presenting your company to a prospective buyer, you should clearly lay out the attributes that make your business a good investment. Financial and strategic buyers have different ways of evaluating a potential acquisition company and they assign different priorities to the evaluation process. While each buyer type will clearly have a unique perspective, it is helpful to understand the common attributes that all buyers look for in an acquisition and also the differences between buyer types. (See the chart below.)

It is important to highlight a mix of quantitative and qualitative measures when presenting data in your initial confidential information memorandum (CIM). While the average buyer is nearly 1.5X more likely to favor quantitative metrics, many strategic buyers will place as much emphasis on the qualitative metrics.

Quantitative vs. Qualitative Metrics

	Strategic	Financial
Quantitative metrics		
Revenue growth	X	X
Gross profit margin growth	X	X
EBITDA growth		X
Revenue per employee	X	
Recurring revenue %	X	X
Qualitative metrics		
Size and quality of client base	X	X
Quality/experience of management		X
Unique value proposition		X
Industry vertical	X	X
Sales and marketing strength		
Core sustainability - no single points of failure	X	X

Fig.1.13

Financial or *quantitative* buyers care about margins and growth above all other metrics because many times they do not have the ability to create economies of scale or cross-sell between multiple companies in their portfolio. As we mentioned above, their objective is to achieve a predefined IRR and to create value in their portfolio for their investors. That said, the quality and experience of management is important but not as critical as the overall quantity metrics.

For strategic buyers, the *qualitative* metrics matter, meaning that the profile of your client base and the quality of your IP are more important than your own revenue or gross profit future growth. While this may seem initially counterintuitive, it isn't. They can take advantage of economies of scale, cross-selling additional IP to an already existing customer base, and thus be able to expand their vertical reach by potentially buying a complementary vertical. Selling into a new customer base or geography can easily outperform the revenue or growth as a standalone entity. Furthermore, additional gross profit margins can at times be realized directly from a vendor by hitting certain sales thresholds, thus allowing for lower vendor-based license fees/purchase prices. A simple 5 percent increase in software margin due to increased purchasing power can potentially drop straight to the bottom line.

When preparing your company for a sale, *qualitative* metrics are just as important to highlight to buyers as *quantitative* ones. The quality of your clients translates directly to the value of your company as well as to the amount of recurring revenue. One could easily say that focusing on your qualitative metrics can greatly affect the outcome of your quantitative numbers.

In Part II, you will learn about 8 key valuation drivers, many of which are qualitative in nature. By taking the assessment you will be able to determine which buyer type, based upon our current score, could be a better buyer for your company. Tailoring your profile to highlight the strengths that meet the demands of different types of buyers is an important step that, in the end, can bring a significantly higher valuation.

The Deal Dynamics

Most sellers are interested in receiving the best possible price for their businesses—well okay, duh! Obtaining the highest sales price, however, should not always be the *only* priority when selling your company. In most cases, sellers are also concerned about the terms of the sale, the culture fit, the future health of their company, and how the business sale will impact their lives and employees' lives going forward.

While receiving an all-cash purchase is nirvana for most sellers, the reality is that 95 percent of all deals have some sort of earn-out or extended payout. There will always be sellers who, for certain reasons, will need a fast sale with an immediate departure from the company. A seller with these motivations may be willing to sell to the first qualified buyer who comes along. They may also be willing to accept a lower sales price rather than holding out for a higher offer with an extended earn-out period.

Other sellers may be slower to exit the company or may be happy to continue on in the business after taking some money off the table to set aside for future retirement. Often these owners are motivated to stay involved in the company and see their legacy remain strong or to work in a leadership role or as a consultant to the new owner for a period of time. This is many times a great opportunity to increase your skills in a large company. The point is to be clear which category you fall into before beginning your process.

Deal timeline

Now that we have covered your personal *exit* timeline, let's discuss specifically the *deal* timeline. Everyone asks, "How long does a typical deal take?" The answer is there is no such thing as a "typical" deal. Each of my company sales took different amounts of time due to the type of buyer and the complexity of the contracts. My first company sale was to my partner and was completed in three months. It took one month to come up with a price that we were both okay with and the next two months to hash out an agreement. My second sale, to a strategic competitor, took only four months—two months to hash out a deal structure and two months to work through due diligence. In both of these transactions, the buyer was familiar with the industry, knew the business they were buying, and had a relationship with the seller, so the trust level was high. This lessened the deal timeline considerably.

At a reasonable pace, with more than one offer to choose from, a seller can anticipate a deal to take anywhere from six to nine months; especially if it is overlapping with yearend or vacation and holiday schedules.

SIX STAGES OF A SELLER'S TRANSACTION PROCESS

Note that there are much more complex versions of this diagram, which you can find in textbooks and online, but I have condensed the process into six stages to keep it simple and easy to explain.

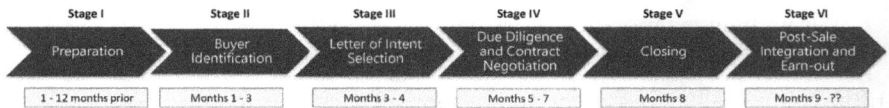

Stage I	Stage II	Stage III	Stage IV	Stage V	Stage VI
Preparation	Buyer Identification	Letter of Intent Selection	Due Diligence and Contract Negotiation	Closing	Post-Sale Integration and Earn-out
1 - 12 months prior	Months 1 - 3	Months 3 - 4	Months 5 - 7	Months 8	Months 9 - ??

Fig.1.14

Let's review each stage in more detail:

Stage I – Preparation

This stage is focused on getting your house in order and finding the broker of choice. It can take as little as one month if you have your financials and other documentation in order, or it can take as much as a year if you need to restate your financials, document your IP, and shore up your contracts. Below is a list of financial and nonfinancial related documents you should gather during this initial preparation phase.

Having your financial statements in order is crucial to beginning the deal process. Be sure to focus on the following:

- Three years of historical financial statements (B/S, P&L, and C/F) prepared with compliance with generally accepted accounting principles (GAAP).
  - If you are recognizing prepaid revenue upon receipt, instead of deferring it over the period that the software or services are being rendered, now is the time to alter that accounting method. At its simplest form, don't recognize 12 months of SaaS revenue in the month it is received. Yes, this seems obvious, but so many people do this because they don't have the mechanism within their accounting system to automatically defer the revenue and flip it to the appropriate months in the contract period. If the income also includes services, the guidelines around revenue recognition have recently been overhauled, so be sure to check with your accountant on proper matching of revenue and expense.

  - The same is true for expenses. If you are incurring a bill from your vendor for 12 months of premier support, be sure to amortize it over 12 months, and not to expense it in the month you paid it. Again, pretty obvious, but a lot of people don't do this, so it's worth mentioning.

  - Proper matching of revenue and expenses in the applicable month is key. If you are still preparing your financials on a cash basis, now is the time to make the change to accrual. Otherwise there is no proper matching of revenue and expenses, and that will surely stop the due diligence process dead in its tracks until a formal review of your financial statements is performed.

- Remove all personal assets from the balance sheet: cars, vacation homes, and other "toys."
- Group all personal benefits into accounts that are easily identifiable. Also, include any other "personal" bonuses, profit sharing, and items that would not normally be paid after the sale. You will need these items for your adjusted EBITDA calculation.

- Properly account for expenses between cost of goods sold and below the line so that your gross profit margin on sales is accurate.
- Properly account for sales and marketing expenses and be able to segment them in your financials. Buyers always want to know how much you spend on sales and marketing.

If you have never had an audit, review, or even an externally prepared compilation, now would be a great time to get one under your belt. While it is very possible to sell your company without one, (i.e., you have a very savvy accounting department that is run by a degreed accountant, who ideally has had a career in public accounting), generally you will instill more confidence in your would-be buyer if you have been through a compilation, at a minimum.

Other important company business documents that should be readied for a buyer, and ideally uploaded to a secure document-sharing site, are as follows:

- Three years of projections
- Complete list of fixed assets and location
- Last three years of tax returns; corporate, payroll, sales tax, property tax, etc.
- 401(k) or ESOP Plan documents
- Updated organization chart
- All lease agreements with landlord or assets (i.e., copier lease, postage machine, etc.)
- Example of customer agreements or contracts
- Complete customer and vendor lists
- Major vendor agreements for products you resell
- Complete list of employees, titles and salaries, locations
- Standard employment agreement
- All signed NDAs with employees and independent contractors
- Human resources manual

Unless you have a close relationship with a broker already (more on that in Part III), you should plan on taking two to three months at a minimum to select who you will use. You can use this time to review data on their websites, listen to past webinars if available, check references, etc. Eventually you will feel comfortable with a couple of brokers, at which point you can begin to make some calls. Obtain copies of their broker agreements and fee schedules in advance and ask to speak to people they have represented in the past. Do not rely on "tombstones" presented on their websites. While they may look impressive, you cannot assume your broker (the person you are going to work with) had any involvement in that particular transaction. If you like one in particular, ask specifically about their personal involvement—see the checklist for broker interview questions in Part III. Be sure to allow time for your legal counsel to review one or more broker agreements before you make your final selection.

As indicated above, this stage could take as little as a month or two, or it could take up to a year. The difference in time is mostly about getting your financial statement in order.

Stage II – Buyer Identification

This stage is all about creating your initial compelling story via a blind profile or CIM and identifying buyers that would be interested in your company. Before your broker sends out feelers to prospective buyers, you should make sure you have prepared a "no contact list" and a "carve-out list" of people your broker should not communicate with. A "no contact list" are those companies you do not want to solicit for any reason, whether that is size, location, reputation, or other (i.e., a close competitor whom you don't want to tip off that you are on the market).

Second, if applicable, create a carve-out list, which is a list of prospects you have spoken to already and who have shown interest in your company and with whom you can continue to negotiate without the help of your broker. This might be other shareholders, joint venture partners, or other interested parties. Not all brokers allow for carve-outs—buyers to whom you will not pay a success fee on because you have already begun negotiations or talks with them. If you have carve-outs, you should negotiate this point early and upfront to avoid conflict later. You may only be able to carve them out completely with no success fee or more realistically be able to negotiate a reduced fee should one of these become your actual buyer.

If you are using an advisor, as soon as your CIM or offering is nicely packaged, they will begin looking for appropriate buyers on your behalf. The more attractive your company is, the sooner interested buyers will appear. Ideally, this stage will take no more than 90 days but it can stretch much longer if you are doing this yourself or if you don't have the appeal that buyers are looking for. A good advisor will try to corral interested parties into a small timeframe so as to keep everyone moving at the same pace.

The following activities should take place in this stage:

- Create blind profile, CIM, or executive summary of your company. Be sure your broker has a clear understanding of your value proposition.
- Prepare a PowerPoint or keynote presentation to highlight the important aspects of your company—more on this in Part III.
- Determine company value through external assessments or formal valuation.
- Review the buyer list with your advisor.
- Determine if buyer websites like Axial and BankerBay are a good fit to upload your profile.
- Finalize the NDA you will be using for buyers. Your broker may have one, but you should review it in advance.
- Once interest with buyers has been developed, begin initial conversations for fit regarding compatibility, culture, and post-sale transition plans (will you remain or exit). Part III contains a list of questions to be used in this process.
- Evaluate strengths and weaknesses of each prospective buyer and settle on your top three.

Stage II, if using a broker, will take up to two months. If selling on your own, this could take longer, upwards of six months to a year. Be sure to minimize this timeline as much as possible, as those who issued you an IOI early on don't want to wait around for months while you round up another IOI or LOI.

Stage III – Letter of Intent Selection

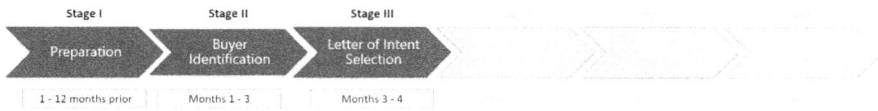

Stage I	Stage II	Stage III
Preparation	Buyer Identification	Letter of Intent Selection
1 - 12 months prior	Months 1 - 3	Months 3 - 4

This stage is about finding that one buyer you feel most comfortable with and who is willing to pay you what you are worth. If you are running a process with an M&A advisor, you should have more than one to choose from. After prospective buyers sign the NDA and review in more detail your company information, they may start initially with an Indication of Interest (IOI). Some buyers, however, skip this and go straight to a Letter of Intent (LOI). (See more on the difference between these two in the next section.) During this stage you should concentrate on the following:

- Get on IOI or LOI from each prospective buyer.
- Travel to meet your top three.
- Receive and review final LOIs.
- Review deal points in the LOIs with your attorney.
- Request proof of funds.
- Commit to one.

Getting a signed LOI is a pretty exciting event. It feels like a validation of everything you have ever worked for and created as a business owner, and you should savor the moment—but only for a moment. From a psychological standpoint, this is when many sellers mentally check out and "go to the beach." Yes, it may have taken a lot of time and effort to get to this point, but *this is only the start*. You cannot relax now that you have a signed LOI. It is imperative that you maintain your focus on the business and not take your foot off the gas.

This is the time to continue to run the business as if it isn't being acquired. And the stronger your management team, the easier this is to do. With so much emphasis, up to this point, on finding a viable buyer, many company's financial performance suffers during the period between creating the CIM and signing the LOI and the closing date. This can make it hard to play catch-up once the deal is closed and to achieve any stated earn-out for the year. If sales or profits go down in the quarter preceding or during the sale so will your purchase price, or worse, the deal may get stalled until sales meet projections.

Do not hold back on normal operating expenses such as insurance or maintenance renewals, regularly scheduled employee raises, or bonuses. If someone leaves or is terminated, hire like you normally would. If your customers have contracts that are up for renewal, stay on top of it, or if anything, be a little more assertive to get them signed in and locked down for another year. If you do have annual agreements with customers that require renewal, the buyer will request a renewal schedule. If the schedule is not up to date and many customers are lapsed, this can delay the closing until they become current, especially if they represent at least 10 to 20 percent of your contracts.

The end of Stage III should culminate in signing one LOI that you are most comfortable with. Ideally, you have more than one to choose from, but even if only one looks promising, the points below are still valid. Comfort can be defined as a *number* of things, not just meeting your monetary goals on paper. They actually have to be realized as well. Here are just a few to think about to help you determine if this LOI's offer can truly be realized:

- How likely is it that you will be able to achieve the earn-out? Is it overreaching or unobtainable without significant assistance from the buyer?
- Will your employees excel in the new organization and remain with the company?
- Can the cultures combine without issue?
- Is the noncompete reasonable should you decide not to stay with the company?

- What is the buyer's ability to fund the deal and still have sufficient capital for future growth?

Stage IV – due diligence and contract negotiation

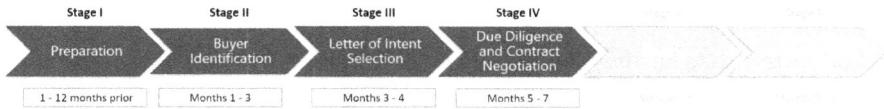

When I received the LOI for my last company, the buyer said to me, "Now starts the ugly due diligence process. You will feel like you are going through the worst IRS audit of your life." He wasn't kidding.

Once the LOI is signed, due diligence will start immediately. As part of your readiness in the preparation stage, you should have all the appropriate documents ready to hand over to your potential buyer via an online document storage application. The resource section of this book provides an extensive due diligence list for you to use, but each buyer will have a slight variation of this. Get these documents together in advance. Your planning and preparation will pay off in this stage. If you don't do the work ahead of time, you will be buried in due diligence requests while simultaneously negotiating specifics in your agreement, which will leave you both exhausted and overwhelmed. It is an exhausting time regardless, so don't make it worse for yourself by not being prepared.

Typically, all LOIs have a period of time that allows the buyer to perform their due diligence and where the seller cannot entertain or negotiate other LOIs. If you don't have all your documentation ready, the buyer may either request an extension or become less interested in your company. Neither is ideal, so I cannot stress enough the importance of preplanning.

Your broker, or you, should recommend a weekly call with objectives that should be completed during that week. This keeps everyone on the same timeline and helps prevent the due diligence from falling off schedule. Everyone should be working toward a close date, which should be defined as soon as the due diligence process begins.

Many buyers also like to begin contract negotiations during due diligence if their initial discovery is going well. PE firms and active strategic buyers often use the same contracts over and over, so they have them handy. Expect the agreement to be anywhere from 25 to 50 pages long. You will be supplementing this with additional disclosures where warranted. Do not underestimate the potential complexity of the purchase agreement and wait until all due diligence is done before you send it to your attorney. Many inexperienced sellers think that all they have to do now is review the purchase agreement and send it to counsel for a few comments and it is a done deal. Oh, if it could only be that simple!

Contracts and agreements typically used in a transaction:

- Asset/stock purchase agreement
- Noncompete agreement
- Promissory note
- Transition services agreement (if not remaining for more than 90 days)
- Employment contract
- Lease assignment

If this is the first transaction your buyer has ever done, they may prefer to wait until the majority of due diligence is done before beginning contracts so as to save legal costs in case the deal falls through in the due diligence phase. However, that is not necessarily in your best interest. By not simultaneously working on contracts during due diligence you can lose valuable time should the transaction not proceed. If you have other interested buyers, they may not wait five months while you go through due diligence only to determine you could not agree on the legal aspects of the deal.

If you are dealing with a delay of four to six weeks, that strategy can work, but usually not for longer periods of time without your buyers either getting wind of a failed transaction or feeling like they are not your primary choice. If the process with the original buyer falls apart after a few months, it just may be better to go off the market for a period of time while you "work on building revenue." This strategy can work, but it does require you to stay off the market for a period of time so buyers view you in a "new light." Again, to potentially avoid this, get contract negotiations going while you are in due diligence even if your buyer is hesitant. A good broker will help with this.

At this stage, you have probably done some investigating of the buyer as well. Your broker should do this for you in the initial stages, but you may want to take this one step further by talking to former owners of other companies that the buyer purchased. This can give you comfort that the buyer follows through as promised.

If the buyer is new to your industry and this is their first transaction, this can become more problematic, as you are under an NDA not to discuss the potential transaction. In the situation where the buyer has made multiple transactions, you may find someone you know well who can give you some insight into how past acquisition integrations have gone. If you have an inside connection that you trust, it is also a good time to find out what the standard employee benefits are, to both validate their benefits and to compare them to your own—for potential adjustments to your EBITDA numbers. You can do this tactfully without disclosing the potential transaction or violating any NDAs.

Even with the consent of the buyer, be cautious when speaking to a seller of a recent transaction. The previous seller may not be in a good place "mentally" to give you an accurate assessment of how the acquiring company is run. On the positive side, they may still be basking in the glory of selling their company for a great price and only have wonderful things to say, or they may hesitate to say anything negative about the owners for fear of consequences. On the flip side, they may be so overwhelmed with integration issues that they cannot yet see the value of the merger (aside from the money aspects). You will have to navigate this one carefully and determine for yourself if the picture that is being painted is an accurate one.

Many buyers want to have a physical inspection of the premises before they sign the deal. Since many times they are buying the assets—furniture, fixtures, and equipment—it is a part of their natural due diligence checklist.

Stage V – Closing and "Wealth Creation"

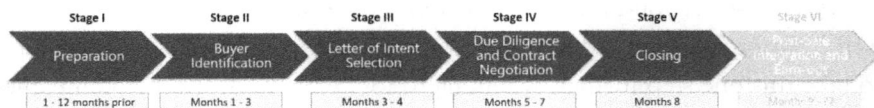

Stage I	Stage II	Stage III	Stage IV	Stage V	Stage VI
Preparation	Buyer Identification	Letter of Intent Selection	Due Diligence and Contract Negotiation	Closing	Post-Sale Integration and Earn-out
1 - 12 months prior	Months 1 - 3	Months 3 - 4	Months 5 - 7	Months 8	Month 9 - 12

By now you should be confident that the deal will get done and be well aware of your buyer's ability to finance the deal. Again, if using a broker, he/she will have already done this due diligence for you. Most buyers have a timeline they like to follow. While this may slip (all three of my company sales did), both the buyer and the seller work toward a definitive close date. Tying a closing date to an upcoming conference or big customer event can help both parties, as there may be media advantages to announcing the acquisition.

While missing closing dates is not uncommon, you don't want it to happen several times. At some point, you may get "deal fatigue." Deal fatigue happens when both parties get exhausted from the constant back and forth and one or both of the parties question if it is really worth the effort. If you are having such a hard time agreeing now, it begs the question of how difficult it will be to work together later. It is also at this point where conversations can get hot and heavy and one or both parties may threaten to back out.

During one such heated exchange, I vividly remember saying, "I don't need to sell my company to you or to anyone." The buyer, in turn, responded, "and I don't need to buy your company." After a brief silent pause on the phone, we both hit the reset button and continued negotiating on a less confrontational point. Nerves can run high during the tail-end of a transaction, but if the deal is worth doing, it will get done. Ideally, you don't want to come to such a point, especially if you have to work closely with the buyer after the deal. This is truly where a *broker* can save the deal and keep everyone moving in the same direction—without an exchange of words that can never be retracted and may damage the relationship going forward.

The last 10 days prior to your close will undoubtedly be your most stressful. Not only are you finalizing the last of contract changes or red lines, you and your team are assembling all of your final representations and warranties, and you and the buyer are finalizing working capital amounts.

If the funding of your transaction will happen simultaneously with the close, the buyer will prepare a mock closing statement, usually 10 days prior to the close. Last minute adjustments like cash, changes in AR, changes in AP (that will be assumed by the buyer), and accruals for payroll and benefits will be calculated at the last moment. But placeholders and line items for such things should be agreed to in advance. Your broker should also supply you with their success fees, which are typically paid out of the proceeds and are included in the settlement statement.

The closing day is either euphoric or anticlimactic but most likely a mix of both. Yes, the long marathon is done and the funds have hit the bank, but for some sellers, they have been working through the final number on the purchase agreement for what seems like an eternity so that when the funds actually hit the bank, they are just plain relieved and maybe even numb.

You should *celebrate*, even if only for a day. Hopefully, you have achieved the financial freedom you had planned, and you have never before seen so many zeros in your bank account. Savor the moment, take a screen print of your bank account, share it with your family if appropriate, and pat yourself on the back. You have done it!

Wealth creation for others.

Many owners want to share in this wealth creation with members of their management team and the coworkers who have helped them achieve their success. Many actually feel obligated to disburse funds to key employees as part of the sale. Figuring out what percentage of your proceeds to use, and then how to divvy that amongst your team, can be a very emotional and daunting task. Cash disbursements can be accomplished via bonuses, profit-sharing contributions, stay-bonuses, future earn-outs, or a combination of these. While every seller will approach this differently, you will ultimately do what you feel is "right" in your heart. Still, you will want to speak to your attorney and CPA before making any disbursements.

Look into the legal documents, such as a formal waiver and release document. These documents should be drawn up in advance of any such "distributions" to employees, as they will allow you to protect the remaining company (assuming an asset sale) against any future employee actions. Many releases, depending on the state, require you to give the employee a certain amount of time to review the release, and then again a certain number of days to retract the agreement should the employee change their mind. This becomes a timing issue, more so in a stock sale as you may want to incur the expenses as part of the closing settlement statement. In an asset sale, you can do this afterwards because the company is still yours and you can disburse funds as you please, but the timing of signing and disbursing funds is still important so be sure to check with your attorney.

An employee waiver/release form will state the amount of compensation the person will receive on the close of the transaction and any specific duties or boundaries they must adhere to prior to the transaction closing. You may need the assistance of key employees to finalize due diligence, or the new owners may want to interview key personnel prior to the close. This is a great way to incentivize management to help with due diligence and thus have a stake in the outcome. It also stops key personnel from leaving before the deal is done. Of course, the financial benefit will only be rewarded if the transaction closes.

Examples of items to include regarding the signing of the waiver are as follows:

- Reiterating the sensitive nature of the transaction and that no disclosure of the transaction other than to a spouse is allowed.
- For a period of XX months, no disclosure of the bonus being received as part of the transaction is allowed—since you may be paying this bonus outside of your legal entity in some cases and therefore any NDAs signed with the company would not apply.
- No social media announcements, other than as directed by the company, can be made using a personal account.
- They must assist in the tasks of preparing due diligence requests as required by the owners.
- They must remain an employee of the company through the sale transaction or (state period) in order to receive the bonus.

Again, I would highly recommend speaking to counsel while you are working on agreements.

If you are working with a broker or have a buyer already identified, Stage II to Stage V can transpire in as little as four months, but on average it takes six to eight months, especially if stretched over a holiday season. Deals under $50 million should typically be completed within a year. Extending beyond that usually means there is a hitch in the due diligence, or the buyer has lost interest in the deal. If that's the case, it is best to walk away from the deal, even if it is your only offer. Otherwise, it will drain you mentally and distract you from running the business efficiently.

Stage VI – Post-sale Integration and Earn-out

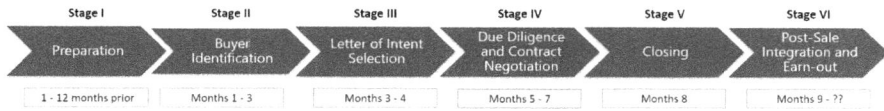

Stage I	Stage II	Stage III	Stage IV	Stage V	Stage VI
Preparation	Buyer Identification	Letter of Intent Selection	Due Diligence and Contract Negotiation	Closing	Post-Sale Integration and Earn-out
1 - 12 months prior	Months 1 - 3	Months 3 - 4	Months 5 - 7	Months 8	Months 9 - ??

As if finalizing due diligence, clearing all red lines, and detailing all final representation and warranties weren't enough, you should *also* be working on what happens the day after the close. A transition team from the buyer should begin putting together a timeline with dates and milestones, and members from your team should be incorporated as soon as possible. There are occasions where the announcement of a transaction is made prior to the funding date due to the size and complexity of the transaction. This is done to help communicate a change to employees, customers, and vendors and to prepare for the post-sale immediate transition.

Buyers who have purchased prior companies may already have a process for what happens next. But if this is new to your buyer, here are some items that need to be ready for the day after the close:

- Press release to the pubic
- Separate notice to your customers and vendors
- Presentation to the team by the new buyers
- New employment contracts – if an asset sale

- New NDAs for subcontractors or close parties
- New employee benefit enrollment
- Transition timeline with dates and milestones
- Transfer of lease
- New vendor agreements if assignment is not possible
- Transfer of ownership of bank accounts, or creation of new ones

If the companies are in the same geographic location, a separate company event bringing together both teams is often a good idea. If not, having photos and bios of each team member to share with the buyer will help get everyone familiar with their new teammates. Some buyers do a great job of this and others don't, so don't be surprised if you have to coach your buyer on good team integration techniques.

The integration of two companies can take up to one year to complete, but most of the heavy lifting is done within the first six months, so be prepared for a busy post-sale life. Be sure to review the bonus chapter on *What are buyers thinking* for additional tips. Post-merger integrations are far more complex than described above and are beyond the scope of this book, so be sure to look for other sources to help with the transition.

ROBERT INSIGHT:

Robert had seen from the sale of his consulting division how practiced the buyer was at post-sale integrations. A press release was approved in advance by both the buyer and seller, communications were ready to be sent to the customers, and customers were already being transitioned into the new billing system. On the day of the close, the lead partner and the head of the HR department were on hand for the initial announcement, and they spent a couple of days in the office meeting with each person individually and reviewing with them their new employment contract, the transition of their insurance and other benefits, and also the additional benefit they would be receiving as part of a larger organization. Everyone had their picture taken, and a picture and a brief bio was immediately posted on the buyer's website, so that their existing team knew all about their new teammates. Everyone received new computers with the new security and protocols explained for both documents and email storage. The process was extremely well organized and made all the employees who were transitioning feel welcome and part of a new and larger family. In retrospect, Robert realized how important this was to the happiness of his former employees and the completion of his earn-out. Robert was also realistic in that once he sold his cloud company, he would no longer be able to dictate future plans as he was not staying with the company. He hoped his new buyer would be just as prepared!

What Is an IOI and an LOI?

In the Resources section of this document are examples of a Letter of Intent (LOI) and Indication of Interest (IOI). While the two appear to be very similar, there are differences between these documents and their respective purpose during the M&A transaction process. Let's review both below.

An IOI is a nonbinding, formally prepared letter written by a buyer and addressed to the seller. Its purpose is to express a genuine interest in purchasing a company. Typically, sellers receive an IOI after an NDA or other type of confidentiality agreement. An IOI should provide guidance regarding approximate target company valuation, and it should also outline the general conditions for getting a deal done. The items you can typically expect to find in an IOI are:

- Approximate price range; can be expressed in a dollar value range (i.e., five to 10 million dollars), or a number ± a percentage, or stated as a multiple of EBITDA (i.e., 3-5X EBITDA)
- Buyer's general availability of funds and sources of financing
- Necessary due diligence items and a rough estimate of the due diligence timeline
- Potential proposed elements of the transaction structure (asset, equity, leveraged transaction, cash vs. equity, etc.)
- List of contingencies

Think of an IOI as the very first written offer for your company. It's usually based on limited information—the buyer typically hasn't had a chance to visit your company and conduct any serious due diligence. Usually at this point all they have seen is either your CIM or a formal PowerPoint with your initial information.

An IOI should help weed out "lookie-loos" and ensure you only invest time and resources with buyers who value your business within your range, have adequate industry expertise, and have the resources to purchase you. This is particularly important if your company has many buyers expressing interest as it helps you to determine the most credible ones.

The LOI is a more formal document than the IOI and it outlines a final firm price and deal structure for your company. Buyers have had more time to review your financials and other pertinent data. Instead of offering a general price range, the LOI gives the final bid for the company in exact dollars or as a firm multiple of EBITDA.

The LOI is also the point at which buyers seek to lock up your company for an exclusive period of time in which the buyer can conduct a full due diligence process before purchasing the company. If you accept and execute the LOI, it most likely will prohibit you as the seller from speaking with other buyers—whereas an IOI doesn't. So be sure you are happy with the LOI and that the main points of the offer are covered.

Additional items that you might find in an LOI:

- An actual purchase price amount with +/- of a percentage of the offer
- Actual transaction structure—asset vs. stock purchase. Cash at close, note amounts, equity into a new company, etc.
- Reserves or escrow amounts
- Definition of how working capital will be calculated
- Management retention plan and the role of the equity owner(s) post-transaction
- Specifics as to the noncompete (i.e., years and general language)
- Timeframe to close the transaction

I mentioned this in Part I, but it is worth another mention here: Just because you have received a signed LOI, do not be tempted to believe that the deal is done and that all that needs to be completed at this point is the paperwork. While this is an exciting time, lots of dollars can move one way or the other after the signing of the LOI—which if not in your favor may cause you to walk away from the deal. It is not necessary for a company to issue you an IOI in advance of an LOI, especially if the buyer knows you well or is a competitor. It may also be the case that you're working with a broker that prefers to go straight for the LOI.

The important thing to remember is that there are many ways to get a deal done. Some deals obtain IOIs, where other ones just receive LOIs. The IOI, while nonbinding, helps sellers refine their buyer list, compare buyers' terms, and review a summary of the buyers' intent. The IOI, though, is exactly what it says—an Indication of Interest—and by no means is it a guarantee that a buyer will progress through the entire transaction process or move to the LOI stage.[9]

If you are selling your company without using a broker, ask the buyer for proof of funds BEFORE you sign the LOI. While it may feel awkward, this is a must. Do not worry about offending the buyer. If they are serious, they won't think twice about the request. Also, don't let the size of the company intimidate you. Ideally, you want a copy of their financials (balance sheet, income statement and cash flow)—not just the income statement, as the issues always hide on the balance sheet (i.e., not enough cash, too much debt, and high AR balances). If the cash is coming from a bank, you want proof of the capacity to fund the deal.

Finally, do not begin an extensive due diligence process without receiving an LOI in advance. If you do, you will lose considerable leverage in the selling process. Tips 88 to 100 in Part III of 100 Tips, Traps, and Tactics are worth reading in advance if you are in this stage.

ROBERT INSIGHT:

Robert was super excited when he heard that someone was interested in purchasing his consulting group. An initial due diligence list request came via an email and he began diligently putting together the documents needed by the buyer. He provided everything requested in a short amount of time and then he waited, and waited, and waited. Robert didn't want to appear to be too pushy or too eager, or frankly too desperate, so he sent out a few feeler emails to see if any "additional information was required" to keep the process moving. Finally, the buyer responded that they were busy "assessing other opportunities" and that they would get back to him as soon as they could. Robert read the email and his heart skipped a beat. What if they were just not interested? What if they were just stringing him along? He was just taking the word of his friend that they wanted to make a purchase.

It was at this point that Robert realized he didn't have a signed IOI or LOI from the buyer and yet he had provided a ton of financial information for due diligence. Robert honestly didn't know the difference between an IOI and an LOI, but he had paid enough attention to a few webinars he had attended on selling your company to know that he probably needed one of them. At this point, he contacted his attorney and asked what to do next. He was quickly counseled that no additional information should be provided without at least an IOI. Robert then crafted a carefully worded email letting the buyer know that he needed some assurance that they were serious and that an LOI was needed in order to proceed. Thankfully the buyer complied and an LOI was attached.

Typical deal structure – show me the money!

When you read a press release that a similar company sold for $9M, you naturally assume it was all cash, and that the owners were sitting on the beach somewhere drinking cocktails. And of course, you are probably a little envious. Comparing yourself to your similar companies is natural, and so is the immediate thought: "Well, if they sold for that much, so can I." Oh, if it were only that simple.

Most announcements, unless the company was purchased by a publicly traded company, don't spell out the specifics of the deal. Most deals consist of a combination of cash and other forms of consideration. That owner who sold for $9M may only be receiving $4M in cash at close after debt repayments, working capital requirements, notes and earn-outs. According to the 2016 Equiteq Buyers Research Report, 91 percent of all deals contain an earn-out. And most deals contain some combination of a note and equity investment into the new company, if it's a private equity transaction. Let's review each in detail:

Deal component breakdown

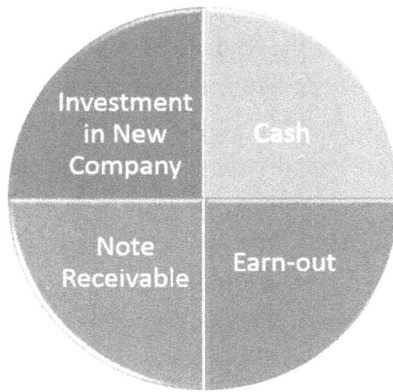

Fig.1.15

- Cash at Closing: Cash at close can represent anywhere from 50 to 75 percent of the purchase price. Of the transactions benchmarked in the last 24 months, this has been averaging around 65 percent.
- Earn-outs: Earn-outs can be one single number or broken up into a number of tranches based upon sales performance, gross profit margins, employee retention, or other metrics. They can be

measured on a quarter, biannual, or annual basis. Earn-outs range from 20 to 40 percent of proceeds and are usually paid out over a 12- to 36-month period. The average is 24 months.

- Note Receivable: A note is the closest thing to cash, which typically is paid out over a 12- to 36-month period. Most notes carry some form of interest, either fixed or tied to a prime or other metric. Notes are more common in strategic deals where the acquiring company pays out of the earnings generated by the acquisition. Notes usually turn into cash but not always. There are far too many stories of sellers accepting notes in lieu of cash with little chance they will be paid. Notes that are paid over time can help defer tax implications. Under the IRS installment sales provisions, sale proceeds from notes are taxed as the principal is paid. You will be able to collect interest if everything is properly structured along the way.

- Stock in New Company: Equity in the new company is typical in almost every PE deal. These on average range anywhere from 20 to 30 percent of the deal amount. Proceeds of this stock will only be realized once the new owners sell the company. This time period is largely dependent on how long the PE Company holds the investment. Most funds hold active investments in the five- to seven-year range. If your purchase is early in the fund, you may find yourself waiting the entire seven years, but if you are late into the fund and the PE firm is looking to sell it soon, you may be able to cash out much earlier. Stock options are also a possibility, but they are outside the scope of this book.

While the four above are the main components to a deal, many deals have an escrow component. An Escrow "hold-back" is an amount that sits in an escrow account to pay for liabilities or shortfalls in working capital that were unanticipated at the close. They are more prominent in stock deals, but they are used in asset purchases as well. The use varies by buyer. Some like the comfort of an escrow account, while others create a mountain of legalese in the document to account for contingencies. Escrow amounts are typically refunded within 12 months.

In the two examples below, we can see how these four components might be used in two types of deal structures: an asset purchase and a stock purchase.

Example 1 – Asset Sale

In this example (below) we have a strategic buyer who makes an offer to purchase the assets of the seller. As mentioned earlier, strategic buyers often incorporate notes and earn-outs into an offering.

Sample Transaction #1 - Asset Sale

Total Transaction Value: $5,000,000		Estimated Expected Payout Range	
		Low	High
Cash at closing **(1)**	60%	3,000,000	3,000,000
Earn-out **(2)**			
No earnout achieved if revenues less than $5.2M		-	
Assumes 100% earn-out achieved at over $5.5M revenue	25%		1,250,000
Payments received on note receiveable **(3)**			
Principal	15%	750,000	750,000
Interest		31,638	31,638
Gross estimated expected payout range	100%	3,781,638	5,031,638
Broker success fees (5%) paid at closing **(4)**		(250,000)	(250,000)
Net total proceeds to Seller **(5)**		**$3,531,638**	**$ 4,781,638**

Fig.1.16a

Deal details: In this example, we have three of the four deal components mentioned earlier. There is no equity being offered to the seller. In this asset sale (meaning the buyer is only acquiring the assets of the company and not the stock). *

(1) The company receives an offer for $5M (5xX EBITDA), of which 60% is cash or $3M.
(2) If the company after the sale is able to achieve $5.5M in revenue, after 12 months post transaction, they will receive their earn-out of 25%

or $1.25M. If revenues are between $5.2M and $5.5M then 50% of the earn-out is achieved. No earn-out is paid if revenues are less than $5.2M.

(3) Starting the first month after the sale and continuing for 24 months, they will receive monthly payments of principal and interest at 4% on a note receivable of $750,000 (note adjusted to prime plus X% and secured by Accounts Receivable of NewCo).

(4) The broker success fee of $250,000 will be taken out of the proceeds upon settlement.

(5) All of Seller's legal, accounting, and other out of pocket expenses are paid directly by Seller prior to closing.

In total the seller will receive between $3,531,638 and $4,781,638.

*An asset sale could have all four deal components, but in this example it does not.

Example 2 – Stock Sale

Sample Transaction #2 - Stock Sale			
Total Transaction Value: $14,000,000		Estimated Expected Payout Range	
		Low	High
Cash at closing **(1)**	48%	6,750,000	6,750,000
Escrow deposit for pre-transaction liabilities **(2)**	2%	250,000	250,000
Earn-out **(3)**			
No earnout achieved if EBITDA less than $2.6M	20%	-	
Assumes 100% earn-out achieved at $3.2M EBITDA			2,800,000
Escrow deposit not returned in low example; used to pay			
unforeseen liabilities		(250,000)	
No deduction for escrow deposit in hight example as the			
deposit was refunded after 180 days of closing assuming			
no additional liabilites discovered			
Gross estimated expected payout range		6,750,000	9,800,000
Broker success fees (4.3%)paid at closing **(4)**		(600,000)	(600,000)
Net total proceeds to Seller **(5)**		**$6,150,000**	**$ 9,200,000**
Equity investment in New Co. equal to 30% of offer **(6)**	30%	4,200,000	4,200,000
	100%		

Fig.1.16b

Deal details: In our second example, the buyer is acquiring the stock of the seller's company. We have all four deal components in this example.

(1) The company receives an offer of $14M (7X EBITDA), of which 50% or $7M will be received in cash at close. ($7M is shown net of $250,000 of escrow holdback.)

(2) A holdback for escrow of $250,000 was stipulated in the deal. Escrow accounts are common in stock transactions and can be found in asset purchases as well. It allows the new owners to set aside money for unforeseen items, which were not anticipated in the agreement but are still a responsibility of the seller per the purchase agreement. Any deposit not used to pay pre-transaction unrecorded liabilities will be refunded to Seller after 180 days.

(3) If the company after the sale is able to achieve $3.2M EBITDA after 18 months post transaction, they will receive their earn-out of 20% or $2.8M. No earn-out is achieved if EBITDA is less than $2.6M. For every $0.1M between $2.6M and $3.2M, $467K of earn-out is paid.

(4) The broker success fee of $600,000 will be taken out of the proceeds upon settlement.

(5) All of Seller's legal, accounting, and other out of pocket expenses are paid directly by Seller prior to closing.

(6) At close, 30% or $4.2M will be invested as equity in "NewCo," which the PE firm has indicated it will sell in the next four to five years. The value of this equity component should grow over time but that won't be defined completely until that transaction takes place.

In total, the seller will receive between $6,150,000 and $9,200,000.

The seller then must wait for the PE firm to sell the company before he receives the final payout —which can amount to an incredible upside or none at all. Hence, selecting the right buyer in these circumstances is critical for full earn-out potential.

Earn-outs

Earn-outs are common in the technology industry, especially where there is a higher amount of consulting (project revenue) associated with the selling company. Buyers structure deals with earn-outs to mitigate the risks of acquiring "people" based businesses, which typically have very little in tangible assets.

What is an earn-out? An earn-out is a contractual agreement between the buyer and the seller in which a portion of the purchase price is contingent upon the "future performance" of the company. The buyer pays a majority of the purchase price upfront as the deal closes, and the remaining is contingent on the performance of the business.

For example, if the seller thinks the business is worth $10 million and the buyer believes it is worth $7 million, they can agree on an initial price of $7 million, and the remaining $3 million can form part of the earn-out. The $3 million may be contingent on factors like future sales, gross profit margin, EBITDA, retention of key employees, etc.

Historically, earn-outs have been spread over 30+ months, but according to many M&A advisors in the sub $50M range, the trend in the technology industry has been moving downward with 24 months now the average, although 12 months is not unheard of. Typically, 60 to 70 percent of the deal is paid in cash, with the remaining amounts as part of an earn-out. A few factors shape this outcome range. For example, the higher your qualitative value, the lower your earn-out percentage and the shorter the period. Similarly, the higher the recurring revenue, the higher the cash at close. The more owners who stay on during the earn-out period, the higher the cash at close. Both reduce risks of future performance.

Below are the benefits of an earn-out for both the buyer and the seller. As you can see, each party has some benefits with a few being shared by both the buyer and the seller.

Benefits of using an earn-out:

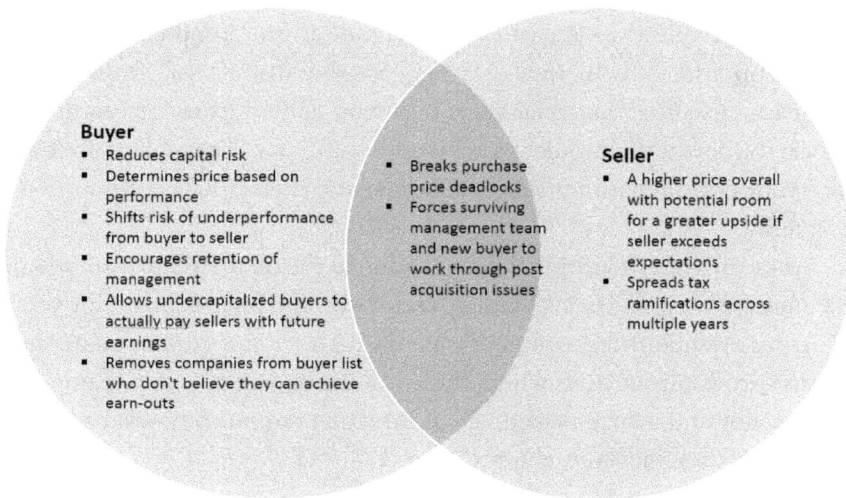

Buyer
- Reduces capital risk
- Determines price based on performance
- Shifts risk of underperformance from buyer to seller
- Encourages retention of management
- Allows undercapitalized buyers to actually pay sellers with future earnings
- Removes companies from buyer list who don't believe they can achieve earn-outs

- Breaks purchase price deadlocks
- Forces surviving management team and new buyer to work through post acquisition issues

Seller
- A higher price overall with potential room for a greater upside if seller exceeds expectations
- Spreads tax ramifications across multiple years

Fig.1.17

Of course, there are downsides to earn-outs as well, and they mostly revolve around the control or lack thereof in achieving these earn-outs. This challenge is most common where the acquired firm becomes part of a larger business and strategy and loses control of how it is operated as a standalone entity. This is a large topic in itself and beyond the scope of this book, but if you are a seller, you need to pay attention to how earn-outs are structured.

If you are an exiting seller, meaning you are not staying with the company that you have just sold, you should be comfortable with the cash at close and view the earn-out as a "bonus." Find a way to incentivize the remaining management team to achieve the stated earn-out objectives, either through incentives offered by the buyer, or your own out of the cash proceeds you received at sale. Otherwise, the likelihood of achieving those earn-outs is low. That said, due to an increase in buyers looking for quality firms, you have more flexibility regarding earn-outs on behalf of buyers.

Some owners find working the earn-out period to be very difficult. Reporting to someone else after having run your own company for so many years can at times be frustrating, especially when you no longer make the decisions. If you are committed to earning your earn-out, you need to negotiate decision-making ability or rights, ideally in your employment contract.

If your acquisition is part of an integration into another company, this will eat up a lot of your time and may possibly distract you from achieving your earn-outs. Your personal focus may have shifted from long term (as the owner) to short term in order to achieve the earn-out. Remember, however, to keep your critical team intact while motivating them, and continue to think long term.

As of the time of writing this book, due to the increased acquisition appetite among buyers in the technology sector and the high demand for vertical, recurring revenue firms, competition runs high for the great firm. More 100 percent cash upfront deals where there is a strong management team, a vertical specialty, and a large percentage of recurring revenue are now prevalent in the sub $35 million revenue space.

Metrics used for earn-outs

Buyers can use a number of different metrics to measure earn-outs. According to the Equiteq Buyers Report, gross margin is by far the most common earn-out metric (83 percent), followed by revenue (37 percent). Retention of key personnel and EBITDA are also used as a metric, but with a lower priority. Buyers often prefer sales driven metrics like gross profit margins and revenue year over year, which focuses everyone on top line growth. These are easier to measure and allows for the buyer to make adjustments in general and administrative expenses without disturbing top line numbers. It is important to understand in advance if your revenues will be combined with the acquiring company, and therefore how they will be tracked. More importantly, if you have the ability to cross-sell services into the acquiring company, make sure there is a way to carve out that revenue. Most of the time, important operational systems such as CRM or ERP applications are consolidated within the first year of acquisition, making it harder to view the revenue and gross profit you are generating as well as specific marketing activities that lead to closed sales deals.

While metrics such as EBITDA are used, sellers should be cautious about being pinned to that metric, especially if the company is being combined with another as part of a platform purchase. These metrics then become increasingly hard to measure and have high potential for disagreements down the road if not clearly outlined in the purchase agreement. To help alleviate this problem, we are now seeing buyers that allow their acquisition to maintain their separate financial and CRM systems in order to keep a closer watch over their numbers during their earn-out period.

Cash-Free/Debt-Free and working capital

The big day has arrived and an LOI (hopefully, one of many) shows up in your inbox. As you intently read the structure of the deal and the purchase price, you might pause at the sentence that reads, "The transaction is contemplated on a cash-free, debt-free basis (CFDF), subject to an amount remaining to cover the target working capital." Wait, what?

Besides negotiating the price and terms of the sale of your company, the next most critical negotiation will be the amount of target working capital and how it is calculated. Not doing this well will reduce your purchase price and create angst between you and the buyer, and it could potentially derail the close or completion of the transaction.

In most well-written LOIs, you will see mention of both the CFDF concept and a "working capital target." Having one without the other typically puts the buyer at a disadvantage because even if the seller pays off all the debts and pockets the remaining cash, the company still has working capital needs going forward, and the buyer doesn't want to put cash in the company to fund them.

The concept of CFDF is simple, but defining a good and fair target working capital is more complex and truly beyond the scope of this book. But ultimately it needs to be a negotiated meeting of the minds between the buyer and seller.

In the next section, the goal is to give you the basics of these concepts, as well as key items to look out for when defining working capital. We are getting into some weeds here, but at a minimum, I hope to convey the importance of getting good advice to calculate these items and how they intertwine.

CFDF

Most deals are structured as CFDF. In simple terms, this means the seller pays off all the *debt* on the books prior to the sale and then can distribute any remaining cash via a salary, dividend, bonus, or other methods. However, if your plan is to pay off all the balance sheet liabilities and keep the remaining cash, you may be in for a little surprise as there are usually a host of other liabilities that the buyer may want you to pay for that may not currently be accrued or may factor into the working capital target. In addition, some liabilities may be accrued based on an estimate, but the final amount may not be known or payable until after the close. See below for examples.

Whether a deal is a purchase of your assets or a purchase of stock, leaving the company with as little debt as possible at the close is the ideal, thus allowing the seller to distribute the excess cash (i.e., CFDF). While this is great for the seller, the buyer will not see it the same way. For the buyer, there are two inherent problems with this: First, by just paying off the current liabilities, either accrued or actual payables, and leaving no cash, will require the buyer to infuse additional cash to run the company immediately after the sale is completed. And this is not usually what a buyer wants to do. Secondly, not all liabilities make themselves known at *close*, which again leaves the buyer paying for items that really are the responsibility of the seller. A savvy buyer will want to mitigate this via either the target working capital, an excess working capital band beyond the target, or an escrow account to capture any deficiencies.

In a CFDF scenario, *cash* is usually simple—checking, savings, petty cash, etc.—but as the seller you also need to consider the differences between what the bank shows and what the books show, as well as credit card deposits or cash in transit. Usually, and especially with smaller companies, this can be handled via a bank reconciliation on the night prior to close. Typically, most owners have a pretty good idea if there is excess cash on hand and they are able to distribute that out of the company (if needed) prior to the close. I highly recommend involving your CPA to assist you with the best way to distribute excess cash from the company, as each may have different tax consequences, especially if you are a C corporation and not a pass-through entity like a partnership, S corp, or LLC.

While cash is usually straightforward, debt in a CFDF scenario can be trickier and usually involves more than just the accounts payable, payroll accruals, and deferred revenue amounts on the balance sheet on the date of close. While most of these can be removed from the balance sheet prior to the sale (except deferred revenue) there are other forms of "hidden" debt that may not have been accrued yet on the balance sheet, especially if the sale takes place early in your calendar or fiscal year-end and you hadn't yet accounted for typical year-end adjustments. We will talk about these more in the working capital section below.

In an asset sale, the **seller** retains the legal entity and usually (but not always) will be collecting the accounts receivable and paying the remaining debt as it comes due or shortly after the sale is completed. An asset sale allows more time for the seller to make cash disbursements for bonuses, dividends, 401(k), and profit sharing after the sale, as the legal entity is still owned by the seller.

In a stock sale, all assets and liabilities are typically taken over by the new owner, so paying debts and distributing cash in advance of the sale are more important. Debts that remain on the books post-transaction (which cannot be paid in advance) are usually accounted for in the final settlement statement, and they reduce the purchase price or cash distributed if they extend beyond the working capital period.

Even though a deal may be structured as CFDF, a buyer will want the seller to leave behind a normal level of working capital to properly operate the business, so they don't have to fund additional cash in the business immediately after the close. Therefore, it is important that you understand your company's working capital needs well before you sell.

Working Capital

In today's more competitive sellers' market and with the speed at which LOIs are being negotiated, in most cases a purchase price is presented in advance of any due diligence, and sometimes the buyer may set a purchase price high enough to win in a competitive bid situation and then use the working capital adjustments as a "sneaky" way to reduce the final purchase price. Since the target working capital is not defined in the LOI, it can sometimes come as a surprise during the negotiation process. The working capital target is usually determined by the buyer and the seller based on the typical working capital requirements of the company and is negotiated after the LOI is signed.

Seasoned buyers will make an attempt in the LOI to address how the "target working capital" will be calculated and what cash must remain in the company to cover it, but the language is usually broad and leaves you, the seller, with an incomplete picture.

Here is an example from an LOI:

> "Working Capital shall be defined as (a) current assets (including but not limited to operating cash, accounts receivable, inventory, and prepaid assets, and excluding all current and deferred income tax assets) less (b) current liabilities (including but not limited to normal course accounts payable and other accrued liabilities excluding all current and deferred income tax liabilities as well as other liabilities.)"

Pretty vague, right?

The accounting definition of working capital is: Current assets minus current liabilities. However, in a CFDF situation, cash, cash equivalents, and interest-bearing debt are excluded from the working capital calculation. Also, customer deposits for future work, or prepaid subscriptions, are usually an exception to the cash-free, debt-free calculation as well, because the seller is required to leave cash in the business to cover those amounts. In a CFDF scenario, it is better to use the following definition of working capital:

> Working capital = accounts receivable + inventory - accounts payable and accrued operating liabilities.

(Operating liabilities also will include unpaid salaries, which is a current liability account, so they count towards the calculation of the company's working capital.)

It surprises many owners that they must leave an amount of working capital "in" the company when they sell, even after all the balance sheet liabilities have been paid. Cash is required, at a minimum to cover the payroll while accounts receivable are being collected, hopefully at the same level as payables are paid. For example, a company that pays its vendors in 30 days but takes 60 days to collect its accounts receivables from customers has a negative working capital cycle of 30 days. Cash will need to remain in the bank to carry this 30-day period, plus payroll.

Current Assets

Many sellers underestimate their current assets when calculating working capital. For example, many technology firms expense all their supplies to get a quicker write-off for tax purposes, or expense hardware or software maintenance renewals when purchased, instead of listing them as prepaid and amortizing them over the life of the maintenance contract (i.e., one year). The same applies for other types of prepaid expenses that a private company owner may simply expense throughout the year. A common list of prepaids are listed below.

Inventory and accounts receivable are generally the largest components of the current assets. However, most technology companies have little to zero inventory, and thus the emphasis will be on the value of accounts receivable, including the accuracy of the reserve for doubtful accounts.

The type of partner organization that you are may also affect the calculation of "collectible" accounts receivable. VARs and custom developers typically bill by the hour and therefore have a higher propensity toward write-off as the accounts receivable ages over 120 days. On the other hand, partners who bill on a monthly subscription usually are more consistent in collections and where possible nonpayment could result in termination of services. This accounts receivable is more secure and reliable and therefore working capital requirements with regards to accounts receivable are easier to estimate.

Regardless of the type of TSP you are, if you have accounts receivable beyond a normal 90-day collection period, a buyer will want to reduce your valuation of working capital for those amounts. Understanding the makeup and staying on top of accounts receivable and cleaning up old straggling balances, or writing off amounts uncollectible in advance, is important. The stronger the accounts receivable, the greater the ability to offset any remaining liabilities for the 30- to 90-day working target period.

In addition to accounts receivable, there are prepaid assets that may need to be transferred as part of the sale. While most of them are usually identified on the books, some are written off as an expense when incurred and therefore need to be reclassified as prepaid if not consumed in full.

Common prepaid assets remaining on the balance sheet:

- Prepaid rent deposits
- Prepaid conference fees
- Prepaid travel
- Prepaid advertising
- Prepaid software enhancement
- Prepaid maintenance/support plans
- Prepaid insurance – commercial, general, life, property, professional liability, etc.
- Proration of rent, parking if closing mid-month

It is not uncommon for the buyer to try to reduce some of the prepaids, as they see no, or only limited, benefit to them. For instance, they may not want to pay for conferences because their own employees will be at the conference, or they may choose not to attend the conference because they see it as not being beneficial to them. They may also have their own insurance coverages for general insurance. In these cases, you should try to get a refund from the vendor, and barring that, negotiate what you think is fair.

Current Liabilities

On the flip side, in addition to accounts payable and accrued payroll, there are a list of operating liabilities, some of which are not as obvious. These less obvious ones become part of the working capital negotiation discussion. Since these items cannot be extinguished prior to the sale, they are either handled as a decrease to the cash proceeds at close, or they are included in the target working capital amounts.

Common unknown or unrecorded liabilities:

- Unaccrued interest or interest adjustments at year end
- Operating lease financing
- Unaccrued employee bonuses/commissions
- Deferred compensation
- Severance payments**
- Pension/401(k) obligations
- Customer deposits
- Unearned or deferred revenue*
- Channel partner commissions or channel partner achievement bonuses at year end
- Deferred taxes (federal, state, sales, property)
- Legal/accounting fees – transaction related

Uncommon, unknown, or unrecorded items:

- CAM charges (common area maintenance) by the property manager; assessed at year end, or assessed monthly based on estimates and trued-up at year end
- Workers compensation overages or underpayments
- Cafeteria plan expense reimbursements (medical/childcare reimbursements)
- Garnishments not handled through payroll
- Accrued excess liability insurance or other insurance subject to adjustment based on revenue or other variable operations metrics
- Deferred rent
- Royalty pass-throughs
- True-up of software license fees
- Margin rebates
- Vendor rebates

*A final thought on deferred revenue: Even though deferred revenue is viewed as a liability and typically added to the working capital calculation, you could possibly make a case for this not happening. To the extent that there are little or no further costs to be incurred in providing the goods or services, it would be difficult for a buyer to justify deferred revenue as debt, therefore allowing the seller to remove it entirely, or in part, from the calculation of working capital.

**If the termination of an employee resulting in severance is requested by the buyer, then the buyer should bear this cost.

Working capital target

After all the items in working capital are identified, the working capital target will be a number that is negotiated during the due diligence process. Typically, a working capital "peg" (an average of your working capital over the last 90 days) is used, assuming your company is not cyclical. If the company is cyclical, then a 12-month average may be the best choice. At closing, if the actual working capital delivered is more or less than that, then usually a dollar for dollar adjustment upwards (if working capital is more than the peg) or downwards (if working capital is less than the peg) occurs to the purchase price.[8]

Working capital adjustments are very common in M&A transactions. As a seller you should understand what your real average working capital is *prior* to selling, in order to ensure that a buyer does not overstate the number. Often buyers use a higher working capital peg to justify a downward adjustment to the purchase price.

In smaller deals, working capital adjustments can occur at the closing date, but as the deal size increases, they are more likely to occur 90 to 120 days after closing. This is because the buyer usually requires this much time to have the auditors review the numbers. By then, all accounts are closed and the more accurate working capital number can be calculated. This final number is the one compared to the original working capital target, and therefore drives the adjustment; and the difference is adjusted to either an escrow account or a working capital target (threshold) account. In addition, to protect themselves from any major fluctuations in working capital between the closing date and when the numbers are finally audited, buyers usually require a holdback, which can be used to make up for any adjustments.

As part of negotiating the sale, the buyer may request that you leave some of the excess cash in an escrow account for any unanticipated expenses, but both buyer and seller should be clear in advance what that escrow account can be used for. While escrow accounts are common, they are not found in every deal, and a threshold captures 90 percent of most unexpected expenses if the buyer and seller are thorough in due diligence. When escrow accounts are created, they remain open for the period of time specified in the purchase agreement, after which any remaining funds are returned to the seller, plus accrued interest earned, if any, and if interest is actually specified in the purchase agreement.

ROBERT INSIGHT:

Robert learned early in his career never to become "the bank," or front for payments to vendors for amounts due from customers. Since most of his subscription customers paid on a monthly basis, he never wanted to be behind in paying his vendors. Occasionally, a customer lost, forgot, or just didn't have the funds to make their monthly subscription payment, which left Robert out the cost of the licenses until he was able to get the customer to pay, or threaten to turn them off, which he did only after a few months of requesting payment. Robert instead decided to use the true rental model, where his customers were required to pay both the first and last month of subscription fees. The last month remained on the books as a liability until the contract was terminated.

Over time, as he grew, so did his deferred income account for all the payments he held for their last month of subscription. The buyers looked at this amount and wanted to include 100 percent of the amount as a liability, as stated on the balance sheet. But Robert made the argument that the deferred amount included the profit margin that had not yet been realized, and that the cost per seat was very specific from a license fee and required no additional labor to deploy it and very little labor to support it. Therefore, he was able to adjust the working capital requirements in his favor and remove a large portion of the deferred income from the liabilities being carried forward.

STOCK VS. ASSET SALE

Everyone asks how a deal should be structured. It is a good question to ask, as the result can have very different short- and long-term consequences. The purchase price of a business can also depend on whether or not the sale is a stock sale or an asset sale.

A stock sale is the purchase of the owner's shares of the corporation. An asset sale is the purchase of the individual assets and possibly some liabilities. Many times, not all the assets are purchased.

Sellers who own corporations always want stock sales, whereas buyers will want an asset sale. Actually, 85 percent of the time buyers will only purchase the assets of a business. When selling a corporation, one must decide whether the company should be sold based upon an asset sale or a stock sale. Partnerships and sole proprietorships have no stock so will only be an asset sale.

Corporations, S corp, and LLCs can get more complicated. While an S corp and LLC are pass-through entities, the C corp is not, and therefore it is more complex. Below is a chart that will quickly summarize the aspects:

Decision Factors for Seller	Stock	Asset
Percentage of deals as:	10 - 15%	85%+
What gets purchased:	Stock	Some assets and liabilities - cherry-pick
Entity records, tax returns, contracts:	Buyer	Seller
Assumption of liabilities:	Buyer	Seller
Amount of due diligence:	More	Less
Transaction and contract complexity:	More	Less
Level of risk and likelihood that deals will not get done:	Higher	Lower
Escrow account used:	More	Less
Tax treatment (federal):	More favorable: capital gain treatment and possible shelter of gain	Less favorable: ordinary and capital depending on assets sold
Leases and licensing:	Remains with buyer	Remains with seller
Assignment of customer contracts, NDA's, employee benefits:	Not required	May need new contracts if not assignable
Buyer will pay:	Less, due to no step-up in basis, and reallocation of purchase price among assets	More due to favorable step-up in basis

Fig.1.18

Aside from the buyer's preference for an asset sale, due to the unknown liabilities of a corporation, the tax consequences for both the buyer and the seller are of primary importance. The buyer wants an asset sale in order to step up the tax basis of the assets, while the seller wants a stock sale to avoid the double taxation (taxation on the asset basis and the stock basis).

That said, as of the writing of this book, there is a nice tax advantage in the US Internal Revenue Code for small corporation stock (less than $50M in revenue) that can allow shareholders to shelter between 50 and 100 percent of the capital gain on the sale of their stock. Look for information on Qualified Small Business Stock for more detail. As mentioned in Part III, consulting a tax professional to look at the different tax consequences is critical. While a seller might take a slight reduction in sales prices to structure the transaction as a stock sale, for reasons mentioned above, the tax consequences of sheltering the capital gain may significantly offset that, Alternative Minimum Tax consequences aside.

PART II
EIGHT KEY VALUATION MAXIMIZERS

This section is essentially about one thing: The ways in which smart people (some of them brilliant, technically) can overlook or misunderstand a wide range of factors that can substantially affect the potential value of a company at its sale. In a step-by-step fashion, we cover the tactical and the practical, and also the short-term and the (relatively) long-term aspects of maximizing your company value. The upshot should be that if you utilize even a portion of what's discussed here, you will be in a much better position to sell, or simply grow, your business.

1. Financial Fitness

*"We won't even begin looking at a business unless we know
we can rely on the financials we are given."*

– Tom Mescall, Partner-in-Charge, Consulting, Armanino LLP

Accurate financial reporting is the foundation of all deals. A set of accurately presented financials (regardless of the bottom line) can set a positive tone for the entire negotiation process. High quality in your financials will lend credibility through the due diligence process—meaning, the level of detail and accuracy in your financial reporting becomes the benchmark by which all other documentation is judged. If a buyer trusts and believes your financials, they will more likely trust and believe everything else you give them. On the flipside, inaccurate reporting will either derail, stall, or just plain kill an opportunity with a buyer before it really even starts. According to many buyers and brokers I interviewed for this book, bad financial reporting is the number one reason deals fall apart.

Here is what we mean by Financial Fitness:

- Accurate numbers in your financials
- Correct use of GAAP (generally accepted accounting principles)
- Correct gross profit reporting
- The calculation of "adjusted" EBITDA (earnings before interest, taxes, depreciation and amortization).

While most deals are valued on a multiple of EBITDA, gross profit margins are equally important as a starting point, especially for strategic buyers who many times care more about the gross profit margin than the bottom line. A company's EBITDA number is the most important information because it is a common benchmark in corporate transactions both public and private.

This chapter will be focused on how you can maximize the quality and accuracy of your reporting and increase the EBITDA you present to a prospective buyer. We will focus on the following:

- Identifying common financial faux pas
- Revenue and gross profit margins
- Projections
- Key metrics used by buyers
- Adjusted EBITDA

CLEANING YOUR FINANCIAL HOUSE AND AVOIDING COMMON FINANCIAL FAUX PAS

Let's start with GAAP and consistent reporting as these are the two biggest areas of concern for buyers.

As part of the "pre" due diligence process—yes, before someone is even willing to send you an IOI or an LOI, you will need to have financials ready to go. In addition to the current year's financials (balance sheet, income statement, and cash flow statement), buyers will want to see the last two to three years of financials to look for upward (or downward) trends in sales, gross profit margins, and cash flow. These need to be prepared on a GAAP basis. That means everything is on an accrual method, and revenue and expenses match each other. The use of deferred revenue and expense accounts are a must if you prepay expenses or receive revenue for multiple periods or months. Even if your tax reporting is on a cash basis (many people who have S corps do this), your books need to be 100 percent accrual based.

If any of this makes you uncomfortable, or if you are unsure how your financials are reported, now is the time to enlist a good external CPA. Not having GAAP financials will stall a deal immediately. The buyer will (via the warranties in your sales contract) require you to represent that the financial statements are presented fairly, in all material respects, in accordance with GAAP, consistently applied.

Any lack of consistency will be a red flag and a possible halt to an IOI or LOI. Consistent reporting over these three historical years is critical. For example, if you weren't reporting annual subscription sales on a monthly basis two years ago, but instead recognizing them in the month you billed them, this will make your financials inconsistent. If you were incorrectly allocating expenses to sales and marketing that should have been included in your cost of goods sold, and you have just now realized this, go back and change the past years' numbers so everything is accurate and consistent. Or if you were using a different accounting package before and then changed your chart of accounts and are now categorizing revenue and expenses differently, you will need to go back and reclassify the financial information in the same format. The point here is to ensure consistency across all years.

Even though the attention initially will be on your profit and loss statement, your balance sheet should not be overlooked. Here are the common issues we see with the balance sheet.

Assets – Now is the time to remove any nonessential or nonperforming asset or assets that don't affect the company's activity. Items such as the owner's cars, art, or real estate unrelated to the operations of the company should be removed. Be sure to distribute those assets prior to presenting financial statements to prospective buyers, in order to present the cleanest balance sheet. Shareholder loans and employee loans should be collected to the extent they can be collected and any uncollectible balances written off so that only customer-related receivables are shown.

Most technology firms have a good amount of hardware in the form of servers, printers, monitors, etc. on hand. And much of it is either not in use or not locatable for whatever reason. Now is the time to remove fully depreciated items or items no longer in use. Unless they are large big-ticket items like storage arrays or large server farms, buyers really don't want to deal with these small assets, especially if fully depreciated or no longer in service. Clean up your fixed assets both in your financials and on your premises before you hand out your financials.

Any accounts receivable beyond 120 days should be highlighted and collected to the extent possible. Leaving these on the balance sheet may affect how your working capital is calculated, which ultimately affects your net proceeds on a sale. Any shareholder receivables, either short term or long term, should be collected and removed. If you know you are not going to be able to collect on a longstanding receivable, now might be the time to turn it over to a collection agency or just write it off if it is not large.

If you have deposits or prepaid items, be sure you can easily identify what they are now. If you prepaid items like maintenance contracts or annual insurance policies, be sure you are amortizing those over the period they cover.

Liabilities – As with the personal assets listed above, all personal liabilities, such as car loans, real estate, and credit card debt should be eliminated from the balance sheet if they are not used in the production of revenue. Showing liabilities beyond 60 days, unless there is a specific reason, can be cause for concern and additional scrutiny during due diligence, so take this opportunity to clean them up. Regardless of whether you sell the assets or the stock of your company, in the end, you will be responsible for any medium- or long-term debt on the balance sheet. If you can retire the debt now, without serious cash flow issues, it would be ideal.

Intercompany – If you have multiple entities and you have intercompany transactions, to the extent possible cancel or remove any "due-from" or "due-to" accounts. If one entity is paying expenses on behalf of another, be sure that these are properly documented and accounted for. This is always a red flag during due diligence and a cause for concern by buyers that you may be hiding transactions in another company.

Expenses – Most business owners have some "personal" expenses that end up flowing through the business. To the extent you can, you should remove these, or at a minimum contain them into special accounts so you can flag them as adjustments to earnings to normalize your net income. This could include items such as season tickets, country club dues, and workout facility dues and any expenses such as maintenance, insurance, and registration on your personal cars. It can also include less easily identifiable expenses like first-class airfare and top-tier hotel rooms. Ideally, you should pare down or eliminate the less obvious expenses that may be more difficult to add back later. Later in this chapter, we will discuss in detail how to deal with "adjustments" to EBITDA.

Once you normalize or remove all nonbusiness-related expenses, how do your percentages compare with the survey results below?

Typical Partner Operating Expenses

As a % of revenue

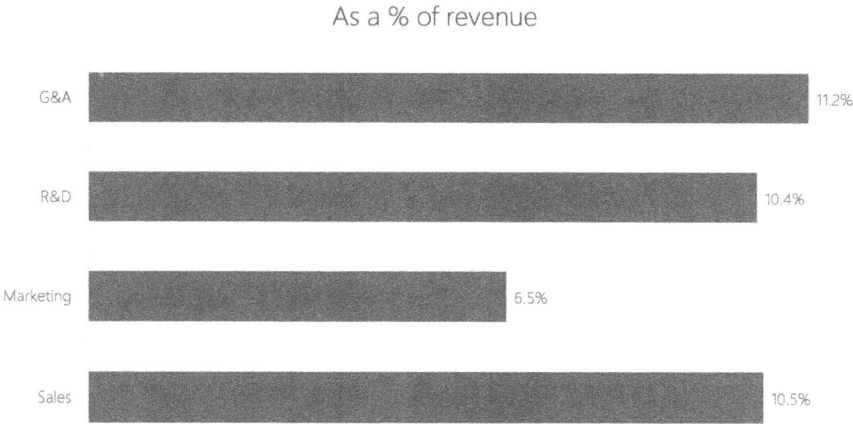

G&A	11.2%
R&D	10.4%
Marketing	6.5%
Sales	10.5%

Source is CloudSpeed Partner Strategy Survey, March 2018

Fig.2.1

Projections – Your future financial projects are going to be reviewed carefully. Most buyers will not only want to see how you performed against current year projections—if only to determine how good your projection calculations are—they will also want to see the next year's projections, especially if your deal is coming close to calendar or fiscal year end. Either way, it is a good idea to include a proforma forecasted statement to show how the year will close so that the buyer can see what the current full year will look like.

For example, if you are a calendar year-end company and you are in negotiation to sell your company in August, you will want to provide proforma forecasted financials through the end of the year so that the buyer can see how the year will end up. This is especially important if your company happens to be cyclical. Historically, many ERP companies sell a predominate amount of software and services in the fourth and second quarters of the year, as their clients plan to begin implementation of this software in their new year. This typically results in second and fourth quarter sales numbers being much higher than the rest of the year.

When presenting your projections and proforma statements, don't be overly optimistic on sales expectations. Remember, next year's projections will very likely be the basis of your earn-out, and the remaining current year projections will be watched closely as the deal nears close. Nothing will stall or kill a deal faster than materially missing the current year's sales projections. Not only will it stall the deal, you will lose credibility with the buyers and you may never regain it. It will also reduce the percentage of cash at close and push more toward future earn-outs. It is better to under-project slightly and then over-deliver.

REVENUE AND GROSS PROFIT MARGINS

Revenue growth year over year (YOY) is a key metric viewed by both financial and strategic buyers. However, the type and quality of revenue is also important to highlight and distinguish. In this section, we will focus on the presentation of revenue. In the chapter on Revenue Readiness, we will focus on the different types of revenue and their value. Ideally, you should separate your revenue by type and have a corresponding "cost of goods sold" tied to each revenue type. And, you should also have separate account numbers in your general ledger dedicated to the different types of revenue and the corresponding costs, which will then allow you to present your gross profit margin by revenue type. Separating your revenue by type, specifically for recurring revenue, will allow you to track a churn rate as well. That's another metric we will discuss later, but an important one to be able to quickly quantify.

If you sell software and that software is available through multiple offerings (i.e. perpetual and subscription), the value to a buyer is very different, especially if it is a subscription on a *contractual* basis (the nirvana of revenue).

Buyers will attribute a much higher multiple to the recurring revenue than they will to the perpetual sales (one-time). Finally, if you are not selling all aspects of your business to a buyer, or maybe only carving out one aspect to sell, this will allow you to easily produce revenue and its corresponding costs of goods sold. In our earlier example, Robert only sold his consulting practice to his initial buyer and he kept the rest. Because he was able to show a separate Profit and Loss statement by type of revenue, (his employees were also segregated by type of revenue) it was easy for the buyer to view exactly what they were purchasing.

Many times, breaking out consulting in the "cost of goods sold" section of your financials may be more difficult, especially if your consultants are working on project revenue and fixed price projects at the same time. This may be especially difficult if you are breaking the consulting cost of goods sold into different corresponding buckets, but with a good cost accounting system, this can be done more easily than you might think. If you don't have that capability, now might be a good time to investigate adding additional modules to your accounting system. Applications as small as QuickBooks already have these features built in.

All revenue is not created equal, so listing your revenue by type can give you an advantage if the revenue is recurring, contractual, or high margin, such as your own IP. Below is a list of the common types of revenue generated by technology service companies and their typical corresponding margins. The most highly coveted is IP that you own and sell as a cloud solution. The least desirable is hardware maintenance revenue, as it is typically low margin and generally dissipates over time as hardware ages.

Value of Revenue by Type

HIGH

Type of Revenue	Frequency	Contractual	Margins
Own IP - Cloud SaaS	Recurring	Y	70% - 90%
Reselling - SaaS	Recurring	Y	25% - 40%
Hosting/IaaS/PaaS	Recurring	Y	40% - 60%
MSP - Cloud	Recurring	Y	40% - 60%
MSP - Break/Fix	Recurring/Repeat	Y	40% - 60%
Custom Development	Repeat		40% - 60%
Prof Services - Packaged/Fixed Fee	Repeat		35% - 45%
Own IP - Perpetual	One-time		60% - 80%
Prof Services – Time & Materials	One-time		25% - 40%
Reselling Software	One-time		15% - 40%
Reselling Hardware	One-time		5% - 20%
Annual Enhancements/Maintenance Renewals	Annual		5% - 20%

LOW

Fig.2.2

Gross Profit Margin

This is also the time to make sure that you clearly understand what belongs above and below the gross profit margin line. Above the line is typically referred to as expenses that belong in your "cost of goods sold" section. Make sure that all of your labor that creates and supports revenue is listed, along with any software licenses that support that revenue. Also, all cloud service subscription fees (i.e., Amazon Web Services, Azure, or private co-location) should be reported in the cost of goods sold, unless they are part of your R&D or selling expenses. Incorrectly showing these expenses below the line, or as general and administrative (G&A), will misstate your gross profit margin, and potentially derail a deal due to a seriously revised "cost of goods sold" number. Research and development expenses should be categorized separately below the line. If you are at all unsure, now is the time to enlist a good outside accountant to review your financials for accuracy.

As mentioned above, the cost of goods sold should align with how you categorize your revenue, which will then allow you to show a gross profit margin by revenue type. If you aren't currently looking at your financials at this level of detail, you cannot possibly know for sure which revenue is producing the highest gross profit margin. Many owners are surprised when they look at this level of detail, as there is usually one area that is outperforming the others. This may also give you a good indication of which line of business or service you might want to eliminate if it is dragging down your overall gross profit margin.

The gross profit margin you achieve will vary by type of product and service. While the above numbers represent a subset of Microsoft Partners internationally, it is important that you understand the margins that are typical in your industry and vertical, and that you are not more than a few points below the typical margins. If you can be above the industry standard, that will definitely be more attractive to buyers.

All buyers pay a lot of attention to gross profit margins, so it is imperative that you correctly and accurately allocate your expenses either above or below this financial line. Meaning: A mis-categorization of an expense in the general and administrative area of your financials, when it should be in your cost of goods sold, can considerably alter the purchase price. Why? While the expense ultimately doesn't change the overall EBITDA percentage, a strategic buyer is usually more focused on the gross profit margin because they can control or create economies of scale in the non-cost of goods sold.

KEY METRICS TO LIVE BY

Once you have your financial statements in order and have accomplished the key identifiers listed above, you may then want to focus on a few metrics.

Rule of 40

As I was preparing my company to be sold, I connected with an industry analyst as a mentor to find out what my metrics should be. While the answer will change slightly for gross profit margin and YOY growth, and depending on your specialty, a rule of thumb I was given was the *rule of 40*.[1] (I have seen the rule of 45 used as well, but it is not as prevalent.)

What is the rule of 40? Growth rate + profit margin should be greater than or equal to 40 percent.

Here is how the rule of 40 looks. If you take your annual revenue growth rate and add it to your EBITDA, that number should be at least 40. Here are a few examples:

And again, for clarity purposes you can assume that the profit margin = operating margin = EBITDA.

- If you are growing 100 percent YOY, you can lose money at a rate of 60 percent of profits.
- If you are growing 40 percent YOY, you should be breaking even.
- If you are growing 20 percent YOY, you should have a 20 percent operating margin.
- If you are not growing, you should have a 40 percent operating margin.
- If your business is declining by 10 percent, you should have a 50 percent operating margin.

The most realistic example in the technology services industry is a YOY growth rate of 25 percent with an EBITDA rate of 15 percent. That is a very achievable number on both ends of the equation and will get your company viewed by a number of qualified buyers. If you subscribe to the rule of 45, as mentioned above, you just need to increase one of those numbers by 5 percentage points, which makes you a superstar—but in today's sellers' market, a rule of 40 will do just fine.

IRR

While many strategic buyers do consider an internal rate of return (IRR), this is a particularly important number for financial buyers, specifically PE Firms. I have yet to meet a PE firm that isn't looking for at least a 20 to 30 percent IRR. That means they are looking to return their entire investment in the next five years, which basically translates to an EBITDA multiple of 5X. Can you receive more than a 5X multiple of EBITDA? Sure, but you will need to find creative ways of structuring the terms of your deal and then wait for your equity share of 20 to 25 percent to pay off, at which point your multiple could be substantially larger.

ADJUSTED EBITDA

As mentioned earlier, the most widely used method of valuation is based upon EBITDA (earnings before interest, taxes, depreciation, and amortization). EBITDA is usually taken as a proxy for operating cash flow. One of the main reasons for the widespread use of EBITDA is that is allows better comparisons between companies. However, a smart buyer will look beyond EBITDA and focus on free cash flow (FCF) to value a business. FCF is a financial metric that includes cash flow generated from operations, minus annual capital expenditures required to sustain the business (maintenance capex). It is a key metric used by buyers to evaluate a business. Free cash flow is sometimes calculated on an after-tax basis. However, most buyers calculate free cash flow before tax because their tax structure may be different than the target company for sale.

Some buyers and sellers use EBITDA and FCF synonymously but technically this is incorrect. EBITDA doesn't take into account the requirement for sustaining capital expenditures or changes in working capital[4]. However, every buyer starts with a calculation of EBITDA and proceeds from there, so knowing how to present as high a number as possible is a very valuable skill to grasp and apply.

Adjusted EBITDA is a financial metric that includes the removal of several of the one-time, irregular and non-recurring items from EBITDA, a process also referred to as *normalizing*. The purpose of adjusting EBITDA is to get a normalized number that is not distorted by owner expenses—not part of operating the business, irregular gains, losses, or other unusual one-time items. This was probably one of the most valuable lessons I learned, and it netted me a million more in the sale of my business just by making some small adjustments to my EBITDA calculation.

Once you sell your company, you will find that there were "perks" you had as an owner that you will no longer have. Once you sell, you may no longer be able to give yourself that great bonus at year end or be able to contribute the maximum to your Profit sharing and 401(k) accounts. Then there are those other little "personal" expenses (cellphones, special lunches, travel perks) that sometime creep into the financials but that will no longer be allowed once the transaction is completed. These can be viewed as "good" adjustments (which add to the sale price) or "bad" adjustments (which detract).

Positive "Good" adjustments are items that increase your EBITDA, so expenses that won't be there or items that are truly nonrecurring and don't reflect future expectations for the business. It makes sense to remove these items, as they won't be representative of your financials in the future. Here is a list of the common good adjustments or add-backs to income:

- Excessive owner salary**
- Owner bonuses
- Profit-sharing
- Automobile/housing allowances
- Country club/gym memberships
- Annual sports tickets/box seats
- Insurance (personal/life insurance) if not staying with the new company or if extraordinary
- Owner travel
- Charitable contributions
- Extraordinary legal expenses, insurance claims
- One-time professional fees
- Severances
- Intercompany expenses
- Extra-ordinary losses and bad-debt write-offs

And a few you should think about, which if you are selling to a strategic buyer, may benefit you: *

- Increase in margins due to combined buying power
- Discounts on purchased items due to buying power
- Commissions/royalties being paid to affiliates that may terminate

*While you will want to highlight these to your buyer, don't expect to get the full benefit of the addback. These are typically negotiated, but you should try to get at least 50 percent of their value.

** Don't go crazy and add back your entire salary if you are required to stay for a year or two while achieving your earn-out.

Negative "Bad" adjustments are items that are being removed for the purpose of inflating or manipulating financial results, or those that don't fairly reflect the economic impact on a business. For example, if you had a one-time sale of an asset (or in the example of Robert, when he sold his consulting company and received payments over time), this would be considered a bad adjustment and the gain would need to be removed from EBITDA. Examples of bad adjustments include:

- Below market owner salary – reduce by shortfall
- Below market employee benefits
- Essential key player salary additions
- Extraordinary gain/sale of asset or IP – one-time (nonrecurring)
- Lease termination costs
- Rent/lease adjustments – free rent for renewing

ROBERT INSIGHT:

#1. When he sold his consulting division, he was still the main rainmaker and selling all of the products and services. He handled the largest transactions, but since he wasn't transitioning to the company that purchased him, the new owner needed to replace his skillset, so a like-kind salary adjustment was added back as a negative adjustment to EBITDA.

#2. Robert realized that he had actually paid a supplier in advance for three years of a subscription fee. He had expensed the entire amount a year ago in order to minimize his taxes. He then went back and adjusted his EBITDA to show two more years of benefit. This was a positive adjustment to EBITDA for two years.

#3. Robert prided himself on being able to coach his son's football team each year and he sponsored a number of fundraising efforts to help with uniforms, field playing time, and recognition events. He had typically shown those as charitable contributions, but he found some buried in other line items as well. These were positive adjustments to EBITDA.

It is important to identify, and be realistic about, negative adjustments as well as positive ones. Even though these adjustments will lower the company valuation, if they are obvious and easily determined, you can enhance your credibility with the buyer by exposing them on your own and thus make for a smoother negotiation down the road. Keep in mind that a buyer is likely to propose various negative adjustments as they work through due diligence, so identifying any such items upfront can help with deal negotiations and help prevent unexpected surprises.

Example of adjusted EBITDA

Here is an example of how to calculate adjusted EBITDA. Below are the line items that both increase and decrease the regular EBITDA and then the adjusted number. Following that is an explanation of each item on the list.

Adjusted EBITDA Example		
Net Income	$	2,250,000
Plus:		
Taxes (Federal and State)		787,500
Interest		5,000
Depreciation & Amortization		25,000
EBITDA		3,067,500
Plus:		
Personal car expenses		15,000
CFO Salary and Benefits (retiring)		175,000
Profit sharing and 401(K)		75,000
Legal expenses to defend company		65,000
Bankrupcy of ABC company lost AR		35,000
Football season tickets		7,500
Charitable contribution to XYZ organization		10,000
Minus:		
Lower than market rent (relative owns building)		(75,000)
Total Adjustments		307,500
Adjusted EBITDA	$	3,375,000
Total EBITDA Adjustments		307,500
Valuation multiple (sample)		6.0
Additional Value Generated	$	1,845,000

Fig.2.3

To arrive at the unadjusted figure, we start by taking the net income of $2,225,000 and adding back to it the taxes (federal and state) of $787,500, plus an interest expense of $5,000, plus the annual depreciation and amortization of $25,000. This produces an EBITDA of $3,067,500.

Moving on to the adjusted figure, we continue to add back more items, including $15,000 of personal car usage; the $175,000 salary, including benefits, of the chief financial officer who will retire and is not needed in the new company, the excessive profit sharing and 401(k) the owner was paying, $75,000, the legal expenses for a wrongful termination suit that was filed against the company for $65,000 and then dismissed, the bankruptcy and write-off of a large accounts receivable of $35,000, and the personal season tickets, $7,500, for the local football team—that won't be transferred as part of the sale. Finally, there was that personal charitable contribution of $10,000 that was made.

The only minus to the income would be the below-market rent of $75,000 that is due to a relative owning the building.

The final result is an adjusted EBITDA of $3,375,000. As you can see, there is a difference of $307,500 if we add up all the line items. If you total these changes and multiply the total by a potential valuation of 6x EBITDA, this increases the sale price of the company by $1,845,000, assuming the buyer doesn't find any additional "bad" adjustments to EBITDA. This is a significant amount, which in this case is in the seller's favor.

The Resources section has a great example of a spreadsheet, but you can also download your own at https://rosebizinc.com/book-resources/.

AUDITS, REVIEWS, COMPILATIONS, AND MORE

Presenting your financials accurately and with relative frequency is the first step in giving your buyers confidence as they begin the due diligence process. A misstep in this early process can taint their view as they wade through your books and records. Meaning they will be more apt to "look" for mistakes if they find some quickly and early in the process. So, spare yourself the audit feel, and present your financials as accurately as possible. Just in case you are unsure, here are the most common issues encountered with the financial statement of technology companies:

- Incorrect revenue recognition
- Incorrect matching of revenue with associated cost of goods sold
- Expensed CAPEX for tax purposes vs. GAAP depreciation
- Lack of accruals for PTO and payroll
- Poor or no tracking of customer deposits or deferred revenue

Even if you feel like you have your financial house in order, you may wonder if you still need a review or audit of your financials. And my answer is always, "It depends." If you are running a $15M+ company on QuickBooks, then I would say absolutely yes! And I would also suggest that you look for a more fully integrated accounting system with internal controls and audit trails. But for those companies already running on a dual-entry accounting system that doesn't let you go back in time and "erase" transactions or change them without an audit trail, the question as to which one is needed is debatable.

A *review* is less intrusive, costly, and time consuming than an audit. During a review engagement, an accountant is required to make inquiries of the client and perform analytical procedures related to the amounts and disclosures in the financial statement. This means they will tie back to bank statements, and accounts receivable and payable agings, review actual to budget variances, and verify contractual obligations. By performing inquiry and analytics, the accountant is able to provide limited assurance that there is no material modification that should be made to the financial statement. A review typically does not require external tests of accounting records or the need to obtain corroborating evidential matter. If your books and records aren't in complete disarray, most buyers will accept a review as sufficient.

An *audit* provides the highest level of assurance and, as such, requires time, work, and effort. It is also the costliest. The most significant difference between an audit engagement and a review is that the auditor is required to corroborate the amounts and disclosures included in the financial statements through testing the accounting documents, physical inspection, the use of third-party confirmations, and/or other procedures deemed appropriate. So, for example, documents will be sent to the bank for them to independently verify your cash. Confirmations will be sent to customers and vendors to independently verify the amount and quantity of transactions. The auditor must also understand the company's internal control structure and evaluate its effectiveness.

The auditor's report provides an opinion that the financial statements present information fairly in all material respects regarding the financial position of the company, and that the results of the operations are in conformity with GAAP. The end game is to make sure to reduce the risk that the financial statements are materially misstated.

Again, for most companies, unless you are in complete disarray, this is overkill.

A third viable option is a *compilation*. This report is the lowest level of assurance issued by an independent CPA. The objective is to assist management in presenting financial information in the form of financial statements without providing any assurance that there are no material modifications that should be made to the financials. No external verification is done, and the information is the "representation of management." Compilations don't require inquiries of management or analytical procedures. Instead, it is really just ensuring that generally accepted accounting principles are being applied. If you haven't been matching your revenue with the associated expense in the same period (a common problem among VARs, MSPs, and CSPs) then this might be the place to start. It is also the least expensive option.

It is possible, however, that you can sail smoothly through due diligence without any of these external reports. In both of my transactions, the buyer asked if I could provide reviewed financials, and in both cases I declined. If you feel confident that your financials are in conformity with GAAP (i.e., not a hybrid of cash and accrual accounting), and you have a process for closing your books on a timely basis, *and* you prepare a review of actual to forecasted revenue and expenses, *and* review the variances, I believe you can forego any audit or review of your financials.

Finally, there is a *quality of earnings (QofE)* report. These are typically prepared when companies want to either sell on their own or want to prepare extensively for a sale in advance. Many of the steps performed in a QofE are completed by M&A advisors who provide consultative services to prepare you in advance for a sale. The QofE highlights the key aspects of your business, include:

- Detailing revenue and gross profit margin by line of business
- Providing a detailed analysis of operating expenses and employee data
- Providing an extensive review of your addbacks for the adjusted EBITDA calculation
- Providing a working capital analysis to operate the business
- Explaining any fluctuations in monthly or annual income

Most companies in the $5M+ range typically have their financials in order or have a degreed accountant on staff who prepares financials in GAAP format. If you feel the person in charge of your accounting may need some oversight, I would suggest getting a degreed accountant to come in and take a look at your books in advance of a review. Remember that auditors cannot audit or review their own work, so the financials need to be in good order before a firm shows up to begin the audit or review. This "pre-work" may take up to a month or more to get things ready for an audit or review. The audit, review, or compilation could take a couple of months, especially if multiple years are involved—remember that buyers want to look back three years. Just be sure to keep that in mind. Being able to point to a set of reviewed financial statements will be well worth the time and expense incurred to keep the due diligence and LOI offer intact.

DOCUMENTS NEEDED FOR THE SALE – THE BEGINNINGS OF THE VIRTUAL DATA ROOM

I cannot stress enough the importance of *preparing* for a sale. The last thing you want to do is have a potential buyer in hand but have nothing ready to show them. If you plan on selling within the next 12 months, begin assembling the items below into a virtual data room (i.e., Dropbox, Google, ShareFile, SharePoint, etc.) that you can share with others (both internally and externally) when the time comes. Below is a list of documents that will be needed initially in preparation for a sale.

- The last three years of financials (profit and loss, balance sheet, and statement of cash flow)
- Current year financials, with budget to actual, and an explanation of significant variances*
- An accounts receivable and payable aging schedule
- Work-in-progress reports
- Details of any deferred revenue
- Fixed asset schedule
- Inventory list or aging report if applicable
- Federal and state tax returns for the last three years
- All payroll and sales and use tax returns filed for the last three years
- Personal property leases and tax returns if required in your city or state
- 401(k) and profit-sharing plans summary
- Employee medical benefit summary
- Summary of year-to-date wages and potential increases for the coming year – include anticipated commissions and bonuses

Nonfinancial documents that also should be gathered in advance:

- Company organization chart
- Sample customer engagement letter or contract
- List of certifications with vendors or others
- Copy of your current lease and any amendments from after initial signing. If your lease is not currently assignable, see what you can do about amending it in advance with your landlord.
- All insurance policies: general, commercial, employment practice, cyber, directors and officers, etc.
- All NDAs for employees and contractors. Now is the time to button this up if you have a few missing. Asking for them in the middle of due diligence usually signals to employees that something is up.
- Significant contracts with vendors: office equipment, software subscriptions, etc.

A more complete list of documents needed for due diligence can be found in the *Resources* section.

* If you are really "off" on your sales projections, and assuming the current year is better than the year before, you might think about reforecasting your projections to something that is achievable by year end. Showing a negative variance on forecasted revenue will highlight to your buyers that something is amiss. It is better not to have that conversation and restate the budget instead.

NEXT STEPS

- Get an independent assessment from a CPA (informal initially) of your financial statements for presentation and compliance with GAAP. If not compliant, then opt for a formal compilation, review or audit, as discussed above.

- Calculate the "rule of 40" for the last three years. Are you close or do you need to either increase revenue or decrease expenses?

- Begin a rough calculation of your adjusted EBITDA. Are the adjustments easily identifiable in your chart of accounts? Do you know the industry norm for your salary? Are you overpaying or underpaying yourself? – this will affect your salary adjustment.

- Start collecting due diligence documents in a separate, secure, online virtual data room.

2. Revenue Readiness

As a business owner, you have spent years focusing on a combination of top-line revenue, net income, and gross profit margins. As you begin thinking about preparing your company for sale, your attention will be more focused on EBITDA and year-over-year growth. While these metrics are all important, savvy buyers look for more when valuing your company. They look at the **quality** of your revenue.

According to the 2018 Equiteq Buyers Research Report, 67 percent of Private Equity firms and 45 percent of strategic buyers consider *recurring revenue* extremely important. And, spoiler alert: The higher the percentage of profitable recurring revenue your company generates, the more comfortable the buyer is with future profits, and thus the more quickly and easily you can exit from a company once it is sold. At a minimum, even in the current sellers' market, you should strive for at least 40 percent of your revenue being recurring.

When we speak of quality of revenue, we mean recurring, repeatable, and ideally cloud. We also mean high margins and geographical dispersal of your customer base. High revenue with low margins is not as enticing as low revenue with high margins. Revenue and margins go hand-in-hand. In addition, buyers prefer software revenue over services, and recurring revenue over repeatable.

For example, a company with only $5M in revenue that is over 50 percent recurring and with $1M in EBITDA will sell for more than a company with $10M in revenue, very little recurring revenue and $1.5M in EBITDA. Why? Even though the $10M is higher in revenue and EBITDA, the recurring revenue is virtually nonexistent. Buyers pay for the *future*, not the past. And the more secure that future is, the more they will pay.

What defines "quality"

As we mentioned above, quality can be viewed as a combination of the type of revenue, the gross profit margin it generates, and where the customer resides. **Recurring or repeat revenue** – Most people think of recurring revenue in its purest form to be software as a service (SaaS) revenue. And while that is the highest valued revenue, it is not the only kind of recurring revenue. Recurring revenue is defined by a contract, which ensures that your customer's agreement is predicated on recurring payments. If they stop paying for any reason, they will lose the ability to use the license, service, IP. or workflow, etc. Therefore, recurring revenue can be packaged as software **or** services. And while most IT companies are comfortable packaging support *as a service*, very few companies are comfortable packaging what was typically viewed as time and materials and fixed fee projects *as a service*. But if done correctly, it (a service) can also be a form of recurring revenue.

For example, ABC company packages the implementation of a SaaS based marketing automation software along with the services to implement it on a monthly fee. The customer is contractually obligated to pay not only for the software (SaaS) but also for the implementation services over that same period of time. The customer doesn't have a breakdown of which part is software and which part is services—just one monthly subscription fee that combines both.

Types of Recurring Revenue:

Own (internally developed for resale) IP software – cloud independent or dependent

Vendor's software – monthly (SaaS)

Professional services – technical support

Professional services – packaged solutions

Managed services – break/fix, disaster recovery, desktop hosting

Hosting services – IaaS or PaaS

Repeat revenue is different than recurring revenue, as it is not based on a contractual obligation or a SaaS-based product. Repeat revenue is defined as revenue that occurs year after year from the same customers and is **not** an annual enhancement renewal (unless it is your own software). As a software developer, repeat revenue might be a long-term plan with a customer for continued services over multiple years. While this is not yet contracted, a past track record may show continued services delivered to a specific customer and thus be considered highly repeatable revenue. Annual enhancements only count as repeat revenue if you are the developer of the software. If you are selling someone else's, it is not.

Selling software can be repeatable as well, especially if it is a 12- or 24-month subscription sold to the same customer for the same software every year. For example, selling a 12-month subscription to Trend Micro antivirus security software (while not on a subscription basis) does require an annual renewal. If you can show a track record of continuously selling this to the same customer year after year, you have repeatable revenue. While repeatable revenue has value, it is not valued as highly as recurring revenue.

To help showcase the value of your repeatable revenue, create a spreadsheet like the one below. Show the last three years of repeated revenue, the date the contracts were acquired, and the life-to-date revenue. With this data, you can perform calculations to determine the average customer value as well as the service length of an average customer. These are all metrics that buyers will want to see, especially if you are relying on the repeatability of your customers vs. a stream of recurring revenue.

Customer Lifetime Value

Customer Name	Begin Date	Revenue by Year and LTD			
		2017	2018	2019	Life to Date (LTD)
1 ABC		$ -	$ -	$ -	$ -
2 QRS					
3 XYZ					
..... More					

Fig.2.4

High gross profit margin (GPM) – The higher the GPM, the more attractive your company. Quality revenue produces, at a minimum, 40 percent gross profit margin. Anything less than this after sales and marketing and general and administrative expenses, leaves very little EBITDA. If you are selling a vendor's software solution that offers less than 40 percent margin, you will need to supplement this with built-in services that can increase the margins. The chart below was created from a study conducted in 2018 of Microsoft partners internationally. As you can see, the margin increases dramatically as companies create their own IP. Even if you don't have your own software packaged solution, a services firm can increase their GPM (38.7 percent – 42.7 percent), as shown below, by moving from project-based services to package-based services. And while four percentage points doesn't sound like much, on $5M in revenue, this can immediately drop an additional $200,000 annually to the bottom line, which could easily equate to an additional $1M in sales value.

Partner Margin Profile

Gross Margin Levels

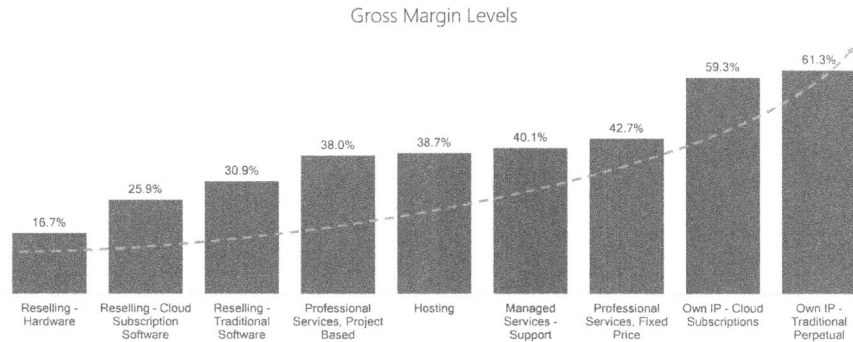

Source is CloudSpeed Partner Benchmarking Database, July 2018

Fig.2.5

Geographic concentration – This aspect can be viewed very differently by financial and strategic buyers. A strategic buyer or competitor may acquire you to increase a presence in a particular part of the country or a presence in a foreign country not currently served by them, so your geographical concentration in a particular area may be very important. A financial buyer may look at this differently and view a smaller market as potentially becoming saturated quickly, and as being more subject to economic downturns, weather, and governmental pressures. For example, a large VAR located in Puerto Rico was ready to sell his company, but the major hurricane that devastated the island in 2018 required him to put the sale of his business on hold. Thankfully, his customer base was geographically dispersed, and after a few months, he successfully sold his business—but not before several qualified buyers passed on this opportunity due to the location of the corporate office.

Cloud deployments allow partners to expand the reach of their customer base, and many customers have now come to expect that deployment and training for new software will be done remotely as well. As you focus on a specific industry or vertical, unless there is a large concentration of that vertical in a certain geography (say fracking for oil), you will naturally disseminate your customers geographically as you deploy more cloud solutions.

ALL REVENUE IS NOT CREATED EQUAL

In the chart below, we listed a number of different revenue line items typical of many technology service providers. Custom generated software (your own IP) deployed in the cloud has the highest value in a quality of revenue analysis, as it is recurring and contractual. The least attractive on the list is annual enhancements or maintenance renewals for either hardware or software. Even if you have a great track record of your customers renewing their annual enhancements or maintenance with you, they are not contractually obligated to do so, and they can decide to either let their maintenance lapse, or worse, switch to a competing vendor and renew with them. This "annual" revenue is uncertain and will be heavily discounted by the buyer. So, while 20 percent of your total revenue may be recurring in your eyes because you can pretty much count on it each year with 90 to 95 percent accuracy, you need to see it in the eyes of the buyer. It doesn't have the same value.

HIGH

Type of Revenue	Frequency	Contractual
Own IP - Cloud SaaS	Recurring	Y
Reselling - SaaS	Recurring	Y
Hosting/IaaS/PaaS	Recurring	Y
MSP - Cloud	Recurring	Y
MSP - Break/Fix	Recurring/Repeat	Y
Custom Development	Repeat	
Prof Services - Packaged/Fixed Fee	Repeat	
Own IP - Perpetual	One-time	
Prof Services – Time & Materials	One-time	
Reselling Software	One-time	
Reselling Hardware	One-time	
Annual Enhancements/Maintenance Renewals	Annual	

LOW

Fig.2.6

As mentioned earlier, most owners have focused on a combination of top-line revenue, net income, and gross profit margins. As you begin thinking about preparing your company for sale, think about how you can move your revenue up the list into higher-valued revenue. This will yield much greater results for increasing the value of your business.

Okay, while this seems very easy to talk about, moving a customer from a break-fix contract to a monthly subscription can take a long time. And as all seasoned owners know, flipping the switch and cutting off all break-fix customers and shifting immediately to a 100 percent recurring model, is not possible, either financially or practically. I use an MSP in this example, but the concept applies to many different technology service partner types. With all these points listed above, there has to be a *long-term* game plan, and many successful partners use a three- to four-year timeline for a smooth transition. Anything longer than that and you are likely to find yourself reinventing yet again as technology continues to change.

Packaged offerings

A packaged service offering is a preconfigured set of tasks to be accomplished for a customer over a specified period of time for a fixed fee. Creating packaged services consists of packaging support previously delivered under a pure consulting arrangement into packages that are predefined in terms of task, time frames, and pricing. This is the first step to help technology service providers bridge the gap between traditional hourly consulting offerings and fully managed services. They also provide an opportunity to create additional sales opportunities and potential new revenue streams by making access to current consulting offerings easier to understand, easier to evaluate their benefits, and easier to purchase. Think bite-sized solutions vs. a massive consulting project.

Packaged offerings of either software + services or just services is what customers prefer today. Unless the project is unique and so specific to that customer, no one wants to pay anymore for an open-ended time and materials project. Packaged offerings, like fixed-fee arrangements, give the customer the ability to budget—ideally, packaged offerings that allow the customer to pay over time, and are charged on a per user seat or some definable metric (providing flexibility as they grow or contract). Customers will pay for a service on a monthly subscription basis if you can prove the business value of your service to the customer and ensure their success.

Why would they pay more for the same solution as a one-time fee? Because as part of your monthly subscription, you will add special features or a greater level of support. I have personally created solutions where the customer will pay more each month if they are given: 1) 24/7/365 support, and 2) a service level agreement (SLA). Here is an example: Let's say you are converting an on-premises data repository to a cloud-based document management solution. You have determined that on a time and material basis, that service would cost the client $12,000 to $15,000. We will also assume that seven people need to be trained as part of this effort. Your packaged solution is charged by the user at $250 per month with a minimum of seven users. The subscription is for 12 months—so there is plenty of time to have the solution implemented and additional user questions answered.

But here is the key: If you truly want to differentiate yourself from your competitors, you need to include in your offering a 24/7* SLA + a guaranteed response time of x hours. If you don't meet the SLA, you will credit the customer some amount of money on that's month's subscription. It is also important to offer them the ability to terminate if you continually miss your SLA. The customer will do the math and see that this solution will cost $21,000—they never see your estimate of $12K to $15K. Since this transition is so important, and you are offering extended services and support with a fixed monthly fee that they can scale when needed, you are probably offering something your competition is not. But more importantly, you are offering peace of mind, low risk, and a fixed monthly solution that they can budget for.

"But wait!" you say. "I now have people working at all hours of the day???"

Yes, someone does need to be on call. And yes, you will need to be prepared to respond to any odd-hour calls during weekdays, but almost no one calls on the weekends or holidays. (And if you prefer, you can carve out certain major holidays.)

"And this will cost me more money in support?"

Not necessarily, especially if you trade days off during the week for someone to cover the weekend shift or at least one day of the weekend. Even with extra overtime or weekend rates for hourly employees, the data shows you can make money if priced correctly. As you create more of these packages, you will be providing better customer support, which means a higher customer retention rate, and you will end up with a much higher gross profit margin. The point is, the more you scale this model, the more money you will make.

Finally, if you add additional training or bonus features (via webinars where you have a one-to-many or on-demand webinars), your customers will see the continued value and may actually extend this beyond the 12 months with an evergreen contract. And as they add users, the monthly fee increases as well.

The offerings you can create are truly endless but adding an SLA and extended support hours is *key* to allowing you to increase the price of your offerings. Many owners are uncomfortable with this kind of an offering, but more products we purchase are doing this and more customers have come to expect this. The sooner you can create a packaged offering with a defined level of support, the easier it will be to sell and the more profitable you will become.

Moving from a one-time offering to a packaged offering requires us to resell the customer every month, quarter, or year depending on how often you bill your subscriptions. Every time a bill lands on their desk, you have an opportunity to reach out, as do they. It increases the dialogue between you and your customer long after the initial services are performed. Remember, the longer you can keep them under subscription, the stronger your relationship with the customer, and the higher your company value.

CONTRACTED REVENUE

Contractual revenue is another component that buyers will often ask about. While you may have one or more of the above-mentioned types of SaaS revenue, if it is not contractual, it will have a lesser value in their mind. That said, contractual revenue does not need to be multiyear to have value.

As Robert was preparing to sell his company, he was given advice by one of his mentors that if he increased the duration of his contracts (which were currently only annual), it would give buyers greater confidence that the revenue would continue post-transaction. While this is true, and buyers do want to see multiyear contracts, it is not necessary. And in some cases, it may be a detriment because it forces the customer to reevaluate and potentially shop the product or service you are offering.

Most large software SaaS vendors like to lock up customers for three years. With large implementations like a CRM or ERP application, this is an industry standard in part because it usually takes a year to get the application fully implemented. Unless you are offering significant discounts for a three-year contract, your customer won't like being locked up with large buyouts to exit the contract. If the industry you specialize in doesn't use multiyear contracts, you should probably not use them either. A one-year evergreen contract, a contract that renews automatically at the end of the 12-month subscription, will suffice in most cases. If the customer wants to terminate the contract before the 12 months, then you can create stiff penalties or buyout clauses. The less risk you put into the contract and the ability to terminate, the easier it will be for your customers to accept your terms. Having a one-year, evergreen contract will overcome any issues with the buyer if you are able to show a strong customer retention rate and low churn rate.

For example, Robert's customer base was mostly in the healthcare industry, and specifically in the life sciences area. Most early-stage life science companies have no idea where they will be in three years or if they will still have funding. Therefore, offering a three-year contract to them would not be attractive and could deter good customers from signing up. Robert knew this about his industry so he designed his contracts to last for only one year, with an evergreen clause that it would renew annually unless the customer gave a 60-day notice. He also provided other areas in his contract where customers could terminate if certain standards were not met. Because of these features, his buyers were very comfortable with his contracts.

CUSTOMER CANCELLATIONS, A.K.A. CHURN

Churn is a term typically used when discussing SaaS, and also general recurring revenue, and it is the percentage rate at which customers cancel their recurring revenue subscriptions. It is a key metric of SaaS business performance and an important parameter in revenue forecasting. An acceptable churn rate is in the 5 to 7 percent range *annually*, depending upon whether you measure number of customers or revenue. It is certainly *possible* to have a lower churn rate, but it is *difficult* because there are things that are out of your control, such as customer bankruptcies, mergers, and acquisitions that will unexpectedly affect your numbers, regardless of how well your product or customer support is working. Can you get a different churn rate if you measure the actual number of customers rather than revenue? The answer is *yes*. So be prepared to offer up either one. But most buyers are interested in the calculation based upon revenue, not the number of customers.

For example, if you lost five customers out of one hundred for the year, then your churn rate is 5 percent, but if you look at those same five customers, depending on the amount they spend with you each month, that churn rate could be higher or lower. If the loss of those five customers represents, for example, 10 percent of your revenue, then your churn rate is that higher number—10 percent.

MAKING THE SHIFT FROM SERVICE TO PRODUCT

The trend has already begun for companies to reduce or minimize "one-time" revenue as the company matures. Of course, that is easier said than done. And that begs the question of how quickly can you transition from one-time revenue to subscription revenue. In the chart below, we show an example of how different margin structures can affect how quickly this can be accomplished.

How quickly can you change profitably? The answer depends on your current gross profit margin, and your selling and general and administrative expenses. The better the bottom line, the more aggressive you can become. According to the Rose/CloudSpeed Benchmark survey: The average channel partner who performs consulting services has a cost of goods sold of 62 percent, with Sales and Marketing at 20 percent, and General and Administrative expenses at 5 percent, leaving pre-tax income at approximately 13 percent. Under that scenario, the most revenue you can convert from one-time to recurring while maintaining a bottom line is about 30 percent. This leaves some cushion for debt service and capital purchases, and a small cushion for margin reductions for subscription software.

Percentage Transition to Recurring Revenue				
	0% RR		**30% RR**	
Sales - Non-recurring	$	100	$	70
Sales - Recurring (1st yr Subscription)*				10
Total Revenue	$	100		80
Cost of Goods Sold **		62		49.6
Gross Profit Margin		38		30.4
Sales and marketing		20		20
General and administrative		5		5
Total Expenses		25		25
Pre-tax Income	$	13	$	5.4

* 30% of the revenue is moved to a 3-yr contract
** Cost of goods sold remains at 62%

Fig.2.7

Why would a customer transition?

Okay, so maybe you are thinking why would your customers give up a license they already own to migrate to a subscription model? After all, they would be taking a product they already own just to rent it back from the vendor. According to a McKinsey & Company study[3], more than 50% of customers are open to making that transition for a number of reasons: The migration gives them an opportunity to clean up years of complex perpetual contracts, to eliminate unused licenses, and to negotiate a subscription contract aligned with the true needs of their business. Most subscription offerings allow for a greater granularity in licensing models (based upon user types or number of transactions) than on-premises solutions. In addition to better licensing options, a subscription offering includes all patching and upgrades, which typically reduces the internal costs of hardware and the staff to maintain it. It also brings a level of security and redundancy which may exceed the current solution on-premise.

NEXT STEPS

- Determine the percent of recurring, repeatable, one-time, and annual revenue in your company.

- Determine the lifetime customer value either on a recurring or repeatable basis using the spreadsheet above as a guide.

- Determine if there are services that could be packaged into a monthly subscription and establish a price.

- Look at your own COGS and EBITDA percentages from a cash flow perspective and consider how quickly you could begin transitioning one-time revenue to recurring revenue.

3. Management Muscle

"You are the average of the five people you spend the most time with."
– Jim Rohn, author and motivational speaker

Management muscle is a combination of all the things you have done or could do to hire and retain the right people, to organize them and document their interrelationships, to create a strong culture, and to ensure that they can function well even when you "take a sabbatical."

And management muscle matters—especially when it comes time to sell.

Impressing buyers is the best way to get full value for your business when you sell, and one of the best ways to impress buyers is by showing them your management muscle—the strength of your organization's management team that guarantees its ability to grow and prosper in the future. A great management team creates transferable value and ensures the company's ability to continue operating successfully with minimal disruption to its cash flow.

Amongst financial buyers, *a strong management team* ranked behind only revenue readiness and customer satisfaction and retention as a value driver. Financial buyers especially look for a strong management team because they are less likely to know and understand the business. Management is important for the strategic buyer, but they already have a seasoned management team in place and may not be as concerned about your team.

For the owner, having a strong management team will allow for you to exit either immediately after the sale or shortly thereafter. Let's be honest, not everybody finds working for someone else to be something they want to do after running the show for so many years. Knowing you have a strong management team in place working to achieve your earn-out gives you peace of mind so you can move on, should you so decide. Secondly, it reduces the risk to the buyer that the company might not thrive without your presence, which in turn allows you to negotiate for a larger amount of cash up front. Finally, having a strong management team will allow them to focus on running the company and making sure sales do not slip while you spend the next six to 12 months consummating a deal. As I have already mentioned, nothing will stall a sale faster than missing the sales forecast.

Unfortunately, one of the biggest misconceptions for many owners is that the value of their business is tied directly to their personal involvement in managing all aspects of the business. This couldn't be any further from the truth. If the business cannot survive and grow without your personal, daily involvement, the value of your business will decrease dramatically. *If you have not already begun, now is the time to begin working yourself out of a job.*

Even if your plan is to stay with the company after the sale, the buyer is still going to evaluate the strength of your management team, as they too want to insulate themselves should you decide to move on.

Buyers are not only looking to eliminate the risk of the CEO leaving and things falling apart, they are looking to maintain growth. Having a seasoned, well-established management team is indispensable to any company's future growth. After all, they will be responsible for sales, customer retention, and employee retention to make it all happen.

Another main worry for buyers, and especially for financial investors, is the commitment of the management team and the question of whether they will remain in the company post-acquisition. The CEO who comes to the table with his senior management already aware and actually involved in the deal is much more likely to have the management team engaged in the due diligence process and it is a sign that the CEO relies heavily on his team, has been forthright with them on the intention to sell, and trusts them enough to expose them early in the process to the buyers. This also gives buyers more comfort that the deal will actually happen and that the CEO will not back out at the end. And buyers also know that, emotionally speaking, it is always easier for a CEO to depart knowing that he/she is leaving the business in the capable hands of his/her management team.

As the seller, you should create incentives to discourage senior manage-ment (if they are not shareholders) from leaving the company during the ne-gotiation stages or within one or two years of the sale. Allocating a percentage of the cash and earn-outs to your management team will compensate these individuals not only for their past performance but for future performance as well.

If they are not already shareholders, your gut will tell you what is right for your team and what percentage to allocate. For those who are not included in these two items, "stay bonuses" are a great tool to keep key performers engaged. And if you are creative, this is one area where you might suggest that you split the stay bonus between you and the buyer because the buyer also has a vested interest in making sure your management team remains.

Remember, you will need everyone's efforts to achieve your earn-out, so why not bring them along for the ride now?

If you are concerned about not having the "right" team in place, you can fine-tune your management team in preparation for a sale. If you are on the three- or five-year plan, take a serious look at your team and evaluate if they can move the business forward without your involvement. If the answer is no, now is the time to start making replacements. Don't let tenure prevent you from replacing someone you know won't work in the long run. Don't wait until just before you are ready to sell to strengthen your management team; otherwise potential buyers will be concerned that you are just "window dressing" before the sale. Sure, it is okay to have one or two newbies on the management team, but if more than 30 percent of your team is less than 18 months in the job, this may cause concern for the buyer.

Tools to hire the right team

Over my 25 years as a CEO, I made more than my fair share of hiring mistakes. The higher the position in the organizational chart, the bigger the impact of a failure. I admit I didn't hire a C-level executive because I made such an epic fail not once but twice. Instead, I filled the role myself, which over time proved unwise. No matter what type of technology provider you associate with, there are at least two or three positions in the organization that are critical to its success.

Regardless of how you choose to source your candidates, whether recruiters, websites, or LinkedIn, in the end it sometimes comes down to a gut feeling if that candidate is right or not. In my opinion, a C-level or any director level position is too important to just rely on your gut feeling. Fortunately, there are a number of tools, such as personality tests, out in the marketplace to assess strengths and weaknesses. I have tried many and considering ease of use, cost and the level of detail provided, my two favorites are DISC and Caliper.

DISC—which stands for Dominance, Influence, Steadiness, and Compliance—helps you determine the personality type of potential hires in an easily understandable way. This test, which has no right or wrong answers, contains 28 groups of four statements. If you answer honestly and spontaneously, it should take you only five to 10 minutes to complete. DISC predicts your behavior toward others and how best to interact with team members, understanding not only your own DISC composite but theirs as well. Although you can take a version of the test for free here at https://discpersonalitytesting.com/free-disc-test/, the paid options may be worth considering.

For example, Your Life's Path (https://www.thediscpersonalitytest.com/) is one of a number of sites that offer the test. They offer multiple paid options as well as consulting. We used the "DISC classic" from Your Life's Path, which runs around $70 per test. We generally used the test after the first interview (either by phone, Skype, or in person) to determine a person's overall traits. A certified DISC provider can review the results with you for an extra charge. We used that service initially but eventually felt we had become so familiar with the tool that it was no longer necessary. However, if you are new to the test, it is definitely worthwhile to engage a certified consultant to review the results with you.

Sample DISC graph:

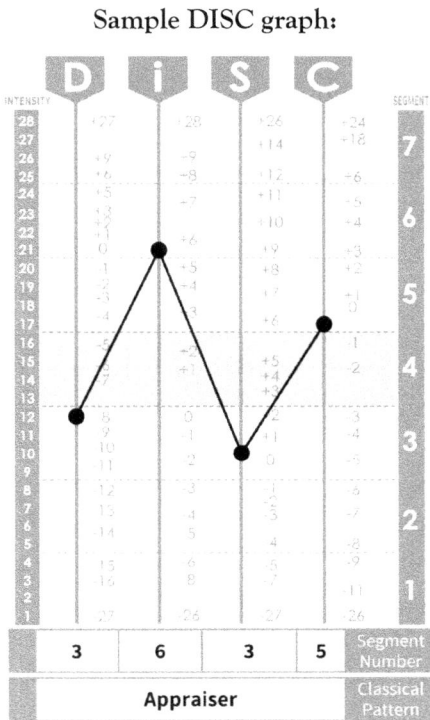

Fig.2.8

The above is an example of a DISC graph. While it is beyond the scope of this book to explain it in more detail, just viewing this one graph can tell me a lot. I can immediately spot if the person is geared toward technical work, or consulting work, or is best suited for sales—just by one small graph.

The second assessment tool, Caliper, is more in-depth (https://www.calipercorp.com/caliper-profile). This is my favorite assessment, as it gave me an accurate picture of what the person would be like 120 days after hire—unlike the DISC test, which a clever person may be able to manipulate. The Caliper Assessment test, which is made up of 180 multiple choice questions and may take up to two hours to complete, is less vulnerable to mental manipulation. Like DISC, it is not a pass/fail test. The Caliper Test is used to measure and report on how an applicant's traits relate to job performance. It gathers information about an individual's natural strengths, motivators, and potential to succeed in a particular role.

Our hiring team found this test valuable for two reasons: First, we could overlay the outcomes of a person's graph results with the graph of their immediate supervisor's report or the management team's reports, to see if there would be a good synergistic or complementary fit. This was invaluable for the management team and built confidence immediately that the hire would be a good fit. Secondly, it would give us a pretty good assessment of the person's ability to pick up on new concepts, their level of risk taking, and their sense of urgency. The need for these traits (and the level needed) is completely different for each team, whether sales, engineering, admin, or professional services. The ability to grasp concepts quickly was especially key for me and my management team, as I was known to explain new ideas at breakneck speed (more due to my excitement than anything else), and I wasn't happy if I had to explain it more than twice. (Personal flaw, I acknowledge, but there nonetheless.)

Caliper is administered directly through the Caliper Corp. organization and by externally trained and certified consultants. We worked directly with Caliper and built up a tremendous relationship with our consultant over the years. She was very instrumental in helping us make great hiring decisions. Unlike DISC, Caliper was typically given after the *last* round of interviews and before reference calls. We used reference calls to validate the report and this made for a much more in-depth conversation. Then before we made a final hire, we would review the results with the candidates to see if they agreed or disagreed with the findings. Rarely would someone disagree, but it made for a great conversation if they did.

Nothing is more painful and costly than a bad hire on your management team, which inevitably leads to employee churn. Do what you can to minimize the chance of that happening.

THE COMPANY ORGANIZATION CHART

As part of your seller package, buyers will want to see an organization chart in order to have a clear understanding of the business structure. Ideally, you do not want a flat organization where everyone reports directly to the CEO, a common practice in smaller companies with less than $7M in revenue. If everyone is reporting to *you*, it does not instill confidence that the company could run profitably without you. If that is your organization chart today, it is something you need to change. Determine if you can promote from within or if you need to hire externally. While this may reduce profitability in the short term, it will add to the value of your company in the long run for the reasons explained above.

Org charts should be created well before you sell your company, and you probably already have one in place. If so, it is important that you share the latest chart with your entire organization so that everyone is clear as to where the solid and dotted lines are drawn. Also, *your* view of the org chart may not be the same as that of the rest of your management team. In other words, what is on paper is not really the way the company is run. Now is a good time to get everyone on the same page and adjust the chart to reflect how the company is actually organized. When a buyer interviews other key personnel toward the end of the due diligence process, you want to make sure that everyone is aligned regarding job responsibilities and reporting structure. Also, be sure to understand who can take over a role in the case of sickness or the immediate loss of a team member. Having only one person on a vertical line is never a good sign, given that there is no one underneath them to take over should they decide to the leave the company. If that is the case, be prepared to discuss who would do their job in the short term or show dotted lines to their immediate successor. Most well-run organizations have cross-trained others to take over key roles during absences or in case of turnover and to develop enhanced skills in other team members.

If positions are open in your organization, be sure to include the boxes on the chart but show them as open. A strategic buyer may see these as positions they can fill with their existing team as part of the amalgamation of the companies. A financial buyer then knows that this is part of your growth plan or that a key role still needs to be filled.

ROBERT INSIGHT:

Before Robert sold his consulting division, he knew he needed to strengthen his delivery team with a services delivery manager. Even though he tried numerous times to hire within the group, many of his best consultants were just not good managers. Thankfully, after advertising for the position externally, he found the perfect person who could take over the team when it came time to sell. Unfortunately, Robert did not think about his own prominent role in sales. When it came time to sell his consulting division, the buyer knew Robert was so involved in new sales that no other person in the group could fill his role. Therefore, the buyer would need to hire for this position. Accordingly, they adjusted his EBITDA downward to compensate for the cost of hiring a comparable salesperson. Robert lost over half a million dollars in value.

Robert vowed not to repeat this mistake and began filling key positions where he needed support. He was not going to let the next buyer lower his valuation for the cost of a replacement position; he was instead going to try to work himself out of a job.

How sabbaticals can strengthen the company

If you are in a key role, such as the CEO, CIO, or COO, and your plan is to exit after a sale, one of the best ways to prepare yourself and prove the company can run well without you, or other key executives, is to take a sabbatical. This extended, and more importantly "unplugged," time can also help an executive step back from day-to-day activities, which allows for creativity in thought and a renewed spirit. From a practical standpoint, it also means someone else has to do your job while you are gone. This works best if you are truly off the grid—no phone, no emails, no texts from the office.

A sabbatical is considered an extended time off, away from the day-to-day work obligations of the company. It is a time for mentally and physically checking out of your normal life. The most successful sabbaticals consisted of either a long walkabout through Australia, backpacking through Central America, or sailing through the Tahitian islands. In other words, the more removed, the more successful. What started as a perk for the C-level became a company-wide ritual that was extended to the entire organization, regardless of position or role. Everyone looked forward to their time.

It also became a major recruiting tool, as not too many companies would pay for their employees to enjoy an entire month off to explore the world, learn new skills, or conquer a major project that they might not have done otherwise—given that normal vacations are usually gobbled up with family gatherings or other holiday obligations. It became a perk everyone looked forward to after their seven-year anniversary

The sabbatical policy required a person to be out of the office for no less than 30 days. Why a minimum of 30 days? Because it was a time period long enough to require that you off-loaded both weekly and monthly tasks. Anything less than a month doesn't require the same level of preparation and documentation because you can come back soon enough to pick up where you left off. Being "MIA" for 30 days requires preparation. I do, however, suggest that C-level execs or key directors take six weeks instead of 30 days because it is a better test to determine if the company can function well in the absence of a key manager.

Employees on sabbatical were required to refrain from responding to any company or customer emails and were required one month in advance to indicate in their email signature the days that they would be absent. That way, anything with a greater sense of urgency would be completed in advance. We let our customers know about our policy and we communicated well in advance who would be absent and who specifically would be taking over their role. Our philosophy was: the better you documented your job and everything that you do, the less likely we will have to bother you while you are gone.

While you might think that only large organizations can afford the luxury of such a policy, that is not the case at all. We started this policy with as little as 15 team members. Clearly, the smaller the company, the more of a burden it is on the people remaining, but I would argue that it is more important the smaller you are.

The policy was put in place for the well-being of our team, and as a great recruitment perk, but little did I know that it would have a very positive effect on the organization as a whole. It also provided proof that the company could function without certain C-level executives if they were absent for an extended period of time. Here are some additional unintended consequences of the sabbatical:

1. It required the person to document daily, weekly, and monthly procedures, which many times is not actually done at every level in a company. The documentation process actually uncovered some IP that we realized was not memorialized anywhere.

2. It required that the jobs then be delegated to other team members, who were then trained in new roles and responsibilities, thus learning new skills and furthering their own careers. This also eliminated single points of failure. More on that later...

3. It required the team to prepare in advance. Since the company announced at the beginning of each year if a team member was taking a sabbatical, everyone knew a process for documentation would need to begin before that person could leave. All documentation and training needed to be completed 60 days prior to the beginning of the sabbatical. This was a great incentive to get the documentation done because when it was complete you knew you could leave without having everything done. One month prior to your departure, the designated team members could begin taking on their new responsibilities and ask any questions prior to your actual departure. It also provided an opportunity for shoring up any lack of documentation, so it turned out to be a crafty way for the company to document the policies and procedures that are not always obvious.

4. Other team members could review what your tasks were and sometimes suggest more efficient ways of doing them, which actually happened naturally because they were taking on a role in addition to their full-time duties. If there was a quicker way to accomplish the additional tasks, they would probably find it.

5.   It allowed everyone to develop new skills. The people who took on the new responsibilities did so because it was required, but the person who came back now had time to pursue new responsibilities as well.

6.   It brought the organization together as a team. The person leaving was excited; the team would throw a bon voyage party to wish them well; and then those team members who were left covering the responsibilities would work closely together to make sure all the tasks were accomplished.

7.   It increased longevity and stability within the organization. Anyone who was close to their sabbatical time wouldn't consider leaving the company unless it was extreme. And upon their return, they were able to take on some new responsibilities as they had ideally shed some of their old ones.

Finally, and most importantly, it shows a buyer that a key member of either the executive team or the management team can be gone for an extended period of time and the company will run well without them. And you, as an executive, can personally have peace of mind that your company can manage if you decide to exit shortly after the sale. It is the most valuable exercise you can do to increase the value of your company.

Not everyone can, or will want to, implement a sabbatical policy, but broadening skills through cross-training, documenting procedures, and having other team members active in other roles during absences will be an invaluable benefit to the organization.

Before we leave the topic of the importance of a strong management team, we should discuss the importance of also keeping intact the employees under management level. We have all heard the saying, *"People leave managers, not companies."* Therefore, having a strong management team will also help to retain the employees. In the technology consulting business, so much customer stickiness and revenue is attached to key individuals. Employees leaving after an acquisition creates a revenue risk that is of real concern to both financial and strategic buyers, but if there is a strong management team in place that will maintain consistency during this transition period, the organization will do well and the buyers will do well.

THE "CULTURE" FIT

As a seller, a good culture fit will be one of the top criteria when deciding between buyers. This is especially true if a large percentage of your sale price is tied up in an earn-out. It probably is obvious, but without a culture fit people leave, profits suffer, and earn-outs fail; never good for a seller.

But a good culture fit is equally important for the buyer. Buyers look for a culture that will attract, motivate, develop, and retain top talent. In the case of strategic buyers, having a strong cultural fit is extremely important because there is a major integration of people, skills, and talent that needs to be brought into the existing ecosystem. A clash of two misaligned cultures will affect both entities. After the sale, two completely different teams will have to come together over a variety of integration challenges such as selling, quoting, and implementing engagements. Many deals die over culture.

Culture fit is not as much of an issue for financial buyers or PEG firms as they tend to leave the acquiring company alone to continue their business as usual. When it does become a concern is when they are integrating a company into an already existing acquisition. In this case, culture fit is as important as it is with a strategic buyer.

But how does a prospective buyer know if you have a compatible company culture?

They will look for the following:

- Low employee attrition rates—less than 10 percent annually. Attrition rates higher than 15 percent creates concern.
- Stated shared mission statement and shared values and beliefs—not just posted on the website or in the office but in practice.
- Team events, reward programs, and other non-cash incentives.
- A strong well-defined process for hiring people; the use of personality profiles.
- How you write your open job positions.
- How employees are incentivized to learn, and training they are offered to develop and increase their skills.
- Bonus structures that incent both individual and company goals.
- Supporting a cause or charity as an organization.

Motivating your teams by giving them autonomy and purpose (doing something that matters and doing it well) while giving them work that has meaning and stretches their skills, and then rewarding them accordingly, creates the kind of environment that binds people in times of difficulty or change. A strong culture will transcend the turmoil of an acquisition.

NEXT STEPS

- Locate, update, or create an organization chart using an MS Word template or Google Docs—include years in the role, and open positions.

- Honestly identify weaknesses—enlist tools like Caliper to assess your current management team's strengths.

- Plan and execute your own sabbatical within the next 12 months. Can't? List all your duties and delegate every one of them to someone else. Give yourself no more than 12 months to complete this task.

- Review existing mission statement and shared values. Don't have them? Create them with your team.

4. Value Proposition/Verticalization

Creating a unique value proposition and specializing in a vertical has been the messaging for several years within various partner channels. While many continue to resist the call to pick a vertical, those that have are now receiving higher values for their companies when they decide to sell. Companies that have a proven track record in a particular vertical are being heavily sought after by both strategic and financial buyers. Strategic buyers are looking to add additional verticals to their portfolio of products, or to strengthen a vertical they are already dominant in, by purchasing your company to complement their existing services. Financial buyers are no longer interested in generalists, as margins erode over time and sales become stagnant.

Equally as important as mastering a vertical is defining your value proposition, which is why these two values are presented together. Kind of like peanut butter and jelly. A statement that is positioned above the fold on your website, and that can define your value quickly to a viewer, is key today in keeping prospects on your website and consuming more content. Buyers know that a company with a strong value proposition will do well in both good and bad economic times as it will be able to set itself apart from the competition while creating higher gross profit margins.

Of course, that is not to say that a large horizontal partner will not be attractive to a buyer due to sheer size; they will, but not at the highest EBITDA multiple.

Value proposition

Your value proposition should set you apart from the competition and provide a WOW factor to clients who can clearly see the value you create with your products and services. In its simplest terms, a value proposition is a positioning statement that explains what *benefit* you provide for your ideal customer and how you do it in a *unique* way, different from your competitors.

If you look just like your competitors and focus only on the features of your service, rather than the value you create for the end client, your growth will become more difficult over time. Most professional service companies are good at describing their services (features), but not so good at talking about *the outcomes and value* that clients will experience.

> **Unique:** What are your unique selling points that set you apart from your competitors? For example, you may be a domain expert in a certain discipline, focused an "inch wide and mile deep" in a vertical niche with a proprietary methodology that delivers rapid results.

> **Value:** What are the business gains or outcomes your clients can reap by using your methodologies or products? Clients are interested in the business gains and are willing to pay more for making their jobs easier. The price they pay for a project will not keep them awake at night, but the risk that they won't meet their business objectives will. Leap right into the head of your client and then jump again into the head of his/her boss. *What business needs and issues do you think the CXO is worried about?* And how will your engagement or product solve their issues and concerns?

> **Proposition:** What are you offering your clients and what are the major components of your service? Use each component to identify how it demonstrates your superior level of expertise and/or how it delivers additional value. Identify features of your solution that *reduce clients' risk*, such as fees contingent on results or reverse the risk entirely—no gain/ no fee.

WAYS TO HELP DEFINE YOUR VALUE PROPOSITION

In case you haven't already defined a value proposition or need to rethink the one you have, below are the keys to a simple yet effective statement:

In a nutshell, your value proposition should contain the following:

1.   Explains how your product solves customers' problems or improves their situation (*relevancy*).

2.   Delivers specific benefits (*quantified value*).

3.   Tells the ideal customer why they should buy from you and not from the competition (*unique differentiation*).

You must present your value proposition as the first thing the visitors (and buyers) see on your home page (up in the hero image), and it should be on *every* landing page.

Be sure to use the language of your customer. It must demonstrate to the customer that you understand their industry, their jargon and their problems. In order to do that, you need to know the language your customers will use to describe your offering and how they benefit from it. Become a member of their community. They will know if you are not, so if you are unclear, interview your target customer to understand their pain-points.

If you have a current value proposition, evaluate it by checking whether it answers the questions below:

• What product or service is your company selling?
• What is the end-benefit of using it?
• Who is your target customer for this product or service?
• What makes your offering unique and different?

Peep Laja, the founder of CXL, has a great article on how to find your value proposition, as well as how to A/B test it if you are unsure how well it will land with your customers. Here is a link to this blog: https://conversionxl.com/blog/value-proposition-examples-how-to-create/.

If you are still struggling with how to create or redefine your statement, Neural Impact (https://neuralimpact.ca/) also has a site that will guide you through the process of what a value proposition might look like. The survey will ask you a few questions, and when you thoughtfully complete the answers, a draft of your value proposition will be emailed to you so you can edit it: https://neuralimpact.ca/valueproposition. Their team of advisors will offer additional services if you are still struggling to create your perfect statement.

Finally, if you are still struggling with your identity or brand story, I highly recommend you read *Building a Story Brand: Clarify Your Message so Customers Will Listen* by Donald Miller. This book does an excellent job of helping you simplify your message. In the book, the author states that your *customer* should be able to answer these three questions within five seconds of looking at your website or marketing material:

1.   What do you offer?

2.   How will it make my life better?

3.   What do I need to do to buy it?

At StoryBrand, (https://storybrand.com) they call this "passing the grunt test." But it is also integral to your value proposition.

INDUSTRY VERTICALIZATION

At this point in your company's journey, you may have chosen a vertical or two to focus on. If you are larger than $10M in revenue, having more than one vertical is achievable, but otherwise stick with one and excel at it. Like your value proposition, hopefully it is front and center on your website. If you support more than one industry, mini sites are typically the best option to uniquely capture that particular industry. Buyers want to see specialization, and that is one of the main reasons why strategic buyers/partners acquire other partners. Many times, they want to expand on an industry vertical or enter into a new one. This is one very specific instance where a smaller partner (in revenue) can earn a higher EBITDA multiple than a larger partner by offering a unique industry vertical solution.

In 2016, nearly three-quarters of companies at the top of the MSP501

Worldwide List and Ranking of managed services providers (MSPs) reported serving clients in specific vertical industries[20].

Of the top 19 companies on the list, 13—the largest share—reported focusing on legal customers. Other key vertical markets included manufacturing, accounting and banking, and financial services, each served by 11 of the top 19 MSPs. Just five of the top 19 firms, or slightly more than 26 percent of MSPs, said they had no vertical market focus. No data was available for vertical markets in 2017 or 2018, but verticalization is on the rise with all TSPs.[5]

There are 19 commonly recognized vertical segments, but for most product and service offerings, these can be grouped together to yield 13 major industry segments:

- Construction
- Manufacturing
- Wholesale trade
- Information technology
- Retail trade
- Utilities
- Financial services
- Educational services
- Transportation and warehousing
- Entertainment, accommodation, and food services
- Healthcare and social services
- Public administration
- Other services

Some software vendors find the above list to be too large. Microsoft and Salesforce specifically focus on six vertical markets with their partners:

- Financial services
- Retail
- Manufacturing
- Government
- Education
- Healthcare

While you might think six is not a very large group, there are subsets within each of these. For example, specific regulatory compliance needs can also characterize vertical markets such as HIPAA and FDA compliance for healthcare and drug companies. Or in retail, a vendor might target the subcategory of cannabis retailers, who have very specific needs as well as regulatory requirements.

How to identify your strongest vertical or subvertical

Maybe you support a few verticals and don't know which one to choose. As I was doing research for this book, I came across a webinar by Equiteq entitled "Quality of Fees"[19]. The chart below, while originally from this webinar, has been modified to more specifically point out how you can quickly determine your existing verticals. To help determine your most ideal vertical, and your chances of success in that vertical, walk through the following two-step process. The results may surprise you.

Step 1: First determine the verticals your customer base falls into. If you are already in just one vertical, niche it down to subcategories to get a better picture. Next, define your top services. You may have *more* than five, but this will tell you that you might have too many and that perhaps you need to focus on fewer. Next, sort your last 24 to 36 months of revenue, by customer, and by the industry buckets you have identified below. Pick the top 25 to 50 customers (or whatever number you feel broadly represents your customer base). Then allocate the revenue by client into the top services. This exercise may take a while if you are not able to create subcategories of revenue by service. Getting the exact revenue by service type is not the goal, so if you need to look at each customer and decide manually based upon your knowledge, that's fine. Ideally, you want to be as precise as possible. At this point, hopefully one or two industries, or subindustries, will emerge.

Step1: Revenue by Industry

Revenue by Industry by Service Offering

Industry	Number of current customers	Service 1 Migration Service	Service 2 Desktop Hosting	Service 3 Office 365	Service 4 DNS Hosting	Service 5 Other	Total Revenue by Industry	Industry as a % of Revenue
Financial Services	12		202,000	37,000	100,000	50,000	389,000	13%
Public Sector	5	12,000		50,000			62,000	2%
Entertainment	8	23,000		75,000			98,000	3%
Distribution	11			28,000			28,000	1%
Manufacturing	9			55,000			55,000	2%
Healthcare	38	39,000	685,000	220,000			944,000	33%
Non-profit	13			130,000			130,000	4%
Life Sciences	35	50,000	487,000	550,000	75,000	33,000	1,195,000	41%
Total	131	124,000	1,374,000	1,145,000	175,000	83,000	2,901,000	100%
Service as a % of Total Revenue		4%	47%	39%	6%	3%	100%	

Fig.2.9

Step 2: Take the top few, not more than five, and then score each based upon the categories below. The total in the second box below will give you an idea of which service and industry would provide you with the highest return. If you feel 1, 3, 5 is too restrictive, then use a larger scale. The result should be similar but more granular if two industries are close. We can see below that the "Life Sciences" industry provides the highest opportunity score.

Step2: Opportunity Score

Overall Industry Score

Industry	Market Size	Industry Knowledge	Reputation in Industry	Competitive Advantage	Win Rate	Ability to Upsell Products	Total
Financial Services	5	3	3	1	3	5	20
Public Sector							
Entertainment							
Distribution							
Manufacturing							
Healthcare	5	3	3	3	3	5	22
Non-profit							
Life Sciences	1	5	5	5	5	5	26

Rank the category: 5 = High, 3 = Medium, 1 = Low

Fig.2.10

Review your totals and see which industry has the highest value. This may be a good indicator of where you need to focus in the future. This spreadsheet is available in our downloadable resource section: https://rosebizinc.com/book-resource.

ROBERT INSIGHT:

Robert knew that life sciences and healthcare were a large part of his customer base, but it wasn't until he created his own analysis that he realized that his desktop hosting services for his life science and healthcare companies were generating roughly 40 percent of his overall revenue. He then took the exercise a step further and analyzed the gross profit margin of this desktop hosting and found that his margins were the highest because he charged more for the services related to HIPAA and FDA application security and provisioning. He now could clearly see he had an opportunity that could set him apart from other competitors. He reevaluated his value proposition and made a major shift to articulating his value to clients who required extra documentation and security for regulated companies, which almost all life science and healthcare companies need. He rebranded his website and changed his color schemes to reflect more of a security look and feel. Almost immediately he saw a change in the type of prospects calling his sales team for quotes.

NEXT STEPS

- Download the *Revenue by Industry* spreadsheet from https://rosebizinc.com/book-resources/.

- List all your customers and assign an industry vertical to each of them, and then determine the total value of that customer—total billings life to date. See any trends?

- Do you see more than one industry that accounts for over 30 percent of your sales?

- Revisit your value proposition—is it easily identifiable on your website and in your marketing materials? It's always interesting to gather a few team members around the table and ask each one to write down the current value proposition. Is there consensus?

5. Customer Satisfaction and Retention

This may come as a surprise to many, but customer satisfaction and retention rank higher than the quality of your revenue for financial buyers. And, it ranks in the top three for most financial buyers. Why? Because studies show that just *a 5 percent increase in customer retention produces more than a 25 percent increase in profit*. Existing customers tend to buy more from a company over time, and happy existing customers refer others to your company. And if you are offering a complex solution or integration service, customers will pay a premium to stay with you rather than switch to a competitor.

How satisfied your customers are is what is going to be most important to buyers. Yet few organizations monitor, report, and reward employees for high customer satisfaction. In order to demonstrate this, you need to quantify the customer satisfaction number.

You also have to be able to speak to how you *lose* customers. If your customers are able to abandon your product or services overnight due to a lack of contractual obligations and with little to no switching costs, this can be a red flag for buyers. If your customer can leave you next week without any pain or planning, that's not a good thing either. This then begs the question of long-term contracts and their implicit value.

Long-term contracts don't necessarily add value to the business if you lose 10 percent of your customers per year. What adds value is the stability of your client base and the class of revenue derived from the technologies and services you offer that are of value to your customers. Contracts no longer guarantee this stability, but customer satisfaction does. Partners who only interface with their customers once a year, perhaps because of an annual enhancement or support program coming due, are always surprised when instead of the customer paying the renewal, they receive a notice that the customer has changed partners. It is not uncommon for partners to get lulled into a false sense of security about servicing the end customer, and they can be completely caught off guard when the customer chooses not to renew.

But here is the problem: Good customers rarely call or email you when things are going well, and unhappy customers (unless the experience was heinous) don't want to have a negative confrontation so they just don't say anything. Every partner has experienced a surprise customer departure. As both competition and buyer awareness continue to grow, customer experience is sometimes the only true competitive advantage, and thus it needs to be measured and monitored continuously.

MEASURING CUSTOMER SUCCESS

Ideally, you are measuring your customer satisfaction in multiple areas and at a minimum on an annual basis. If you are a project work-driven organization, it is best to be able to measure and monitor your customer satisfaction on an ongoing basis. Typical times to measure customer satisfaction for project work are as follows:

- Completion of an upgrade
- Conversion of data to your platform or cloud
- Completion of onboard, especially if moving them from a competitor
- Completion of any project lasting more than 100 hours

For customers who are on annual support contracts or SaaS contracts, the following work best:

- After the completion of onboarding
- After the upgrade of an application in the cloud
- Ninety days before an upcoming annual renewal
- If an unusual amount of tickets is issued in a month
- A change in the customer's account executive

So, what is the best way to measure customer experience? Measuring customer satisfaction doesn't have to be complicated or expensive. In fact, it's fairly simple to incorporate customer satisfaction measurement in your current customer success strategy. Three excellent tools for measuring customer satisfactions are as follows:

1.   Net promoter score (NPS)
2.   Customer satisfaction (CSAT)
3.   Customer effort score (CES)

The net promoter score is a customer experience metric that surveys customers based on one question: "On a scale of 0 to 10, how likely are you to recommend us to a friend or colleague?" Based on their rating, customers are then classified in three categories: Detractors, passives, and promoters. Customers who are promoters score 9 or 10. Passives score 7 or 8. Detractors score 6 to 0.

As you might be able to infer from the names of these groups, promoters are enthusiastic, loyal customers who will tell their friends about your business and bring in new customers. Passives are indifferent and could become promoters or they could switch to your competition. Detractors are unhappy customers and not only are you at risk of losing them, they could do damage to your brand by sharing their bad experiences with other people.

To calculate your net promoter score (NPS), subtract the percentage of detractors (customers who wouldn't recommend you) from the percentage of promoters (customers who would recommend you).

Add up the responses you earned in each category and subtract your detractors from your promoters to determine the net likelihood your typical customer would recommend you to a friend. Passive responses are left out of the equation because they can't be counted on to either recommend or give negative reviews.

For example, imagine you surveyed 100 customers. If 40 percent were detractors and only 50 percent were promoters, your NPS would be 10 (50 percent - 40 percent = 10).

Since NPS is nothing but a vanity number on its own, it is impossible to give you a single number that represents a good net promoter score, especially when you are starting out. The best way to find out if your number is "good" is if it's better than your scores in the past—your most important benchmark.

The best way to start measuring progress would be to compare your NPS against your score over the last quarter or six months. If you notice *an increase of at least 10 percent*, you are heading in the right direction and progressing toward building a successful business driven by organic growth. On the other hand, if you notice a significant decrease, something is wrong, and you must quickly identify the cause and take appropriate measures.

This tool is popular because it not only measures customer experience but also customer loyalty, since it transcends a single experience. It asks the customer to draw on the sum total of their experiences with your company, not just the most recent, making it a good indicator for future projects and purchases. If you pair it with an open-ended question like "Care to tell us why?" it allows you to also get detailed qualitative feedback that can provide specific insights as to your team's performance. While NPS surveys are deployed once or twice a year, there are ways to deploy a "drip NPS" to keep an ongoing pulse on your customer satisfaction, thus allowing you to react to issues quickly before they become pervasive. SurveyMonkey has made this easy by creating a predefined NPS template that is ready to modify and use: https://www.surveymonkey.com/r/Net-Promoter-Score-Template.

Customer satisfaction score ("CSAT") is the most popular transaction metric, and it is the most straightforward of the customer satisfaction survey methodologies. It's calculated by asking a question, such as "How satisfied were you with your experience?" There's a corresponding survey scale, which can be 1-3, 1-5, or 1-10, and it's flexible and highly customizable. You can also ask multiple questions to create a longer survey.

A big strength of the customer satisfaction score is its simplicity: It's an easy way to close the loop on a customer interaction and determine whether or not it was effective in producing customer happiness.

If for some reason the experience wasn't satisfactory, it's easy to pinpoint that moment and take actions to remedy the experience. The survey can also be used to track customer satisfaction across *a project lifecycle*. Since it's such a quick survey, you can ask it across multiple experiences during a customer's journey and get a big-picture view of how your customer feels at various touch points in the process. Just be sensitive not to "over-survey" your customer. We provided gift cards for coffee and ice cream as an incentive for our customers to take the survey.

CSAT Score by Lifecycle Stage

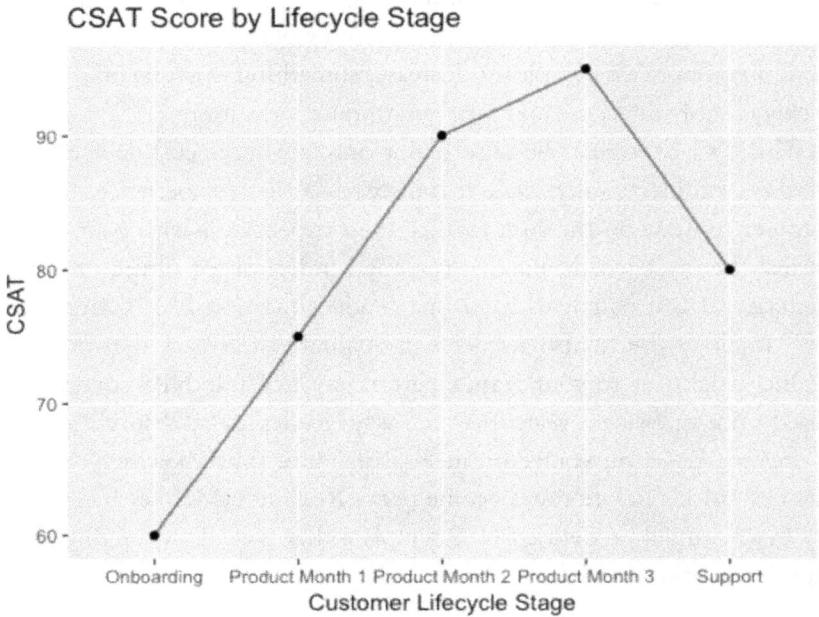

Fig.2.11

(Source: https://blog.hubspot.com/service/customer-satisfaction-score.)

We used this format for project, consultant, and company performance and were able to combine all three in one survey. This helped us determine if an issue was with a consultant, the project as a whole, or entirely with the company by how the person scored each section.

Customer effort score (CES) is where you change the question and instead of asking how satisfied the customer was, you ask them to gauge the ease of their experience. You're still measuring satisfaction, but in this way, you're gauging effort (the assumption being that the easier it is to complete a task, the better the experience). Making an experience low effort is one of the greatest ways to reduce frustration and disloyalty.

An example of a question would be: "How much effort did you have to expend to handle your technical support request?" and it is scored on a numeric scale. It's a customer service metric that is used to improve systems that may frustrate customers. Their belief is that "effortlessness" is the most relevant attribute of customer satisfaction. If you have a software solution that is deployed via a "click, try, buy" method, this is a good program to use because you typically want that experience to be as effortless as possible. A CES survey is typically deployed after a support interaction, but it can also help gauge the effort required to onboard a customer. According to the Harvard Business Review, CES can predict repurchasing even better than CSAT, making it the go-to metric for SaaS companies that depend on successful onboarding.[6]

Let's face it, highly satisfied customers are usually less price sensitive than other customers because they believe they're getting good value overall. They tend to buy more add-on features or products and will be the first to act as a referral if needed.

Tracking your retention metrics

Calculate your customer retention rate (CRR) – the percentage of customers you *keep* relative to the number you had at the start of your period. This does not count new customers. It is the reverse of customer churn. To calculate CRR, you simply use the following formula:

$$CRR = ((E-N)/S) \times 100$$

Take the number of customers you had at the END of the period (E), subtract the NEW customers you gained during the period (N), and this gives you the number of customers you kept.

Then, you simply divide that number by what you STARTED with (S). Then multiply by 100 for a percentage.

For example, let's say you started with 1,000 (S) customers, ended with 1,100 (E), and added 200 (N) new customers during that period. ((1100-200)/1000) x 100 = 90 percent.

You can also use churn rate (CR), which is simply the inverse of CRR. In other words, CRR is the percent you retained, while churn rate is the percent you lost. CR = L/S x 100.

For example, this is customers lost (L) divided by customers at the start (S). (100/1000) x 100 = 10 percent.

In other words, one tells you that you kept 90 percent, the other that you lost 10 percent.

While tracking these metrics is good, and I would recommend you do this at least twice a year if not quarterly, it is not a complete picture. For example, if you are replacing lost customers with customers who are paying you more each month, the attrition is not as important. Also, if the customers you are retaining are paying you less than the customers you are losing, then a high CRR might be misleading as well.

Ideally, you would like your CRR to reach 100 percent, which means you never lose a single customer. That's quite improbable even with the best team, as businesses get bought, or go bankrupt, or merge, sometimes leaving you in the cold. You should aim for 90 percent or at the very least 87 percent CRR. Again, this will vary from business to business, which is why it's important to track your own rate and try to improve it every month.

You will also want to track the same metrics using revenue dollar retention rate and not just number of customers. As opposed to CRR, which measures the customers that renew, dollar retention rate (DRR) measures the revenue you retain and is generally measured on an annual or semiannual basis.

The important point here is that dollar retention rate focuses only on the money, the actual revenue you retain, rather than on customers. So, if your existing customers start paying more, through upgrades or other purchases, your dollar retention rate might grow even if you've lost some customers. This doesn't mean you should focus only on DRR and ignore CRR. If you are consistently losing customers, at some point you will start losing revenue, no matter how many times your existing customers upgrade.

On the flipside, you might see a drop in dollar retention rate but a rise in CRR. This would happen if your existing customers start downgrading to lower-cost subscriptions or service plans. For example, if a customer changes from a $100 per month plan to a $50 per month plan, even though you retained the customer, you lost 50 percent of the revenue generated by the customer.

Ideally, you want your dollar retention rate to be above 100 percent. This means you're earning more every period and your company is growing. Many people aim for 110 percent, but again this number will be unique to your company and services. Essentially, both measurements need to be used hand-in-hand to get a complete picture of what is happening with your business.

As you are preparing your company for sale, strong customer satisfaction scores should be announced via press releases or social media to ensure potential buyers can learn about your company. Furthermore, if you sell a SaaS based solution, having your customer retention rate displayed prominently on your home page adds to your appeal. Finally, having a documented internal program for rewarding employees for excellent customer satisfaction also tells buyers you actually monitor, care, and reward.

NEXT STEPS

- If you are not already surveying your customer base, pick from one of the tools mentioned and send out a survey. If you are using one already, when was the last time you polled the customer base? At a minimum, it should be annually.

- Calculate your customer retention rate: both in numbers and dollars.

- Create customer satisfaction rewards for team members or an overall company goal with a reward at the end for achieving those milestones.

- Already have customer satisfaction metrics in place? Issue a press release on your achievements, if noteworthy. Mention this on your website as a metric you track.

6. Sustainable Success

Just as buyers want to see that the company can operate without the CEO running all aspects of the company, they also want to see that no single point of failure (SPOF) can threaten future earnings.

Think of sustainability in terms of four pillars: Employees, customers, vendors, and infrastructure. No single person is responsible for a critical action, no one single customer drives a large portion of your revenue, no single vendor provides the majority of your products, and no single piece of hardware or greater infrastructure could ultimately negatively affect the growth and profit of your company. You could also view this as eliminating all major single points of failure within the business. Doing so will make your company a more sustainable and viable company for acquisition.

Employee SPOFs

We have all done it—sat at our desks and wondered what would happen to the company if employee X were involuntarily absent from work for an extended period or decided to leave. Most businesses have a select few people that drive the organization forward, while others play a supporting role. This is a normal and healthy balance. But when sales are going well, employee morale is high, and customers are buying, it is easy to take your employees' longevity for granted. TSP's generate more than their fair share of *single points of failure*. It is a very easy trap to fall into because many systems or applications require specialist knowledge to resolve problems, support developments, and provide recovery. It is not possible to make every team member an expert for every system or application, plus people just have different skills, knowledge, and aptitudes.

You have seen it many times: One or two team members become the experts during the implementation phase but then quickly move on to new tasks or clients once the project is completed. Whether by accident or design, the organization is then left with one person as the best person to speak to and after a few months they actually become the *only* person who can support that skillset. It is an easy way for clients to walk out the door if one very talented consultant decides to leave. This lack of sustainability is not just limited to the IT staff. It could be your controller who is away ill, and then a commission check or sales tax return is due one day and no one else has a clue how to handle it.

Of course, most of the time having only one person able to perform a function is unintentional but on occasion it's by design. Signs of fiefdom building are as follows:

- They avoid documenting their processes and procedures, even after being asked multiple times.
- They rarely take time off.
- They insist on being available 24/7.
- They feel no one else has enough experience to carry out the solution.
- They have little desire to train others.

Having these single points of failure may make what looks like a large company appear small and risky to a buyer. And while an organization chart may hide this, as the business owner you need to make sure these issues don't develop.

Okay, so maybe some of the points above resonated with you and you have some single points of failure—now what?

- Require EVERY employee to create their own job/position manual. *While this might seem like a boring task that people won't want to do, you can turn it into something fun with rewards for quality, thoroughness, and diagrams. The manuals (either physical or virtual) can be reviewed by external judges to help determine a winner.
- Have each person present their weekly duties to other department members. This requires the person presenting to begin the

documentation process. Team members then become more educated about their role.

- Tie bonuses to completion of job/position manuals.
- Use the "sabbatical" approach and encourage people to begin documenting their work before their extended absence.

*Even though you may have multiple people in the same role or position, each person will have a different spin on how they see their role and how they execute their duties.

Preparation is the key to not getting into a situation where an offer is on the table and you know the success of your earn-out is tied to one of these key people. At that point, it may be too late to get all the tribal knowledge out of the head of your single points of failure; and in order to make the transaction work, you may need to create specific stay bonuses or earn-out incentives tied to documenting their role.

A "stay bonus" can either be paid by you, the seller, or possibly split between you and the buyer (assuming the buyer understands how critical this person is to the success of their future earnings). The theory is: You will pay the person 50 percent of their bonus on the close of the deal, and the remaining 50 percent after one year. Ideally, you would want to tie this to your earn-out period, but if that goes beyond a year, it becomes impractical and less of an incentive to the person receiving it. If you are forced to use a stay bonus as part of the final bonus payout, the key person has to have all their knowledge documented and communicated to the team, as mentioned in the chapter about IP.

Hint: If you find yourself in this situation, you probably don't want to discuss this potential issue until you are close to finalizing the deal. But you don't want to hide it completely either. If you don't want to openly admit that one person has the keys to your kingdom, you may have to front the entire stay bonus out of your sales proceeds!

Vendor SPOFs

The consolidation of vendors is nothing new and it continues in the technology space. The big giants like Microsoft, Google, Salesforce, etc. purchased a number of competitors as well as add-on solutions over the years. Where you may have been supporting multiple vendors in your area of expertise, you may now find yourself with one main vendor/supplier and thus be at their mercy. While vendor consolidation has benefits, such as increased purchasing power, fewer relationships to manage, and higher perceived sales transparency, vendor consolidation is not without risks. While it is unlikely that one of these large vendors will go out of business, you are at risk for the following, which can quickly affect your bottom line:

- Margin erosion
- Security breaches
- Brand abandonment

Margin erosion is the most prevalent and most feared by all technology owners from their largest vendors. Usually, you have some time to react to the news (ideally the announcement is made with six-months' notice), but even then, if all your eggs or substantially all your eggs are in this basket, can you really make a change that quickly? Probably not.

Let's take, for example, a 5 percent reduction in margin due to a vendor repricing of product/licenses or because you didn't make the threshold in annual revenue with the vendor. Say you are selling $1.75M top line in sales of that vendor's product. That 5 percent is a direct hit on your bottom line and EBITDA. A 5 percent hit in margin would represent a $87,500 direct hit to the bottom line, multiplied by a 6x EBITDA, which means a $525K hit in valuation. To bring home this point further, if your annual retirement salary is $125K per year, you just shortened your retirement payout by 4+ years!

Spreading your vendor love

Understanding and being able to support multiple ERP, CRM, or any other large application solution is costly, difficult and impractical, and not a viable solution in the short term. To protect your business from losing value, aim for no more than 40 to 45 percent of your offering associated with one particular vendor. Ideally, you want to spread the love among multiple vendors, but the size of your organization sometimes doesn't allow the ability to support multiple large vendor products, and that's when add-on solutions to the core product can make this diversification easier to swallow. Let's say you are a substantial CRM consulting firm and you are aligned with one major software vendor. Find two or three high margin add-on or complementary products that can be sold with the core application. This will not only help to round out your industry experience and potentially bundle a unique solution that can be priced higher, it will also insulate you from potential pressures from your main vendor.

In the example below, we show how additional revenue, generated from complementary products, helps to buffer a margin decline by any one particular vendor. In this case a 5% margin decline from the largest vendor equates to just 1.8 years of retirement vs 4+ years in our previous example.

Multiple Vendor Example		
Software Vendor	Gross Margin by vendor	% of sales
Main Vendor	750,000	43%
Additional Product #1	333,000	19%
Additional Product #2	333,000	19%
Additional Product #3	334,000	19%
Total Software Sales	$ 1,750,000	100%
5% reduction in magin - Main vendor	37,500	
Reduction in Value @ 6x Multiple	$ **225,000**	
Years of retirement @125K per yr.	1.80	

Fig.2.12

The trend has been for many software vendors to reduce margins by as much as 7 to 15 percentage points by transitioning their products from a one-time perpetual license to subscription pricing, which has lower margins. While this is great for long-term recurring revenue, you need to have a substantial amount of new recurring revenue to make up for the margin loss. If you are selling your company while in the transitional period, it could be greatly affecting the valuation of your company. Again, this is where additional complementary solutions can help soften the transition.

Another reason to spread your reach across multiple products is the threat of security breaches. Security breaches are a common threat and will continue to surprise even the savviest of software companies. Several large tech companies and large retailers have faced scrutiny by the public after it was determined that personal information was compromised. A company's stock price and reputation can take a substantial hit overnight if a breach is determined. If your main service offering is providing cloud services to your customer, the above rule applies but for different reasons. Most cloud service providers align themselves with one major public cloud provider such as AWS, Azure, and Google. Even though these are major vendors with significant backups, they are not impregnable. Your company should have a secondary cloud such that should there be a major threat or breach, you can quickly and easily transition your customers to an alternate cloud. If you are procuring your services in a private cloud, spread that love as well to protect yourself from outages and other breaches.

Brand abandonment or rebranding, while uncommon, does happen. In the last five years alone Sage, SAP, and Microsoft announced significant rebranding to an extent that all the content on your website could be obsolete overnight. All the SEO you have worked hard to attract through numerous blog posts can be wiped out once a vendor decides to rename their software and products. While it takes the public a while to catch up with the new name, it may take Google even longer to re-index all your prior posts for the new names.

CUSTOMER SPOFs

Customers are one of the most important assets that buyers will check out. Customers can be a direct relationship or through a channel. Your blind profile and CIM will have a section dedicated to your customer concentration and partner concentration (if selling through the channel). It's a very important section, as every potential acquirer will want to review what percent of your business would cease if you lost one or a few of your largest customers. Once due diligence begins, a schedule of revenue by customer will be a key schedule that is viewed by a serious prospective buyer. If you are not already generating metrics of revenue by customer, and average customer long-term value, you should begin to do so immediately.

Generally, no one customer should represent more than 10 percent of your revenue, and no three customers combined should represent more than 20 percent. Anything more than this will catch the attention of the buyer's due diligence team. They will want to dig into how consistent that customer will be for years to come.

There are advantages and disadvantages to high and low customer revenue concentration. Advocates of *high concentration* point to the ability to develop long-term relationships with fewer large customers and contractual agreements that can be tailored to each client. Customer service can be focused on fewer clients, so more resources may be applied in getting to know and meeting each client's needs better. Often, large customers will provide valuable input to a supplier to improve products or services because of a vested interest in supplier success. Some companies and their largest customers function similarly to partners in many ways.

On the other hand, high customer concentration carries substantial risks that can far outweigh any benefits in the long term. As your sales team scrambles to achieve their sales numbers, they want large customers to help fill those quotas. This is done with little respect to what percentage of your gross revenue may be concentrated into your top volume customers. Obviously, it is difficult to turn away business from a large customer, especially in the growth phase of a new business, but the risks involved should be understood before committing to such an arrangement.

Potential buyers view *high volume customer risks* as follows:

- Losing a customer can have a devastating effect on revenue, profit, and cash flow in a high concentration scenario. While agreements are entered into with the best of intentions, changes in the economy, pressures from competition, and other factors outside your control can result in the loss of a key client. Losing any client is undesirable but losing 10 percent or more of revenue at one time can have a long-lasting effect on a business.

- Large customers can command large price discounts, which for small customers are difficult to match. This results in decreased profits and lower EBITDA. This is also true of large channel partners who command higher margins.

- Large customers can, although not always, take a disproportionate share of resources away from a larger number of smaller ones. Management then feels the need to cater to the needs of the few or the one top buyer. This can take away some of your best resources from other customers and/or the creation of new offerings.

If you are selling your product through a partner channel, some of the above factors don't necessarily apply because the selling channel partner is not the end customer. But you don't want an overconcentration of customers buying from one partner either. If you are selling to the customer through a channel, take steps to maintain a strong relationship not only with the partner but with the end customer as well. While your channel may be supporting the customer directly, you want to make sure you don't lose a customer because of inadequate partner support or a relationship gone bad. Also, once a partner has completed a deal, they may not be as engaged with that end customer over time. While this is more prevalent in a perpetual model, we see it in a subscription model as well. Always have a way to be able to interact and have a relationship with the end customer so that if things are not going well, they have an opportunity to reach out to you directly.

Be prepared to present a customer matrix by selling partner as well. A buyer will be concerned if there are too few partners reselling your product, especially if one partner resells the majority of your products. Below are a few common reports requested by buyers. Create and monitor these in advance to look for trends (both positive and negative), and act on the negative ones before they become an issue.

Schedules of customer activity you should be tracking:

1. Revenue by customer (over a 12-month period) listed largest to smallest.

2.   Customer lifetime value —revenue generated over the life of the customer. Include in this schedule the total life in months of the customer to determine average customer life.

3.   Customer loss report—buyers will ask for the last 12 months of lost customers, their annual revenue loss, and the reason the customer was lost.

4.   If selling through a channel—revenue by partner.

Finally, if you are discounting your highest-volume or largest customers, you should calculate the gross profit margins (GPM) of those customers and compare them with your smallest customers. It should be fairly easy to pull the information out of your accounting system to create a spreadsheet to see how customers compare. If you see some large discrepancies, you may want to consider making adjustments now. If your GPMs are around the same for all your customers, this is a sign of a well-run business, and you should be promoting that as well to your potential acquirers. Keeping this in mind, as you land the big ones, remember that margins count to potential acquirers.

INFRASTRUCTURE REDUNDANCY

Hopefully this will never happen to you, but in 2011, someone manually turned off the power to all of southern California. It is referred to as the Great Blackout of 2011, and it affected areas south of Orange County including areas into Mexico. The blackout left nearly seven million people without power for more than 11 hours. The affected area was so extensive that you would have to drive for hours to find an area that had power. There was no escaping it; we were beholden to the battery life in our phones and laptops, and desktops were useless. Since our primary datacenter was running on auxiliary power, we all headed there. This example, however, is minor compared to cities that have been destroyed by inclement weather, leading to days if not weeks of outage.

Extensive power outages due to weather or grid overload happen, yet so many people are unprepared. Let's face it, unless it's your business to be fully redundant (i.e., a data center), you are probably vulnerable in this area.

If you are preparing your business for a sale, consider the condition of the technology side of your business. It seems obvious since that is our line of business, but if you answer "no" to any of the questions below, you might not be that ready.

If your entire office and the surrounding area loses power for more than 24 hours, can you do the following?

1.   Answer your IP phone?
2.   Respond to email?
3.   Enter data in your CRM system?
4.   Enter data into your ticketing system?
5.   Create and send an invoice or, better yet, collect credit card payments?
6.   Power your cell phone or laptop?

Clearly, the example above was an inconvenience for our team, but it could have been huge for customers (most of whom were located outside the affected area) had we not had our core infrastructure sitting in our datacenter. Almost every item on this list is now available in a SaaS solution by a reputable vendor. If you have a homegrown system that is key to your product and services, be sure to have a redundant site in the cloud that you can count on.

Today, almost every reputable datacenter has a SSAE 18 report, which warrants for most redundancies, but this is only *one* part of a redundant infrastructure. If you provide any sort of cloud solution, you must also have redundancy of servers. If you read the fine print of every SLA provided by a major cloud vendor (i.e., Amazon, Microsoft, and Google), they are not responsible for the redundancy of the servers within their own datacenter—*you* are. Those who dabble in IaaS at the request of their clients usually do not have servers redundant in the same datacenter, let alone in another one. If you say you are a cloud provider (meaning you are supporting your customers' applications infrastructure), NOTHING will destroy your credibility quicker in the due diligence phase than not providing redundancy. This, however, does not extend to vendors who support their own applications like Office 365, Salesforce, NetSuite, or other large vendor solutions over which you have no control.

Closely related to redundancy is the necessity of knowing, and being able to document, the infrastructure and assets on which you depend. Business owners should prepare a software and hardware inventory listing the servers, networks, software packages, and third-party software, hardware, and cloud vendors that are being used by the business. When you list the hardware assets, note if they are leased or owned, and what is under warranty and for how long. Buyers are not as concerned with laptops used by consultants as they are pretty expendable. But if you have an investment in servers—in either a private datacenter or on-premise—that are serving up applications to customers, these are critical in creating revenue and will be the most heavily scrutinized.

While this is slightly off topic, it is worth mentioning here. For the software used to run your company, list the software with the license it uses. Some software is purchased outright, and you usually have a license key (make sure of this!). Other software may be leased from a larger vendor, in which case you are probably paying for that on a monthly or annual basis. Be sure to know the length of your obligations, as some of what you are now using may become obsolete as part of an acquisition.

If you are selling software to end customers via a subscription model, be sure to have a schedule of payments due to the vendor by day, as you will need to calculate a good cutoff number based upon a close date. Also, find out in advance if your vendor will require you to pay off any outstanding software balances prior to a change in ownership. Not all, but some, vendors do require this.

Doing a presale internal license audit can save time and potential embarrassment if the acquirer finds you deficient in the licensure of your software. And having a comprehensive IT system inventory ready to go at due diligence will speed the process and make a favorable impression on your acquirer.

NEXT STEPS

- Look at your last three years of customer sales data and sort your customers by sales. Do your top three customers represent more than 20 percent of your revenue? If so, is there a way to break up the contracts?

- Look at the last three years of vendor payments. Is there one vendor that represents more than 70 percent of your product purchases? Can you negotiate better margins? Is there another vendor that gives you higher margins? Can you shift some business there?

- Ask your team what would happen if the power went out for eight hours? What is your contingency plan? What if you lost connectivity for a week? How would this affect your business? Determine ways to increase redundancy of services.

- Looking at your team, is there one person who if gone tomorrow would negatively impact your business? Do you have documentation to teach someone else what they do?

7. Sales and Marketing

A well-run sales and marketing engine is critical to the future profitability of the company. Therefore, every potential acquirer wants to know two things: First, do you have clear, well-defined offerings that are easy to quote and sell, allowing a sales team to scale post-acquisition? Second, is there enough depth on the sales bench without the owner(s) to continue the momentum? Also, with buyers often 70 percent of the way through their buying journey before they will speak to a salesperson, the marketing team is more critical than ever. Actually, I might argue that they are more important than the sales team, especially if you are selling an online product. Therefore, make sure the website clearly presents the value proposition and leads the buyer far enough down the sales funnel for the sales team to close deals with a greater than 50 percent close rate. Is your website delivering the hits to your site? Are you monitoring the hits? These are the initial areas that *your* potential buyers will want to understand immediately.

Sales

Suffice it to say that without a sales engine, growth stagnates, buyers become unhappy, and earn-outs become unachievable. The lack of a well-structured sales process can be seen early in the due diligence process. Absent a good sales engine, while the seller focuses on getting the company sold, the revenue starts to decline because it is not being managed by a capable sales team, or worse, the owner is also the rainmaker. Unfortunately, what happens next is that the forecast given to the prospective buyer is not achieved and the deal gets stalled, or worse, falls apart.

Rethinking your sales and marketing department isn't an option, it is a must for building the value of your company, not to mention a successful recurring revenue business. Solutions must now be broken down into small consumable packages that customers can easily implement and consume. Sales teams need to focus not only on new buyers but also on upselling products and services to happy existing customers. The right mix of salespeople (hunters and farmers) with a great sales manager to lead the charge are key to a successful sales team.

Repeatable packaged solutions

Strategic buyers will be more accepting of long sales processes, as they are more likely to understand the products and services that your company sells. PEGs, however, want to see a very streamlined approach with consistent pricing models, or if you are offering a SaaS solution, a "click, try, buy" approach to selling software.

If your organization still sells a good amount of services, they should be packaged into easily digestible solutions and not long, drawn out consulting quotes that require multiple people in the organization to review and bless. Ideally, your solutions should provide three options with three different price points that give the prospect just enough variability from both a pricing and services options (i.e., the bronze, silver, and gold packages). Below is a great example of products, services, and response time options in three concise packages.

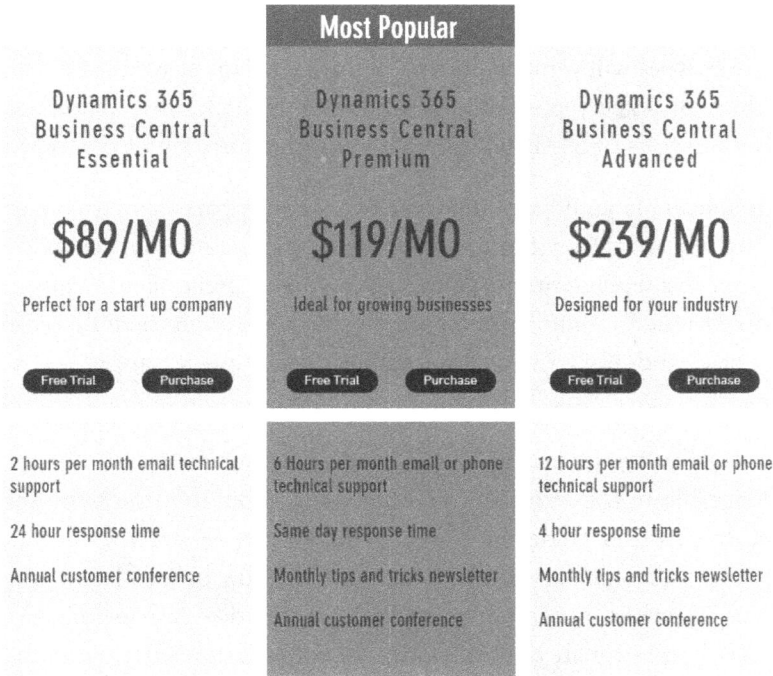

Fig.2.13
(Source: https://www.theknastergroup.com/pricing.)

The days of presenting open-ended estimates where you list out all the steps and give a high/low bid for the number of hours are long gone. The one exception to this would be for an application development project that may be unique, but otherwise all services should be nicely packaged into fixed fee solutions that are billed out in monthly, quarterly, or annual increments. Most sales departments typically create a standardized quoting template that allows for fast, easy delivery of quotes for products and services. Creating this internal "selling IP" will show a buyer that your sales team can scale quickly and easily once acquired.

Sales team

Both buyer types will want to understand the makeup of your sales team and what they can expect post transaction. As a general rule, companies with revenues in excess of $5M will want a sales team consisting of the following:

Sales manager: Is your sales manager (who is not part of the management team) actively engaged with each salesperson and assisting to help win deals, or are they just feeding numbers into a pipeline? A great sales manager needs to be able to set the right goals for their teams, give them the tools to achieve those goals, and hold them accountable. And hint—it cannot be *you* the owner.

Account executive (hunters): These people are not technical, but they are knowledgeable in the industry you serve. They shouldn't touch the software you sell but instead guide the buyer to the correct solution. It should be a consultative sale and these individuals need to know how to listen and solve problems. Your historical salesperson who has sold the big one-time perpetual deals may have a tough time migrating to subscription offerings, which are typically lower priced and are not a big pop on commissions, so be prepared to add new blood into this role. Many companies revisit their sales team and do one of two things: Either teach the old dogs new tricks, or get new dogs. You probably already know the answer. Now is the time to act on any changes that need to be made. Not doing so may jeopardize your future earn-out.

Commissioning your sales team not only on software and service will smooth this transition a bit, but it will still bite initially. You will, if you don't already, need to front-load the commission on your subscription deals so that your salesperson is incentivized to sell cloud solutions. That said, your salesperson shouldn't continue getting compensated on the second and third year of a subscription renewal. They need to stay hungry for commissions.

Inside salesperson or customer relationship manager (farmers): After the first year, transition your customers to your farmers. This is a "nurture sales" role. This inside sales role has a more "caring" approach, as your customer doesn't want to feel sold again. Add-on solutions, either within your own product set or other third-party complementary solutions, can drive significant additional revenue if done correctly. From my own experience as both a VAR and a cloud provider, more than 25 percent of sales for the year can easily be generated from your existing customer base, if mined well. The number of inside salespeople you employ should be in direct relation to the number of customers you serve. That ratio will be dependent on how many additional solutions you have to sell and how much of a "customer care" role this person will assume.

Solutions engineer: Ideally, this person should handle all technical questions, act as a complement to your account executive, and create content with the marketing team (i.e., videos, case studies, blog posts). This person should never have any billable requirements. The more time they spend creating content with your marketing team, the easier it will be to attract the perfect buyers.

The quantity of each of the above is dependent on the volume of sales, but if your revenue is north of $5M, you should have at least one person in each role, and increase this numbers, by a factor of one, for every $5M in revenue. If you are not yet at that level, you might not yet have a sales manager. The CEO or COO most often fills that role. This is acceptable as long as the owner is not the one selling for the company. If you are, then be prepared for a good portion of the sale to be tied to an earn-out which again is fine as long as you are good to stay after the sale.

Key sales metrics to track

To give buyers confidence in the sales team, you should track a number of metrics in addition to a comprehensive forecast. The following items should be well-defined, documented, and communicated to the entire team.

Annual sales forecast: This should provide a clear analysis of how many leads it takes to win a deal, what the average size of each deal is in revenue, and the number of deals required to meet the annual sales goal for the year. This forecast should be prepared in advance of each year, and the team needs to be held accountable for achieving it. The forecast should include new deals and additional add-on revenue to existing customers. Note, if you have at least 50 percent of your revenue in subscriptions, be sure to include some percentage

for churn—5 to 7 percent are good conservative numbers. However, if historically it has been higher, you will need to use that instead.

Discounted sales pipeline: You should have a sales pipeline with applicable
win-rates updated weekly by the sales manager. It should be generated directly
from your well-implemented CRM system, which is then compared to the
forecast to make sure there is a sufficient amount of pipeline to meet the
sales goals for the month, quarter, and year. Reward accuracy. Not so great
salespeople put everything in the pipeline to make it look good so it looks
like they are busy. Good, but insecure, salespeople like to keep things in their
back pocket and pull out deals at the end of the month or quarter, which
makes them look like the hero. Neither allows for accurate pipeline and sales
forecasting. This pipeline should be reviewed on a weekly basis in your sales
meeting. Find ways to reward accuracy, if you are not getting it currently. A
good due diligence team will scrutinize your forecast and its accuracy.

Win rate analysis: Do you know what your win rate is? Win rates below 30
percent present a problem. Win rates should be north of 50 percent if the
sales and marketing teams are in sync. If win rates are low, determine why. Is
it your offering or the person working on it? Answering these questions can be
difficult, and sometimes even the most seasoned sales managers will struggle
with how to fix the problem. If you feel you need to reach out externally, there
are several outside sales organizations that can work with you.

Cost of sales tracking: Tracking the direct cost of sales as a percentage of
the average deal size is important. Microsoft conducted significant research
over the years with top performing partners, and with business process and
business transformation consultants, including IDC, and 10 to 12 percent
seems to be the number that successful organizations achieve. Here is an example of how best to calculate this number: COS = the complete cost of your
sales rep (including base salary, commissions, and benefits) divided by the
annual revenue they added to the business in the current year. So, basically
for every $100K you pay your salesperson, they need to generate at least $1M.
This, of course, assumes that you don't have a sales manager or solutions
consultant that you have to pay or that they don't have their own quotas. If
so, you will need to add quotas to those roles or increase your sales quotas

per individual salesperson to cover the overhead. Ideally, you want to remain below 20 percent if you have additional overhead but only if you are able to keep churn very low.

Cost to acquire a customer: Customer acquisition cost (CAC) is a metric that has been growing in use, especially for companies selling SaaS or cloud-based solutions, whether their own product or that of a vendor. Investors look closely at this metric. You can calculate this by taking the entire sales and marketing budget divided by the number of new customers acquired in a given period. This works really well if your sales cycle is short, and where your sales and marketing costs can be tied to new customers in the same period. If it's longer, you may want to stagger your costs and new customer wins to get a more accurate picture. Here is the actual formula:

Cost to acquire a customer = sales and marketing costs/new customers won

For example, if you had total annual sales and marketing expenses of $500K and you acquired 40 new customers in a given year, the calculation would look like this: $500,000/40 = $12,500 CAC.

*Costs should include all sales and marketing related expenses + salaries and benefits.

Customer lifetime value (CLV) is another important metric to calculate. This metric determines how much your customer is worth. CLV is the estimated *net profit* a customer will provide over their lifetime as a paying customer.

If you combine the two ratios, you can get at the more important question: To what extent is a customer worth their cost? In other words, what is the true value of a customer to your business? An ideal CLV: CAC ratio should be at least 3:1. The value of a customer should be three times more than the cost of acquiring them. If the ratio is close, i.e., 1:1, you are spending too much to acquire a customer. If it's 5:1, you are spending too little.

So, in our example above, if our CAC = $12,500, our CLV should be at least $37,500.

Ideally, you want to recover the cost of acquiring a customer within the first 12 months or so. In other words, if the average customer brings you a net profit of $15,000 over 12 months, you should be spending about $5,000 to acquire customers. This is a lot easier to calculate with subscription customers or monthly fixed fee customers. It can be calculated for consulting and non-subscription customers as well, but it requires a deeper analysis.

While this calculation is simple, many business owners have never gone through the effort to figure it out. You need to know these numbers to articulate the value and cost of a customer to your business, which in turn gives your buyers more insight into the value of your company. Will every buyer ask you if you know these numbers? Probably not. However, the larger you grow, the more sophisticated the buyer becomes and the more metrics you will need to track.

There are so many metrics you can use to manage your sales team but describing them all is beyond the scope of this book. The point here is that you have a forecast, you are tracking against it, and you know what your costs are to achieve your goals. If you are doing this and have a capable team that can continue to sell products and services without your daily involvement, you are on the right track.

One last note on forecasts. I have mentioned this already in another section, but since each section stands on its own, it's worth mentioning here as well. If you are in the process of selling your company, or if you have a potential buyer looking for a forecast, this is *not* the time to reach for the stars in your forecast. That means if you have consistently hit 20 to 25 percent YOY growth and you can show a track record of that, don't go crazy and present projections with 30 to 35 percent growth, which shows the majority of the growth in the last quarter—unless you are tracking this growth all year long, meaning month-over-month from last year. Dial it back, regardless of whether it is achievable. What? Yes, you read that correctly. Two things will stall a deal: the first one we have already mentioned, namely, a drop in sales, and the second one is an unrealistic (or viewed as unrealistic) forecast.

If you want to continue to use an aggressive forecast with your sales team to keep them pumped and motivated, that's fine. Sending that same forecast to someone who knows little about your business and can only look at historical numbers, can send waves of disbelief when you need everything to remain calm. They may still will want to believe you, but this will stall the deal or shift more weight to the earn-out.

If you feel strongly about achieving your numbers, you should look for creative ways to extend the due diligence process to allow for greater clarity. A good business broker will help.

ROBERT INSIGHT:

Robert was a little worried. While his existing customer base remained stable, his first quarter sales numbers had fallen off. He suspected that this was because it was an election year and the primaries had not yet been decided. The stock market was also at a standstill as investors weren't sure which candidates from each party would ultimately win. Robert altered his projections for Q2 and Q3 so they were not as aggressive and dropped his growth rate down 5 percent. He felt that he could explain to a buyer why he had not projected a 25 percent growth rate, and that he would have time during the due diligence process to hopefully catch up and exceed the new revised projections.

Marketing

All the talk about sales is empty without a strong marketing department to fill the sales funnel. Marketing is the new sales because buyers now self-educate about your solution long before they give you their email address or pick up a phone to speak with you. Without a strong marketing department in today's buying behavior, sales are almost impossible. Marketing creates leads, which creates sales, which in turn creates clients. Then you use customer case studies, testimonials, and videos to have those customers be a large part of your marketing effort. It is now all about the quality of your marketing and it becomes increasingly more important as your company transitions from services to product sales. As your product transitions from the large one-time capital expense to a monthly recurring operating expense, the stronger the emphasis should be on marketing. In the diagram below, you can see how a services company (no products being sold) depends more heavily on the human interaction of a salesperson. As the services transition into a one-time product, the mix between marketing and sales are equally important. Finally, as you transition completely to a product, marketing becomes paramount to your continued success.

Transition from sales to marketing as services move to products

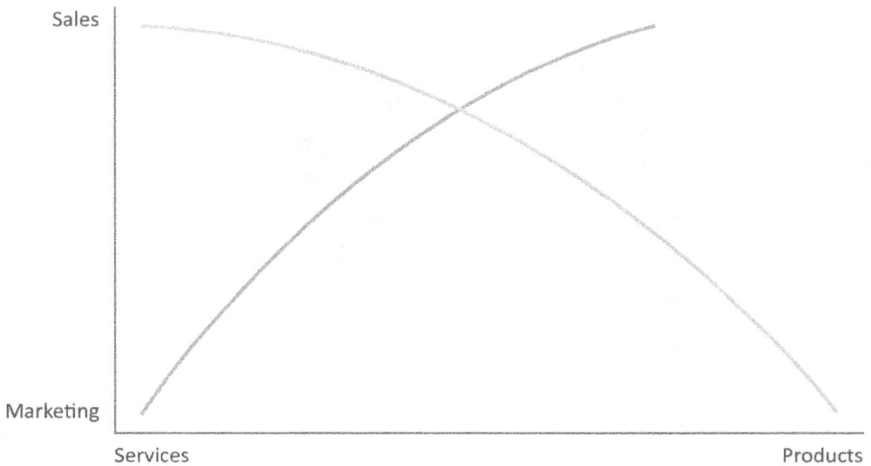

Fig.2.14

Savvy buyers will look harder at a marketing department with SaaS products than they will at a services-based organization. These potential acquirers will look for a combination of inbound and outbound marketing efforts. Clearly, you already have a website, but how effective is it?

- Is your value proposition front and center in your hero image?
- Are you speaking to your audience or just talking about yourself as a company?
- Have you identified the personas of who is visiting your website?
- Do you have a clear and concise message with a call to action on every page?
- Do you demonstrate your industry expertise via white papers, videos, and case studies?

- How many emails are being delivered to prospects monthly?
- What is the bounce rate?
- If you have answers to these questions, you are well beyond most marketing departments in your ability to execute, even if not perfectly.

The team

If all this seems overwhelming, it can be. That said, a good marketing plan can be executed with just a few key team members, and 81 percent of technology service providers have between one and four people on their marketing team[17]. Ideally, every organization generating revenue in excess of $5M should have at least three people in marketing.

Marketing manager: This person is ultimately responsible for the marketing activities of the company. He/she must create and manage a marketing plan that identifies the long- and short-term objectives and strategies, including a nurture calendar for prospects in the self-service mode. Ideally, this person has a strong enough technical background so they can implement and run your marketing automation software. If not, work with your technical team to implement a system your marketing team can then take over.

Content creator/social media expert and blogger: If you have limited resources, you might be able to find a qualified person who can do all three, since all three require great writing skills. Content is what drives traffic, and this person will be creating it. Don't rely on consultants or your technical team to create content for you on a regular basis. It is a good way to get you started, but in the long run you need a person whose sole responsibility is to put words out into the ether, including a press release about something newsworthy on a monthly basis.

Graphic designer: Ideally, this person has an eye for art and design and should have the skills to create new designs in Photoshop, InDesign, Canva, or something similar. Once the branding for your company and products has been established (either internally or externally), this person should see that branding is carried out for all content published on the web, at tradeshows, or on brochures. If you aren't finding the right person immediately, you can outsource some of this to external sites such as www.99designs.com, www.fiverr.com or www.upwork.com. These and other sites offer a variety of freelance workers if you are short on internal talent.

Even the most successful and mature marketing department sometimes finds itself short of resources, and outsourcing is certainly an option. If you are less than $5M in revenue, outsourcing large components of your marketing may be the best option. A graphic designer, content creator, or social media expert can be outsourced efficiently. If you do outsource some or all of your marketing efforts, I cannot stress the importance of finding people who truly understand your products and services. You should not have to spend significant time explaining your value proposition or services to your outsourced marketing department. Thankfully, there are a number of organizations that specifically focus on technology service providers of all varieties. While I have not personally worked with every group listed below, these four teams do come highly recommended by other TSPs.

> **The Partner Marketing Group**: https://www.thepartnermarketinggroup.com/ is a group of tenured marketing professionals who have devoted their careers to technology partners and vendors. They help companies by providing experience-backed guidance and industry expertise, combined with high-quality content to fuel your inbound and outbound marketing campaigns. Services include: marketing planning and strategy, content development and design, campaign creation and management, channel marketing, SEO/SEM, and more.

> **Marketing Monarchs**: https://www.marketingmonarchs.com/ is a marketing bureau that works with technology partners to overcome digital marketing challenges, leverage the power of social platforms, maximize social footprint, and ultimately drive more leads. Services include: Social Media Strategies for LinkedIn, Twitter and Facebook. Training, Social Media Campaign Creation and Management,

Content Creation, LinkedIn PointDrive Services, Lead Tracking, Social Media Analytic Reporting, PPC Campaigns, and more.

Lionfish: https://www.lionfishcreative.com/channelmarketing/ focuses on effective marketing, positioning your company for immediate and long-term future advantage. Ranging from small resellers to global partner networks, their approach is to empower channel partners by providing marketing tools that make it easy to engage audiences and support sales. Their "teach them to fish" philosophy ensures that marketing toolkits, step-by-step guides, presentations, thought leadership assets, sales tools, and campaign resources are easy to use and customizable to fit the partner's specific needs. They also offer a lead generation model that leverages traditional, social, and news media to help channel partners fill their sales pipeline and attract and retain customers.

Extra Mile Marketing: http://extramilemarketing.com/get-acquired-for-millions/ is a team of "marketing perfectionists" who work to help companies stand out in a crowded marketplace. They have worked with more than 7,000 tech companies around the world to help build content that tells a unique and memorable story. They assist with marketing planning, sales enablement, customer experience, and comprehensive go-to-market campaigns.

Every marketing department needs some software to run effectively. While there are books and websites galore for all the tools you can use to monitor, track, spy, or whatever you want to do, a marketing automation software tool is a must. Marketing automation usually includes analytics, tracking, online forms, and even email marketing. Marketing automation suites give your visitors customized content, facilitate sales and marketing, and much more. There are a number of solutions to choose from, but some prominent ones are: HubSpot, Salesfusion, ClickDimensions, Claritysoft, Eloqua, and Infusionsoft. All are priced differently and work well for different budgets.

Some of these connect with an existing CRM system and others are stand-alone, which is fine, too. The point is: You need a marketing automation software to have an effective marketing department. No one will take you and your department seriously without one.

Marketing budget

The US Small Business Administration recommends spending *7 to 8 percent* of your gross revenue on marketing and advertising if you are less than $5M in sales and your net profit margin is in the 10 to 12 percent range. Most technology service providers spend significantly less than this. Per benchmark studies done by The Partner Marketing Group in 2019 of over 100 technology partners worldwide, the average was about *1 to 5 percent*. In the chart below we can see that 50 percent of technology companies spend less than 5 percent on marketing. This does not seem to increase with the size of the organization. That said, most of these companies increased their spend as they realized that more people are spending time reviewing content on their website than speaking to their sales team.

Marketing Budget Percentage
of Annual Gross Revenue
Not Including Salaries

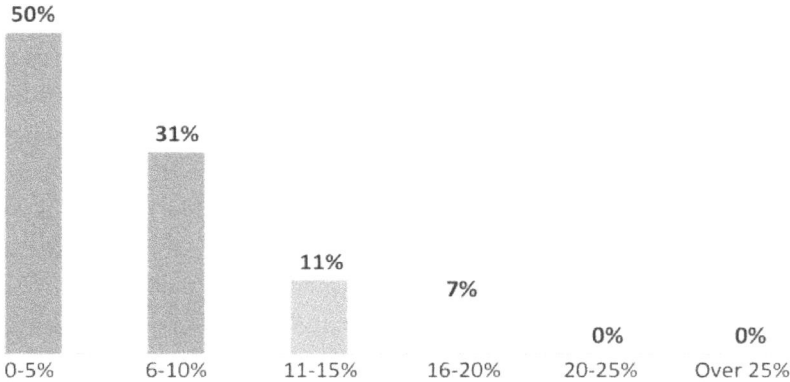

0-5%	6-10%	11-15%	16-20%	20-25%	Over 25%
50%	31%	11%	7%	0%	0%

Fig.2.15

Source: 2019 Technology Marketing Benchmark and Trends Report

(http://www.technologymarketingreport.com).

View of the marketing department by strategic vs. financial buyers

As we discussed earlier, having a strong marketing team is key to the success of the sales team. So, what I am about to say next may come as a surprise: Unless you are in a very niche vertical and can demonstrate that sales will falter greatly without a dedicated marketing department in most acquisitions, the marketing team is the department that will see the most attrition. Why?

Strategics will see it as redundant, especially if you are a competitor or the purchase is made to acquire your customer base. In these cases, it is very likely that your website will be merged into theirs, eliminating the need for the people and the applications that have been running your website. Even if you have a unique vertical, that messaging will be integrated into their existing site. This can happen in as little as 30 days, and usually in no more than six months. Economies of scale prevail with strategic buyers.

Financial buyers will attempt to do the same if you are going to be "tucked" into an existing company. Even if you remain as a stand-alone, many have external marketing companies they use to run all of their portfolio companies. Of course, this doesn't happen all the time, but more often than not, cuts will be made in marketing over time, as most financial buyers do not see the value of the department. I do believe the tide on this is starting to change as they see the changing habits of prospective customers. If a large part of your purchase price is associated with an earn-out and tied to sales, be sure to understand in advance the plans for this department, and how that may affect sales in the long run. Be prepared to explain the value and ROI of your marketing budget line items, as well as the value of each team member. The stronger the team and the more unique your marketing, the more likely it can survive the post-merger consolidation.

Finally, if you know you plan to embark on the sale of your company in the next 12 to 24 months and you are a little light in your marketing department, either with staff or applications, outsourcing to accomplish projects is ideal. Also, if you feel you are lacking tools internally, only consider applications that are available on a SaaS basis and that do not require more than a 12-month upfront commitment. Even if you have to pay more, monthly usage fees are better than having to buy out a contract. You want to be as nimble and agile as you can in this department, as you never know what the buyer may bring to the table regarding the strength of their own marketing department.

Getting your message out and being recognized

In addition to your marketing team creating content for your website, your management team should also get on the marketing bandwagon. They should be speaking at conferences and trade shows and creating thought leadership blog posts to attract customers and prospective buyers. Note that I said management team and not the owners specifically. If your goal is to exit shortly after a sale, make sure your *management team* is engaged in the speaking and presenting opportunities, and not *you*. It is time for you to fade from the spotlight and let your competent team members shine.

Create and disseminate surveys to customers or your partners (if selling through a channel) that allow you to identify trends regarding the products and services you support. Then engage the people from your team who have subject matter expertise to create and present videos. You can use these for marketing your company on your website, at conference speaking opportunities, and/or on your company YouTube channel.

Every new large customer should be celebrated via a win-wire or press release. Now is the time to amp up your wins in whatever form. Buyers will read your press releases, especially regarding customer acquisitions, awards, new management additions, and superior customer retention metrics.

Apply for and nominate your organization for every award available in your channel. Even if you don't win, many awards also give publicity to the finalists. This can mean consistent and positive press about your organization that may attract a potential buyer. Ideally, a year should never go by that your organization isn't either nominated for or wins some sort of award or honorable mention. Not only do the major software vendors issue awards, but a number of channel affiliates also offer mentions or awards (e.g., Redmond Channel Partner, Computer Reseller News, Inc., 500/5000 awards, Best Companies to Work For, Deloitte Technology Fast Awards, local business journal awards, etc.).

Now is the time to get out and market your company with other well-known technology providers at events, and to talk about how you can strategically work to partner on projects. More than one discussion over a drink in a bar late at night has ended up in a very happy merger.

NEXT STEPS

- List your offerings like a menu at a restaurant. Are there set prices for services and products? Does everyone on the sales team adhere to this pricing schedule?

- Review the last 12 months of customer sales. Are there recurring services that might be packaged into a fixed fee solution?

- What do you have that is repeatable and can be used across multiple customers?

- What are your win rates as a sales team? What are your win rates by person? Do they align with your goals? Are they greater than 50 percent? If not, can you look at the data to determine why?

- Are you tracking CAC and CLV? You may be surprised at what you find.

8. Intellectual Property Presence

"Our industry does not respect tradition.
What it respects is innovation."

—Satya Nadella, *Hit Refresh*

Product intellectual property (IP), a unique product that is sold on a subscription basis in the cloud, should be viewed as the nirvana of all intellectual property. Why? Simple—companies that have product IP receive more offers at a higher price and with better terms. Buyers are willing to pay premium prices for repeatable unique product IP, ideally one that sits in the cloud and is sold on a monthly recurring basis; and furthermore, benchmarks show that product IP has a higher growth rate than professional services of traditional software resellers.

Product IP also carries the highest margin because it is disconnected from labor. We don't have to pay a person for each product we sell. Once we develop it, the margin structure only gets better. Buyers are looking for future profits, higher margins, and increased sales, and product IP is their answer. Ideally, you need to anchor your IP on to a cloud solution, if not your own; this is key to building a profitable business in the cloud and to the value of the business.

In Part I we saw that ISVs can receive anywhere from 1.5 to 2X higher multiples than other partners. In the chart below, we can see more specifics about partner activities and the profit margins they generate. You can see that the last two columns on the right are ISVs that have either an on-premises or cloud subscription product, and you can also see that they are substantially higher in gross product margins.

Gross Margin Levels Across Revenue Type

Gross Margin Levels

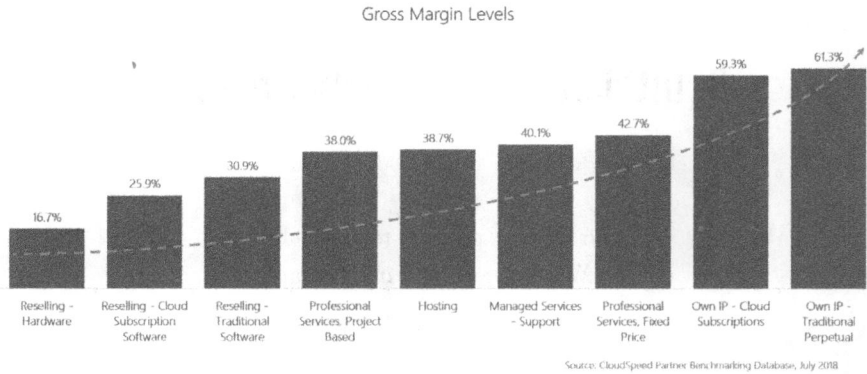

Source: CloudSpeed Partner Benchmarking Database, July 2018

Fig.2.16

If 75 percent or more of your revenue is generated from selling your own IP in this way, congratulations!—you can stop reading this chapter now. For everyone else, and that is the vast majority of you, there are other forms of IP that exist in your organization today that you can monetize. If you have run a company for more than three years, you most likely have already created IP and you just don't realize it. But, by not taking the extra steps to identify your IP, you could definitely be leaving money on the table. A survey of buyers in 2017 shows that over 70 percent of sellers do not make their IP apparent to prospective buyers[1].

Now is the time to identify and monetize what you have and to develop IP that if you have a long-term plan to sell. And there are steps you can take today to turn the know-how of your business into a package that can increase the value of your company. Some of these steps take time, but others just require you to look for and identify your current processes and nicely wrap that solution into a package. To help you discover and monetize your own IP, we will cover the following:

- Discovering your own IP
- Managing and packaging your IP
- Moving from services to packaged IP

The message is clear from some of the largest software vendors: Develop your own IP and either attach it to a major software vendor or run it as a stand-alone. It all began with the Apple Apps Store, but now major vendors like Microsoft and Salesforce provide a platform for traditional channel partners to create and sell their own apps via online marketplaces such as AppSource and AppExchange, respectively, which combined serve up over 8,500 apps (and growing daily) to end customers. Most of these apps were created by channel partners who initially started as consulting firms. Let's take advantage of these platforms and promote your IP so you can increase the value of your company.

DISCOVERING YOUR "ORGANIZATIONAL" IP

This next sentence may sound ludicrous to you, but it is not. Everyone has IP, but not everyone knows it. How is that possible you ask? Most people view IP as an invention or a piece of software or a program. But IP is more than that. For the context of this discussion, the definition of Intellectual Property is: The ownership of an idea. Unlike tangible assets to your business such as computers or your office, intellectual property is a collection of ideas and concepts. The key word here is "ideas." Note that I didn't say software, programs, or code but ideas. We will get to what this means in more detail in a minute.

Organizational IP is important because, if managed well, it allows for greater profits. Once you realize you have this type of IP, you need to make sure you can demonstrate its use, protect it, and measure its results. The more you can do this, the more valuable your company will be. But owners often get hung up over what is truly IP. Maybe you are not a software development firm and haven't created a fabulous app out in the marketplace or on your own website. But that is not the only IP out there. Let's start by identifying what IP actually is.

IP basically falls into four categories: trademarks, copyrights, trade secrets, and patents.

1. **Trademarks**: A trademark or service mark prevents another person from offering a similar product or service confusingly similar to yours.

A logo can be a trademark and many times they are used as such. But a trademark can also be a symbol that is from the logo of the company. This typically covers logos and names. If you have named a process or a product, you should make sure it is trademarked. If you have begun the trademark process through the US Trademark office, be sure to use the ™ symbol (which stands for Trademark) or the ᔆᴹ symbol (which stands for Servicemark). Once approved, you can then change it to the ® symbol (which stands for Registered Trademark).

2. **Copyrights**: Copyright protects most creative content you produce that has been written down or recorded. This includes things like websites, brochures, software code, software programs, databases, technical designs, workflow, and emails. It is basically the rights you have over different types of work. Be sure to always assign copyright on your websites and documents, even though common law provides some nominal protection without official documentation. And be sure to register more substantial works like eBooks or major white papers.

3. **Trade Secrets**: Most consulting firms' IP consists of trade secrets, and there are few legal protections for this. A trade secret is a formula, practice, process design, instrument, or compilation of information (that is not generally known or reasonably ascertainable) by which a business can obtain an economic advantage when it comes to competitors and customers. Trade secrets are more challenging to identify but important nonetheless. They are usually protected by an NDA, confidentiality agreements, and employment contracts or passwords or restricted access. Many times, a trade secret in our industry is a precursor to a patent but not always. In actuality, most IP, in the technology services area, is just a trade secret. Most ISVs do not have a patent on their IP that underlies their product.

4. **Patents**: A patent is a grant of protection for an invention. It's granted by the US Patent and Trademark Office (PTO) and has a term of 14 to 20 years. Owning a patent gives you the right to stop

someone else from making, using, or selling your invention without your permission. This provides the greatest legal protection and costs the most but is not typically found in technology companies, even those that have developed a significant solution. Most ISVs that I interviewed, including those who sold for significant amounts of money, did not have patented IP, but instead a solution that was a combination of trademarks, copyrights, and trade secrets that were bundled into a named solution.

ORGANIZATIONAL IP VS. PACKAGED OR PRODUCT IP

The easiest IP to clearly demonstrate is a packaged software solution (product IP) that you sell either as a standalone solution or as an integrated solution in one or more products. Product IP that sells on-premise or in the cloud on a monthly recurring basis drives the highest valuation for your company. If the sale of this product drives the majority of your revenue, you are an ISV. If you already have product IP, you should continue your efforts to develop it. If not, your IP journey needs to start with identifying your organizational IP.

Organizational IP is a form of IP that makes the running of your company more efficient and predictable. This form of IP drives higher processes, procedures, and ultimately higher profitability. Identifying this IP is key, as it shows the buyer you have a methodology that you adhere to that increases sales, reduces costs, and drives repeatable results. Here are four common areas of organizational IP of the trade secret variety:

1. IP to market your service,
2. IP to sell your service,
3. IP to deliver your service, and
4. IP to operate your business.

Marketing IP: If you take a look at your website, I am sure you will find videos, webinars, white papers, reports, case studies, eBooks, presentations, articles, blogs, logos, etc. This type of IP demonstrates thought leadership and allows you to separate yourself from the competition and not be viewed as a "me-too" firm. It helps you demonstrate that you have industry or domain expertise. It helps in the sales process and expedites the prospect through your sales funnel. Also, think of it this way: If you don't want someone else to steal or copy your marketing products, you have IP. Which is why you put a copy mark or trademark symbol on your creations. Buyers do not want to have to create from scratch when they can buy what you have already created. Consider this as marketing IP.

Sales IP: Your sales team probably doesn't create a quote from scratch each time a customer requests a proposal; that would be costly and inefficient. Someone over time has probably created an easy way to push out proposals or detailed quotes. Or maybe you have created an online quoting tool where prospects can enter data and get an idea of the cost of your service or annual subscription. Do you use email templates to communicate to prospects once they have been passed over to sales? Or do you use nurture emails to continue to follow up on prospects that are pushed out by your CRM system? All of these should be documented and stored so they are not lost if a salesperson leaves. Consider these tools as sales IP.

Delivery IP: If you reach out to your services delivery manager, I am sure he/she uses IP to deliver your services—like implementation, on-boarding, and go-live methodologies. Workbooks, templates, process maps, project plans, software tools, integration tools, and questionnaires to assist with the deployment of services are other examples of delivery IP. Almost every consulting firm has developed these over the years, but they don't necessarily view them as IP. For example, if you have developed a superior way to procure a cloud instance, based upon a combination of code or macros that have been written to allow you to significantly reduce the time involved, it is IP—because it allows you to scale your business and create profit due to the fact that there is less labor involved to do these tasks. Would you want this trade secret to walk out the door with an employee? Probably not; consider it your delivery IP.

Operational IP: Finally, let's not forget the IP to run your business beyond sales, marketing, and delivery of services. Buyers buy management teams first and consulting teams second. If the management team has a business plan that maintains sales forecasts, provides compensation plans, and creates budgets, they have IP. If the management teams uses such tools and can report the results, they are viewed more positively in the eyes of the buyer since they can continue to grow the company. If the company maintains a comprehensive CRM database with metrics on how often clients are communicated with and their level of satisfaction, and a database of all proposals and contracts as well as a competitor analysis, they have a form of operational IP. Whatever tools you have created to manage, monitor, and help report your company's results are considered operational IP and should be identified as such to potential buyers.

Packaged IP will always drive more value for your company than organizational IP. But if you don't have a product you can monetize now or you want to sell your company in the near future, demonstrating, documenting, and assigning value to your organizational IP can convince a prospective buyer you are worth more.

ROBERT INSIGHT

Over the years, Robert had developed an internal system that tracked the licenses purchased by customers to the licenses that he needed to purchase from Microsoft to deploy his solutions. As the company grew larger, and as the solutions he sold became more complex, so did the need for an ability to track and report accurately. While he was on the honor system to report his license usage to Microsoft, he knew that would one day be up for an audit by Microsoft. While there were applications that could track the licenses that he was using, since many licenses were sold only as computer core or processor licenses, tracking the usage back to specific clients was sometimes very difficult. No package at the time could handle all the different scenarios, so his team of engineers wrote an internal solution that could accurately gather the data for monthly reporting back to Microsoft. Then, just as he was entering the due diligence phase with his buyer, his company was notified of an audit. Had he not had the internally developed solution that could track his license usage, he might have over-reported—or worse, under-reported—his licenses usage, which would have affected his cash at close. His internally generated program was his IP, and it proved its value by ensuring the accuracy of his license usage.

MANAGING AND PACKAGING IP

Now that we have identified some of your existing IP, we need to manage and package it to protect and maintain its value. Unprotected IP has a tendency to leave the organization and fall into the wrong hands. Also, IP that is not identified cannot be assigned a value. As we noted above, 70 percent of IP is not identified to buyers, and therefore cannot be assigned a value. Let's not let years of work go unrecorded and unidentified. Here are a few important steps to take that will help quantify and validate the use of IP in your organization.

1. Brainstorm with your sales, marketing, delivery, and support teams on the tools and methodologies that they use daily but that are not documented. Have each team come up with a list. Don't worry yet if it is truly IP or not; just get it all down on paper. You will probably be shocked when you see how much your team uncovers.

2. Assign value—for items like workbooks, templates, process maps, project plans, software tools, questionnaires, determine how much time is saved by using these tools. Determine how often they are used and multiply the numbers together to get an annual value for your tools, and then sort them by most valuable to least valuable. This will also determine which tools are meaningful and which are not. For example, if you have created a training session on how to import data into a system and you sell that training system for a fixed fee, quantify that. Or if you have a template that saves hours of time but you still charge a fee to do the work, quantify the delta between what you charge and what your costs are.

3. Document and name each of the above discovered items and determine, on a scale of one to five, how unique it is to your business. If

you are borrowing a vendor's video of a product on your website, that is a one, not really unique and probably deployed on multiple competitor sites. But if your team has created a video on how to [fill in the blank] that is unique to your industry or area of specialization, that's a five! By going through this exercise, you will be able to determine which assets are of value and which are not. Tribal knowledge is common in every organization, but it is valuable information that needs to be shared with the team via knowledge sessions.

4. Store and protect. Just like you store and protect your customer list from outsiders, you need to do the same with your other trademarks, copyrights, and trade secrets that you identified above. Original documents, templates, pieces of code, or videos need to be stored in a secure location, either in the cloud or on-premise (with offiste backups). SharePoint, Dropbox, or other programs that allow security by user are ideal. In order to keep this information confidential, you need to be clear about what can be stored on laptops and what can be stored only on a secure site. And this has to be enforced. If people leave, the IP cannot leave with them. Remember, what is hardest to enforce are undocumented trade secrets. Some ways to protect these trade secrets are as follows:

   a) Enter into legal contracts with your employees, agents, consultants, contractors, vendors, and anyone else who is likely to create IP for you or have access to your IP (*or any other confidential information*). It is important to specifically state that all IP created by an employee, agent, consultant, intern, etc. shall remain with your company. Similarly, strict confidentiality obligations need to be carved out. Do not wait until you are in the middle of due diligence with a buyer to get all your agreements signed. By then, you may find yourself unable to connect with old employees or subcontractors, or other people who may no longer have an interest in fulfilling your need for documentation.

   b) Execute NDAs with vendors, customers, and consultants (especially external developers) who are likely to know details of your business, clients, financials, IP, etc.

c) Change the passwords on these protected sites as key managers or employees leave. This includes external storage locations that may not be authenticated to your active directory—meaning that when you terminate someone's access to email, that same username and password may be used to access other sites. If not, you need to remember to remove that access. This is very often a forgotten process, as HR is not always made aware of the external systems used by a company.

5.   Communicate your IP to the team. Often IP is created but not shared amongst the team, so some people are taking advantage of it while others are not. Technical IP must also be shared with marketing and sales so they can show the benefits the IP can deliver to the prospect and customer.

6.   Finally, IP must be measured constantly. IP can become outdated as new releases of software are available, or as features retire, or as new software prices and packages are updated by vendors requiring you to update tools. Each year review your IP list and measure it to determine if there is revenue acceleration or reduction of expenses by using your IP. Those metrics will need to be communicated to future buyers.

Now that you have identified the organizational IP, we need to make sure it is documented. The documentation is not just to keep it safe, or to prove to a buyer that you have IP; it also serves to increase the efficiency of your company. Here are the benefits you can immediately realize by codifying IP:

- Reduces delivery failure rates – Documenting a process step by step eliminates errors or missteps that can increase delivery failure rates.
- Leverages more junior associates – Getting new staff up to speed is tough, but if all process is well documented, they now have a guide so they can accomplish work typically done by a more senior employee. Delivery costs are then less, allowing for a higher gross profit margin and increased profitability per consultant.
- Increases employee satisfaction – Happy customers make for happy employees. By reducing failure rates and reducing implementation

time and costs, customers are able to realize their ROI sooner. Your consultants are praised for their efforts in keeping costs under control. Your senior engineers and consultants can remove themselves from less challenging tasks to create new IP for your company or continue to document or update existing IP.

- Allows for faster employee growth – Consultants and engineers can learn and implement new tasks faster because they are well documented. Therefore, new employees can progress faster towards working on higher dollar value projects.
- Builds scalability faster and at a lower cost – IP gives you the ability to scale faster by onboarding new people quickly and getting them billing sooner. It also allows you to move more senior consultants and engineers into other tasks where their assistance is needed, thus reducing bottlenecks in delivery when only a few people know how to perform a task.

MOVING FROM SERVICES TO PACKAGED IP – THE IP STAIRCASE

Now that we understand why IP is so important—efficiency, scalability, repeatability, and increased valuation—let's turn to how you go about creating it if you are not yet at this point within your company.

Making a transition from a traditional on-premises VAR or MSP, to a CSP or ISV that relies more on recurring revenue, can be a long and arduous task. If done organically, without any outside capital infusion, it can take as long as four to five years to complete if you are trying to stay cash flow positive. But it can be done in as little as two or three years if you tackle it aggressively. However, this requires either draining your existing working capital reserves or looking for outside capital to fund the project. Most partners opt for the slower three- to five-year transition plan, albeit at the risk of being too late to the game.

Moving to a packaged IP solution also requires new sales and marketing execution. The goal is then to educate the buyer via your website with videos and quick demo vignettes, while offering up bite-size solutions with little risk to the end customer. The sales team must gear up for volume and for providing the best onboarding experience possible to the end customer. This new sales strategy may also involve changing players on the sales team, typically to younger, less experienced talent. This is a lot of change in a short amount of time, and for some organizations, it will prove to be *too much* of a change. For others looking to increase their company valuation, it is a necessary transition.

In practice, creating your own IP is best thought of as a progression rather than an event. Through extensive work with resellers, CloudSpeed (https:// cloudspeed.co/) has distilled this progression into a framework called the "IP Staircase" (as seen below). Essentially, it is a "fast track" roadmap for partners who are looking to transition from a service to a packaged solution focus.

IP Staircase

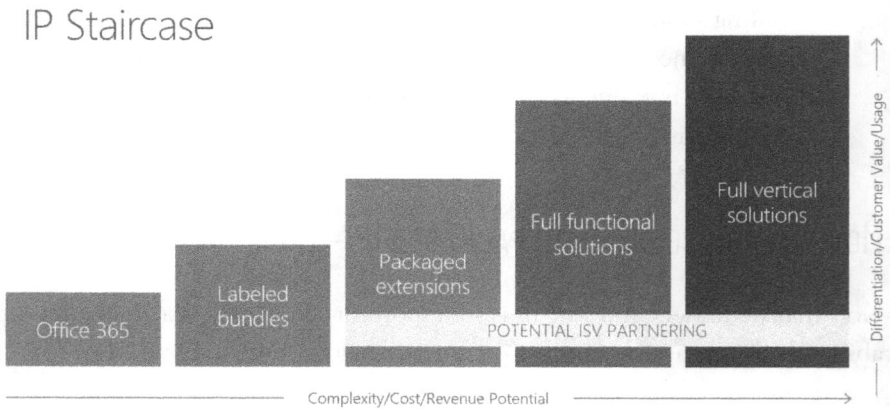

Fig.2.17

To start with, a packaged offer is always grounded in a vendor product. Office 365, Dynamics 365, and SharePoint are examples of common "anchors" within the Microsoft channel, but other products can be used instead. Ideally, the foundational product is cloud-based to allow for subscription pricing and greater sales growth over time.

From there, a reseller typically ascends the IP Staircase in four stages, as follows:

Step 1 – Labeled bundles

A labeled bundle is usually little more than a packaging exercise. It takes what a reseller already does in the way of services, "bundles" it with the anchor vendor product, and "labels" it in a manner designed to appeal to a specific target audience. The key here is that the labeled bundle is focused on addressing a specific business issue and delivering a meaningful business outcome to the customer.

Vertically specific labeled bundles are the most common, and they typically leverage industry expertise that a reseller has accumulated in past projects. But some labeled bundles can address specific business functions that cross industries, for example, human resource management or procurement. Either can work, so long as the business outcome promised to the customer is meaningful to them. Articulating the value proposition using terminology the target segment understands is pivotal to ensuring that the labeled bundle sells.

Finally, the best labeled bundles generate at least some recurring revenue. Many resellers achieve this by folding in ongoing support for their solution. Ideally, labeled bundles also take a "tiered" approach—some version of silver, gold, platinum—whether for one-time or ongoing (recurring) offers.

Step 2 – Packaged extensions

The next step is typically to "extend" the packaged offer by connecting it with other pieces of the technology puzzle, so that it delivers a more valuable business outcome to the customer.

A common example is to connect the labeled bundle with external databases and combine it with industry-specific dashboards that enable better management control at all levels of the customer business.

It is important to note that this *should not* require extensive development time. Think in terms of hours or days at the most, using your existing team of consultants and engineers to work on the implementation of your labeled bundle.

Ideally, any initial development required is billed to the first end customer. In other words, the initial customer funds any needed R&D to the greatest extent possible. From there, the extension is priced based on the value it delivers to the next customer, not on the cost of its delivery, which will be low. This is key to generating good margins and also to ensuring that the extension is in fact viable. If you can't convince subsequent buyers of its value, you don't have a compelling offer and you're not ascending the IP Staircase.

Another key is to fully leverage any customization a customer might request, making sure that it is in fact repeatable and can be added to a "library" of extensions that builds over time. Avoid one-offs wherever possible.

Finally, don't forget to fold in ongoing support for your packaged extensions, wherever possible, to increase both recurring revenue and overall margin levels.

Step 3 – Functional solutions

As we move on to these last two stages, it is important to note that you can build a very nice repeatable recurring high margin business with increased revenue growth by just creating a number of packaged extensions. However, as time goes on, you may see some trends in the packages you have created that might lead you down the path of these last two steps in the staircase. You may see a pattern emerge either within an industry or a functional efficiency (see below). It is really this fork in the road between industry and efficiency that leads you to the last two steps.

As you move toward your "own" IP, the margins significantly increase and the more valuable your business becomes to a prospective buyer. (We saw this at the beginning of this chapter, in fig 2.16.) While the best differentiation of your IP is built on a vertical solution, you can very successfully monetize a solution that is purely functionally oriented and not vertically oriented. It is more important that you *leverage* what you have already created and build around that, rather than trying to create a vertical that you don't have or don't know. Your customer base and the work you have already created will make this decision easy for you.

Here is a quick example: My last company was a cloud infrastructure company that hosted a variety of Microsoft ERP and CRM solutions for our customers. The solutions we offered were not industry specific; in fact, if we looked at our customer base, we served at least a dozen different industries, so we were initially very horizontal. What we did see, however, was a recurring theme within our customer base—an interest in added security due to regulatory requirements such as SOX, HIPAA, FDA, etc. This "extra" level of compliancy required us to step up our services to allow for extended backup retention, additional audit trails around user access, and additional procedures and reporting that was performed by our team. This became the base of our *functional* differentiator. Very few, if any, other providers were offering the same level of "compliance" that our company could provide. We then saw a trend toward attracting more financial services and healthcare clients, as well as publicly traded companies, that needed this extra level of compliance. From there, we began marketing this extra layer of compliancy and we were able to charge at least 50 percent more than our competition. Our margins increased dramatically, even though generic cloud hosting services became more commoditized over time.

A functional solution is an offering that increases efficiency or removes risk from a business function that crosses industries, rather than a solution for a specific industry. Functional does not mean horizontal; it must solve a business problem. In addition to the example above, functional solutions can link together several solutions that align together nicely but don't clearly link together out of the box.

A good example of a simplistic solution is an expense reporting system that might need to link to an ERP or CRM system and can also then store the data in a SharePoint for nonfinancial reporting to business team members.

A more complex example is a solution called *PowerGPOnline* (https://powergponline.com), which combines a Microsoft accounting system with other industry solutions (i.e., Dynamics GP, Power BI, Excel, Word, and Jet Reports, all sitting on an Azure cloud). It solves the problem of a complex accounting solution with easy to use reporting for both financial and business intelligence, not only within the application, but also by using industry tools, such as Excel, Power BI, and Jet Reports, where the tools are already configured to look at the correct tables within the accounting software. The combination of these toolsets with preprogrammed links provides a powerful solution that would otherwise be difficult and costly to create and maintain. All of these applications are bundled as a single package and sold on a sub-scription basis as an Azure cloud-based application.

Again, this type of solution is typically built out over time, usually around a few key customers who support the development efforts. Typically, few external development costs are incurred, and if some are required, they are typically outsourced or created internally. Over time, you continue to build out your solution by adding functionality to create multiple solutions with different price points or additional small add-on features that customers can procure as needed.

As you do this, gross profit margins increase even more, and the amount of professional services decrease, all the while increasing the average annual growth rate. This type of IP will grow sales organically within the customer base, in addition to the added growth of new sales. As customers become more comfortable with the application and business outcome, they purchase additional seats within the application. As a point of reference, we were able to count on at least 18 to 22 percent growth from our existing customer base. Even with a 5 to 7 percent customer attrition rate, this is a nice add each year to the sales growth goals.

Step 4 – Vertical solutions

The final step on the IP Staircase is a full vertical solution. This is the most valuable packaged offering. Although it usually involves more complexity and development cost, typically a group of customers are funding this R&D over time. As you work with companies in the same sector, each project you com-plete creates additional IP. Use each customization as the core of repeatable code that can be used for the next customer by adding to the library of code that they can then reuse each time. Typically, this type of IP is built over time, hence the four- to five-year period, but as we will see in our example, it can be done in as little as two years. Deploying the solution in the cloud reduces the costs of deployment and support as new versions are rolled out to users. The customer receives the greatest business value, and this IP delivers the strongest possible ongoing revenue steam for you, as well as the highest margin. But also, and more importantly from a valuation perspective, the value of the company is increasing dramatically.

A great vertical example is a solution called *365 Cannabis™* (http://d365cannabis.com). The product was built specifically for the growing (no pun intended) cannabis business specifically designed to help their customers smoothly manage their seed-to-sales process and maximize yield and profitability. The system combines the Microsoft Dynamics Business Central accounting system with other industry solutions (i.e., LS Retail, Agriware, nHanced, Office 365, Power BI, and Jet Reports), all sitting on an Azure cloud. It solves the unique problems of the cannabis industry by combining the needs of a grower, nursery, or producer with a tailored accounting solution, including a point of sale with extended reporting and field enhancements. Additional code was added to specially meet the needs of their particular industry. The combination of these toolsets with preprogrammed links provides a powerful solution that again is bundled as a single package and sold on a subscription basis as an Azure cloud-based application.

While both a couple of the examples above are built on accounting packages, any packages that have an open API can be used as the bases for your own staircase.

NEXT STEPS

What can you do next? Spend some time to define what packaged offers you can identify that you might already have or could turn into a package quickly.

If you aren't sure which solution to pick, and perhaps you currently have a few options, for each package offering you identify, answer the following:

- What stage of the IP Staircase would each packaged offer be at today?

- What is the focus of your IP—function or vertical?

- What market does it target?

- What business outcome does it deliver?

- Where are your referenceable clients?

- How large is the addressable market?

The IP Staircase is a proven framework for developing and monetizing packaged IP, but there are certain practical keys to ascending it quickly and successfully. For more detail on that, check out https://cloudspeed.co/ip-staircase/.

Having codified IP enables companies to deliver services of higher quality—more reliably and typically at a lower cost than their competitors. To be able to present to a buyer the list of IP that has been created, documented, and protected, and with its monetary results tracked, is huge! And yet so few organizations do it. It also suggests to a buyer scalability and capacity—both of which are important factors for future growth. Every firm that has been in existence has developed processes and procedures as IP. Just find it and document it to add additional value for your company when it comes time to sell.

PART III
ADVISORS, ADVICE, AND RESOURCES

This section covers three primary topics. It defines the key advisors you should engage in the selling process. It dissects the real and potential value of these advisors and offers possible criteria for selection. And it offers comprehensive tips for carrying the process forward and taking your initial steps with a potential buyer on your own, if you choose to do so.

Advisors – the big three + "The Coach"

Selling your business is probably the most complex sales transaction that you may ever have in your life, so getting it right the first time will be especially important. Selling your business will affect not only your shareholders and immediate family members but also your employees, customers, and vendors. For this reason, it is imperative that you surround yourself with the best advisors and ones that you unequivocally trust.

If you are on the "1-year plan," as we discussed earlier in the book, this is probably the most important section of the book for you to read now. Researching, interviewing, and selecting your three most important advisors takes some time and effort. While many people go with referrals from other sellers who have been through the process, others listen to webinars and podcasts, and read blog posts written by advisors. Give yourself enough time to do your own research and begin to develop a rapport with the key players before you need to make a final selection. Whatever method you use to choose your advisors, you never want to feel in the end that you made a hasty decision in selecting your team.

As an avid backpacker, I loved experiencing the wild for multiple consecutive weeks, as I did when I hiked hundreds of miles on the Pacific Crest Trail, and it requires proper planning and equipment to make the journey. No experienced hiker would contemplate a long-distance hike without seriously researching their "big three:" tent, sleeping bag, and the perfect backpack.

Selling your company is very similar: It's a journey into the wild that requires planning, preparation, and the "big three:" a tax CPA, an attorney, and an M&A advisor or coach who specializes in your size company and your industry. Like preparing for a long-distance hike, not having dialed in your big three could result in serious problems when selling your company: lost revenue, minimized acquisition value, increased taxes, and a host of other potential difficulties.

There are many instances, as we will discuss below, where you might decide to proceed without a business broker and use an M&A coach instead; but do not forgo the counsel of a good attorney to review your contracts, or a CPA who can explain the tax ramifications of how the deal is structured. I sold two of my three companies without a business broker (mostly because I knew my buyers well) but never without my attorney and a CPA.

CPA

There are two types of CPAs that you may need during a sale transaction and possibly even three:

a) One to review your financials, either formally via an audit, review, compilation, or quality of revenue audit. This CPA would also perform an assessment called Quality of Earnings (QoE), which will give the potential buyers the information about how risky or stable your stream of revenue is. This assessment is not required prior to going to market but definitely valuable information for a buyer.

b) One to advise you of the tax ramifications of the sale.

c) And potentially a third who intimately understands sales tax law. Rarely is this the same person and sometimes not even the same firm.

Larger CPA firms can usually provide all these services, including succession planning. Smaller firms sometimes specialize in a particular practice area and can typically provide only some of these services but usually at a lower cost. Therefore, if you decide to take the small-firm route, you might need to enlist more than one firm. For example, sales tax is a very specialized area and not every firm offers that service. On the other hand, audit, review, and tax services are usually provided by the same firm.

The Tax CPA

While there is always much talk by politicians about simplifying the tax code, it seems like every attempt to do so creates more complication. Understanding the tax ramifications of either a stock sale or asset sale is best left to those people who can run "what-if" scenarios through some very sophisticated tax planning software. Don't attempt this on TurboTax yourself!

Whether you are a C corp, S corp, LLC, or something in between, there will be tax consequences to your sale on a federal and state level. Most transactions will qualify for capital gain treatment, but with the onset of alternative minimum tax, it is a nightmare to figure out actual tax liability without qualified help. This is one of those times where you might look beyond your existing tax preparer (assuming he or she is a CPA or CA) and speak to someone who is thoroughly knowledgeable about large asset transactions. If the sale includes a note payable over multiple years, you may have to add an installment calculation to the equation. Add an ESOP into the mix and everything gets even more complicated. Once you have an LOI in hand and have a good idea of how your transaction will be structured, get your CPA to prepare a proforma tax return to see the tax implications of your deal. This way, you will have a better understanding of how much cash you will have (after tax), and if it makes sense to finalize the current proposed structure or the deal in general.

It is critical, however, to get the advice of your CPA *before* you enter into the sale transaction. The due diligence for a stock sale is much more involved than for that of an asset purchase. The buyer usually dictates which offer they are willing to make, but there is the rare occasion where you may be given either option. Therefore, it is important to understand in advance which one benefits you more (cash in your pocket). This pre-transaction consultation will also give you an idea of how knowledgeable your CPA is on the subject. If you are not feeling convinced in this early phase of discovery, you won't be happy later when you get the surprise of an unexpected additional tax.

The Financials CPA

It is possible that your buyer will request audited, or reviewed, financials. If your plan is to enter into a transaction in the coming year, have your previous year's financials reviewed or compiled (not audited) in advance if you don't feel completely comfortable with the financials you are producing. I would especially recommend this if you use an accounting package where historical amounts can be changed easily without an audit trail, or if you have a substantial amount of deferred revenue or complex multiyear subscriptions. A buyer will typically require you to represent in writing that the financials are prepared in accordance with generally accepted accounting principles (GAAP), so if you are not that knowledgeable about GAAP, you should have someone who can review your financials and accounting policies and make any appropriate adjustments before you present your financials to a buyer.

If you use a midlevel accounting package with good internal audit trails, and your reporting is accurate, then you might be able to do without a review or an audit. I highly recommend creating a budget to actual variance report that is examined each month for unusual activity. This will give you and your buyer comfort in your projections and the accuracy of your financials. Not all deals require CPA prepared financials, although most every buyer will ask. If you can show strong audit trails, detailed budgets, and GAAP accounting, then you may be able to avoid this.

Remember, if you do need to issue reviewed or audited financials, you should use a different type of CPA, not the one you will use to advise you on your sale. One type of CPA performs strictly accounting and audit, and the other type focuses on tax. They are two very different disciplines. Not many CPAs do both, and if they do, they likely do not have in-depth expertise in both.

The Sales Tax expert

It is possible you may need a third type of CPA or sales tax expert. The complexity of sales tax and the rules regarding when to apply it and when not to, have increased dramatically over the years. If your company sells software/

services or a subscription of any sort, and is selling it directly to the end customer, be sure that you have your sales tax fully considered and accounted for. Do not assume that you must charge sales tax only in your state and not for out-of-state sales. More and more states have revisited the concept of *nexus*.

Nexus, also called "sufficient physical presence," is a legal term that refers to the requirement for companies doing business in a state *to collect and pay tax on sales* in that state.[21] In the past, you truly just needed physical presence (i.e., an office or an employee in that state); now, however, the rules defining physical presence have become much more complex.

If you feel you have not completely complied with all the sales tax initiatives in each state in which you sell, it might be worthwhile to have a mini audit prepared to assure yourself of your level of compliance. You will want to know this *now*, and not when you are in the throes of full due diligence with the buyer, as a sales tax audit later can delay, alter, or kill a deal.

Keep in mind that, in an asset sale, you are still responsible for the liabilities of the company prior to the sale, so any pending sales tax issues that arise will be your responsibility. Even in a stock transaction, where you are no longer responsible for the ongoing liabilities, for sure there will be language in the definitive agreement that will bind you should a liability over a certain amount arise.

ATTORNEY

As a business owner, I relied on three different types of attorneys: Employment practices, trademark, and contracts. As with CPAs, each one provides completely different services and areas of expertise; they do not overlap, meaning even a great attorney cannot do it all. Also, do not assume that the attorney who incorporated you many years ago is your go-to attorney to help you wade through sales/purchase agreements. A typical deal not only includes the buy/sell agreement, but can also include: a noncompete, a note receivable, a transitions services agreement, and an employment contract.

There are two big points I would like to stress here. First, find your M&A attorney *before* you enter into a deal. You should start by having your attorney review your Sellers Agreement with your M&A advisor (or M&A coach), or if you are not using an advisor, then the LOI (Letter of Intent). While most LOIs are provided by the buyer, there is that rare occasion where the seller writes the LOI, in part because the buyer has either never done one or else feels they don't need one. It is best if the LOI is written first from a business perspective, as it is the basis of your purchase agreement (on the larger points), but then have your attorney review the LOI for legal issues.

Your attorney will become heavily involved during that last 60 to 90 days of the process. Make sure he/she has the bandwidth, as they may be working on this *exclusively* toward the end, as final red-lines are challenged and rewritten for the nth time. If you find yourself looking for new counsel, here are some questions you can ask a prospective attorney:

- How many of these transactions (buy/sell agreements) have you worked on in the last 24 months?
- How many in the technology industry?
- What is the average size transaction you work on? Largest? Smallest?
- If IP is relevant: how many companies had IP as part of the transaction?
- Will there be anyone else in the firm who will be working on this?
- How much do you anticipate this deal will run in fees?
- What is the hourly rate and fees by person who will work on the engagement?
- Will you cap your fees at a certain amount?

Which brings me to my second biggest take-away for this section: Your attorney is there to mitigate your risk, *not* to negotiate your deal. Do not confuse your attorney's role with that of your advisor or broker. Your attorney needs to stay focused on the contracts. Also make sure you have him or her review *all* your disclosures, so they are properly worded, don't blow up the deal, and still cover you. In addition to the disclosures, your attorney should perform a critical review of the representations and warranties in the contract. He/she will be able to identify what risks and potential liabilities (e.g., think sales tax!) may remain your obligation and for what period of time.

There are a number of M&A advisors who suggest their own attorneys (either in-house or on retainer) who are willing to work for a fixed fee. There is some merit to this, especially if they have done a number of deals in the past with your broker and they have extensive experience working with technology service providers. However, on the flip side, no attorney works for free. While a fixed fee sounds appealing initially, the attorney has a number of hours in his or her mind that they plan on spending on the contracts. Once they hit their limit, they may not be as engaged. Keep that in mind when you are making this decision.

Speaking of fees, for a well-seasoned attorney that bills hourly, you can expect fees on average to range from $25K to $75K. A stock transaction will be on the higher end as the agreement needs to cover more areas of law. The fees will also vary by the number of separate documents that need to be reviewed—employment contracts, non-competes, etc. Is it possible to over-lawyer? I guess it depends on which side you are on.

M&A ADVISOR/BROKER

The marketing and selling of your business will require meticulous planning, marketing, and the preparation of financial and legal documents to properly complete the transaction. Even if you are approached by a buyer, you may still want the advice of either an investment bank, an M&A advisor, or a business broker to help review the deal points and keep the process flowing.

Most companies in the lower middle market (firms with annual revenue less than $250M) will use an M&A advisor instead of an investment banker who usually services larger private and publicly traded companies. Since investment bankers typically require formal licensing as broker-dealers, their success fees are higher and they offer a broader range of services, like fairness opinions, private placement memorandums, public offerings, etc.

A business broker typically works with smaller companies that will likely sell to an individual buyer versus a corporation or private equity firm. Business brokers typically work with companies that sell for less than $2M, and in many states they are actually required to be a realtor in order to sell the assets of your company. Unlike an M&A advisor or investment banker, a business broker does not consult extensively with the company owners to prepare them for sale, other than listing them on a number of small business websites featuring companies for sale. They typically work with a predefined "canned" advisory agreement.

Most M&A advisors offer services similar to investment bankers in preparing a **private** company for sale. These services could be valuation work, or a review (not in the formal accounting sense) of financial, managerial, and corporate data in preparation for a Confidential Information Memorandum (CIM) and a blind profile. Services can also include preparing a detailed working capital calculation and the gathering of due diligence documents and post-merger acquisition integration services. A good M&A advisor will typically work with a company for a few months in preparation for meeting with potential buyers.

Even though these services may overlap those of investment bankers, most lower-market to middle-market transactions do not require the M&A advisor to be formally licensed when working with private companies, and you will find that most are not. In recent years, the SEC has seen a number of important developments, via case law and no-action letters, related to the activities of "finders" or nonregistered broker-dealers; and most M&A advisor activity can be done without violating these requirements.

Now that we are clear on the differences between investment bankers, M&A advisors, and brokers, we will use the term "advisors" and "brokers" synonymously throughout the rest of the book.

Benefits of using an M&A advisor:

Business owners always underestimate both the actual time and the mental energy needed for selling a company. Unless you have a very strong management team that can just go about business as usual, it is very likely your business will feel the effects. Smaller organizations, where the owner is involved in sales, usually feel it the most. Therefore, if you are a smaller company (under $25M), the more you can hand over to your M&A advisor, the better, as sales *cannot* slide while you are looking for a buyer.

Once you decide you are going to sell your business, the entire sales process can take up to as much as 9 to 12 months. This is a long time to juggle attention between your ongoing business operations and negotiating the sale of your business, so picking an advisor who is competent, whom you trust, and who has your best interests in mind, is critical.

A well connected and experienced advisor will know the most active and reputable buyers in your industry, keep the process on track, make everyone feel heard, and keep your deal from falling apart. And more importantly, he or she will insulate the buyer from your "less professional moments" as nerves fray and tempers get short.

The benefits can be summarized as follows:

- Owners can continue to focus on increasing the value of their company. The last thing you want to do is take your foot off the accelerator while you are hashing through prospective buyers. In addition to the mental bandwidth required to run the deal, there is also the emotional aspect that comes with it. Hand off as much as you can, as your plate will be full enough negotiating your contracts.
- Maintain confidentiality. Customers, employees, and competitors will find out quickly if you are selling your business. As the seller, if you can keep your company name a secret until you have a signed NDA with a target buyer, then you are in good shape, but in practice that is very hard to do. It is much easier for an advisor to make calls and not disclose the company name while ascertaining the appropriate buyers. Having an advisor will allow you to create a blind profile that will only be distributed to prequalified buyers after an NDA has been signed, protecting you completely as the seller.
- A good advisor will have access to many more buyers than you will. If you have chosen well and have selected one that works specifically in the technology industry, you will have many options. They will be able to screen out the buyers who are just looking but don't have sufficient funds. They will present you with their list of potential buyers, but you should then perform your own due diligence to screen out candidates that you know would not be a good fit based on your knowledge of the industry.
- Managing the sales process. The goal is to get every buyer to align around the same timeline. Some buyers may come to the table earlier than others, but the goal is to keep everyone within a few

weeks of one another. That way you are not stalling earlier IOIs—or worse, LOIs—for weeks while you are waiting for others to arrive.

- Just like a leasing agent for a building, your M&A advisor becomes that buffer between you and the buyer. You can say things to your advisor that you may never want to say to a buyer. Let them be that delicate go-between so you can maintain a positive working relationship throughout the deal process.

Selecting an advisor

Selecting the right advisor can make the difference between a great sale and a waste of time. More than one TSP has shared stories of not selecting the right advisor. And in most cases, revenue took a downward slide as the owner was fully occupied with the wrong deal or constantly updating quarterly financials and projections while waiting patiently for their advisor to bring them qualified buyers. In some instances, no qualified buyers ever emerged because their M&A advisor did not have the appropriate list of buyers to solicit. Even in a great economy, this can become a detriment to the seller.

Pick someone that you are professionally "comfortable" with, as you will be working together extensively for a few months. This doesn't mean you pick the person you "like" the most. Competency trumps "like," so look for someone who you feel comfortable working with, and who is numbers savvy and completely confident around legal teams. Nothing is more embarrassing than having the attorneys and buyers talk over the head of your advisor.

Select an advisor who understands your business and the services you are offering. One of the advisor's most important role is to represent your company to the buyers with the specific information regarding your services. There are numerous conversations before a buyer will sign the NDA to talk to you directly; and while maintaining your anonymity, the advisor has the power to convince a buyer to talk to you if they are on the fence. An advisor who understands your services, the markets, and the potential growth for your company will be crucial in bringing the right buyers to the table.

Obviously, trust is a key factor, and in most cases, you will have to "trust your gut" on this, even after checking seller references. Be sure when checking references to also ask about responsiveness and their availability throughout the process. Your advisor should be there for you 24/7. After all, you will be thinking about a pending sale 24/7 and so should they. If they are not quick to respond while going through the selection process, chances are they won't be quick to respond later either.

When interviewing a business advisor, consider questions around the team that will be working with you. The extent and degree of their marketing efforts, and how fees are calculated and earned, are all important. Here is a list of questions to ask regarding their team, their marketing efforts, and their fees:

Team

1. Who will be working on the engagement? Roles?
2. What credentials/certifications does the broker have, if any?
3. How many transactions have they closed over the past 24 months in this industry?
4. What was the range of revenue of the companies they represented? Largest, smallest?
5. Have they sold companies that you have heard of, and are they willing to allow you to speak to those former owners as a reference?
6. What was the range of multiples for companies similar to yours?
7. How many were unsuccessful and why?
8. Did they receive offers for each company they took to the market, even if unsuccessful in the sale?
9. MORE IMPORTANTLY, can you speak to someone they represented and failed to sell?
10. Are they willing to travel to meet you in person (should you so desire)?

Marketing

1. Do they already have a list of buyers in mind, and if so, how many?

2. Of this list, what percentage of buyers do they anticipate will review your blind profile or CIM blind profile (i.e. what conversion rate do they expect)?

3. How many buyers will they actually phone vs. email?

4. What is the split between strategic buyers and financial buyers?

5. How many of these are currently in the technology industry?

6. What is their detailed marketing approach? Do they have a process timeline document for each week?

7. What will they be preparing on your behalf? Do they have examples to show you?

8. Is there a sample solicitation letter and/or seller profile they can share with you?

9. How will a "do not market to" list be handled?

10. What are the ramifications of accidentally marketing to someone on this list?

11. Can they provide an example of the reporting you will receive on buyer contacts?

12. Will there be a weekly call for updates on the process once the company goes to market?

Fees

1. What are the terms of the engagement: Is there a retainer? Is there a monthly fee? If so, how much?

2. How is the success fee calculated, and what are the percentages being used at different levels? Ask for an example calculation.

3. What is their minimum success fee?

4. Can the retainer or monthly fees offset the success fee? (This can be negotiated if not written into the agreement.)

5. How are earn-outs handled in the success fee? Are they paid at close or later when earned?

6. If fees on earn-outs are paid at close, are they discounted at NPV?

7.   What is the tail period of the engagement—if you disengage, how long will you continue or on what terms are you obligated to continue to pay them a success fee?

8.   How are carve-outs handled (in other words, people who you have already approached in the past)?

9.   What happens if you sell to one of these carve-outs—are you still obligated to pay a fee?

A download of this checklist can be found at www.rosebizinc/book-resources.

Big and even medium-sized firms tend to roll out the managing partners or directors of the firm at the first meetings, but typically have junior or less-experienced staff members to do most of the work. Know the entire team that will be working on your engagement upfront, and who will be on the call with the buyers once the NDAs start rolling in. Make sure that everyone on the team can articulate your value proposition and what makes your company unique to a buyer.

Industry experience

This is not the time to pick a friend who happens to be an M&A advisor in another industry. I would even say that a general "technology" advisor may also not understand the particulars of a channel partner or IT business, or even who the buyers are (both financial and strategic) in this area of specialty. There are buyers specifically looking for Microsoft, Salesforce, NetSuite, or AI partners, etc. Others are specifically looking for MSPs or ISVs. Find an advisor that knows your buyers well and not just someone who has an extensive list they procured from some website that they subscribe to. I affectionately refer to this as the "spray and pray" method. Most emails are never opened, and those that do, may not be qualified or know anything about your business.

Size matters

There are all sizes of M&A firms. Just because you are on multiple webinars with a large firm who can speak to your industry doesn't mean they are the best fit. Also, a firm that has a broad range of clients they service, say $1M to $250M, is not going to be all that engaged if you are less than $10M in revenue. Conversely, picking a firm that has never done a transaction larger than $25M may also not be a good fit if you are larger.

Per the recent 2018-2019 M&A Fee Guide published by Divestopedia, 77 percent of M&A advisors work on less than 10 deals per year and are defined as boutique firms.[12] Of this group, 61.4 percent work on deals with a minimum transaction value of less than $5M. If your revenue is in the $3M to $25M range, picking a boutique firm will be your best option. You will get much better service and attention to your deal.

Acquisitions over $50M typically have more people involved both on the buy and sell side. Deals over $100M should involve brokers with certifications offered by the International Business Brokers Association (IBBA) or other state broker associations. A $50M deal may not require the credentialing, but typically, the larger the transaction, the more complex the negotiation and terms. Credentialing as mentioned above via a CBI certification at least gives you peace of mind that the advisor knows what they are doing. In general, it is good to avoid being either on the low end or the high end of the range of an M&A firm's transactions.

THE "+" CHOICE – THE M&A COACH

There are a few instances where I would advocate not using a business broker or M&A advisor but instead *an M&A coach*. An M&A coach typically has similar skills (sans any certifications), has been through a few of their own transactions so they have been in your shoes, knows the industry buyers well, and probably has several resources to bring to the transaction (accountants, attorneys, etc.) if needed. They can either guide the transaction with the buyer and seller, like a broker, or stay behind the scenes and guide the seller through the process. Coaches typically operate on a fixed monthly fee, hourly rate, or fixed transaction fee, and therefore are a more economical solution. An M&A coach may be a better option when the potential buyer has already been identified and you just need an extra independent guide. M&A coaches do not typically source buyers for you but some do via close contacts or their private network. Consider an M&A coach in these situations:

- **You are selling to an existing shareholder, employee, or family member** – All players are familiar with the business, customers, and vendors. In this instance, you may want some independent, arms-length guidance.

- **An unsolicited offer has been presented by another strategic partner** – The number of sales that occur with the start of an unsolicited offer is higher than most estimates, and more than half of all transactions in a particular partner channel are completed this way. In an active vendor channel, businesses get to know each other, and those looking to acquire companies are attending industry conferences and other partner events, and networking over drinks. The opportunity may start as a partnering discussion but many times subsequently leads to an offer. In many situations, two companies have worked together in the past, have a shared customer base, and therefore have a trust level that makes an unsolicited offer compelling. While many brokers still advocate using their services to bring other offers to the seller, this can be detrimental if a deal is already being seriously contemplated between two owners who know and trust one another.

- **A vendor or customer presents an offer** – Many times strong preexisting relationships are developed between the seller's customers or vendors where an acquisition is an obvious move for growth. As discussed earlier, many large software vendors routinely purchase complimentary ISVs that help round out their solution.

- **You already have a couple of buyers in mind, but your company revenue is below $5M** – Most knowledgeable advisors will charge at least a $100,000 to $150,000 minimum "success fee" in addition to a retainer to get the process going. This may prove to be too high for the overall value of the deal. For example, a company with $3M in revenue and $400,000 in EBITDA might sell for 4x EBITDA or $1,600,000. With a minimum $100,000 to $150,000 success fee and another potential $20,000 in retainer, you are basically paying $120,000 to $170,000, or a 7.5 to 10 percent fee, to sell your company, which most sellers would consider to be too high.

ADVISORY AGREEMENTS AND FEES

The Advisory Agreement is the document between your company and your M&A advisor or broker. It states the activities that will be performed and the fees that will be charged to accomplish those services. Understanding the Advisory Agreement in detail and how all the fees are earned and calculated, in advance of signing any agreement, is key to a successful relationship with your advisor. If you are uncomfortable with legal agreements, now may be a good time to engage counsel and have your attorney thoroughly review the agreement. This is also a great test to see if you have chosen the appropriate counsel to represent you in this upcoming sale. Unfortunately, I see too many sellers sign these agreements without fully understanding all aspects, and then finding out later that they are required to pay their advisor even if he/she was never involved in the final sale of their company! Don't let that be you.

Breaking down the fees

You will typically see three types of fees for M&A advisory services. They can work independent of one another or in combination, so you may see only one, or all three, in an agreement. Here are the three most prevalent fees:

Commitment fee: A nonrefundable deposit to get the process started. Fees range from $10,000 to $25,000.[2] This fee is used when an advisor is participating in assembling the data needed for a blind profile and CIM. The size of the fee is dependent on how much work they will put into this effort. This fee also begins the process of contacting potential buyers, either via personal connections, email blasts, or posting your profile on certain buyer websites, and, of course, running the buying process.

Monthly retainer: Many advisors charge a monthly fee to more thoroughly prepare your company for sale and determine value through a formal valuation process, in addition to creating the blind profile and CIM. For some companies, this is money well spent and can yield a higher sales price in the end. Monthly fees typically range from $3,000 to $7,500 per month, depending on the size of the company. This monthly retainer can also extend into post-sale transition items—prior to the completion of the sale. Some advisors will net this against the final fee, but most do not.

Success fee: This is the fee that is earned upon the sale of your company, at closing. In general, these run between 3 and 5 percent of the transaction price.* There is usually a *minimum* stated success fee (the fee that must be paid regardless of how little the company sells for), which typically ranges from $100k to $250K.* The success fee is independent of the monthly retainer or commitment fee, although we have seen brokers that reduce their success fee by the upfront commitment fee or monthly retainer. This is usually negotiated and not the standard practice. Also, if you feel the project dragged due to the advisor not finding an adequate number of prospective buyers, netting the monthly retainer or portion thereof against the success fee is an option, but make sure you negotiate that ability upfront in the agreement.

*Per RoseBiz survey of M&A advisors selling technology service providers under $100M, conducted in 2019. Outlier numbers were removed.

Advisory Agreements

When negotiated and structured properly, the Advisory Agreement should align the broker's interests with yours. In order to successfully negotiate this agreement between you and your advisor, you should understand the factors that create a successful outcome for everyone. Equally important is structuring an agreement to allow for early termination should you find that you are not a good fit for one another. Be clear on the following terms with no uncertainty: minimum transaction value, success fee structure—specifically on future earn-out or equity interests, monthly retainer, break fees, and termination requirements.

A well-structured Advisory Agreement should contain the following elements:

Fee Structure: As mentioned above, the agreement should be clear on what type of fees will be charged, when they are due, and how the success fee is calculated. For example, let's say the final deal includes cash at close, a note receivable, payable over three years, a holdback for an escrow account, and an earn-out over the next 24 months. It is very important that you understand if the entire amount is calculated as part of the success fee or if there is a discount factor for items that are not yet earned. Again, I always like the advisor to prepare an example if there is any ambiguity as to how these are calculated.

Covered Transactions: A sale process can result in a wide range of outcomes, from selling the entire company, to selling only a portion of the company, to merely raising working capital. In order to ensure that certain transactions are not unintentionally included or subjected to inappropriate fee structures, it is important to clearly define the scope of services provided and the transactions covered.

Transaction Value Definition: Understanding and clearly defining what is considered the "transaction value" is imperative to a positive outcome with your broker. Given that many items, such as earn-outs or milestone-based payments received by seller, are contingent on performance, it is important to understand if you may be required to pay a success fee on these at close based upon some present value calculation, or (a less likely outcome) your broker may delay receiving payments until they are earned by you at some future point. Items to define include excess compensation to owners, the value of any real property of other assets that are distributed, securities in the new company, and all liabilities being assumed by the buyers. It is very important that you pay close attention to this section, so you are not surprised at the close.

Exclusivity: Nearly all brokers will require that you work with them exclusively, meaning they are the only advisor that can market your company. Since your broker is going to be putting a significant amount of time, thought, and effort into preparing your team, and your offer to the market, he or she will want your commitment. Exclusivity is a reasonable request given that it takes a considerable amount of time to bring the right buyers to the table (resulting in several LOIs), and to calm troubled waters between the parties as you negotiate the deal over several months. Most agreements, however, contain a clause that will allow you to terminate the agreement should you find that this wasn't the best broker match for you. Make sure this is in place before you sign an agreement.

Carve-outs: Sellers at times come to a broker with some specific buyers already in mind. In some cases, they may have already begun a dialogue. Whether these potential buyers are competitors, internal employees, or long-time business relationships, you should specifically identify these and have them addressed in a carve-out section. If your company is sold to one of these predetermined or already-in-negotiation buyers, the success fee may be eliminated, or a reduced success fee may be assessed. Carve-outs typically do not affect retainers as those are typically paid regardless. The more detailed and specific these carve-outs can be, the better. On the other hand, coming to the table with an extensive list of names for inclusion in the carve-out will not be well received by your broker. Limiting this to a handful or less is optimal and should include only people with whom discussions have already begun or are about to begin.

Length: The agreement term length specifies how long the engagement period will last. A 12-month term is standard. This allows sufficient time for your broker to position the company, including time for them to prepare a confidential information memorandum, send out summaries to potential buyers, solicit interest, receive offers, and negotiate a deal. The engagement term you negotiate should be driven, however, by how much time your broker needs to close your specific deal. In today's technology market, buyers are moving very fast, as sellers in the IT industry typically do not have tangible assets that need to be valued and thus the process can be much quicker.

Termination and Tail Period: The engagement letter should explicitly state a right of termination after the term of engagement. In some cases, the agreement may automatically renew on a monthly basis after the initial 12 months (engagement term) until canceled in writing by either you or your broker. If for some reason you decide to move forward with a transaction after signing your Seller agreement, be sure to check if you have a termination clause that specifically needs to be cancelled in writing.

Additionally, agreements also include a "tail period"—a period after termination during which, if a transaction is completed by a broker induced buyer, then the broker will still be paid. Typically, the tail period is two years, although business owners can push for a shorter period. The purpose of a tail period is to make sure that the broker is compensated for their work should a deal get started but not finish during the agreement period (say 12 months). This prevents sellers from going behind the back of brokers after the agreement period is over and finalizing a deal, thus eliminating the success fee to the broker.

Some brokers may try to include the rights to a fee, regardless of whether they introduce you to the ultimate buyer. This is a gray area which you should negotiate with your broker before signing the agreement. For example, if you sell your company to one of your carve-out companies, as discussed above, but the offer was higher than the initial IOI or LOI represented due to a bidding war created by the broker, the broker may ask to be compensated on the difference (or increased value created by bringing multiple buyers to the table).

Expenses: Your broker most likely will incur some reimbursable out-of-pocket expenses such as travel, research, and material preparation during the sale process. Make sure the engagement letter allows you the ability to exercise some control over these expenses, and make sure the engagement letter requires them to obtain your prior written approval before incurring such expenses, or expenses over a certain dollar amount.

Break Fee: This is a fee that a broker will charge should you elect not to proceed with an offer they have procured for you. Most brokers (61 percent) do not use this, especially if they are charging a monthly retainer.

Confidentiality: All agreements have some level of confidentiality statements as to how the data you will be sharing with them will be kept and who will be able to access your data.

Additional items such as disclaimers, guarantees, warranties indemnifications, limitation of liability, governing law, and venue, etc. should also be covered in the agreement.

Once you have found a group of brokers that work in your industry and revenue range, you might assume that the only thing that differentiates them from one another are their fees. That couldn't be further from the truth. A broker's services range from marketing and finding you a buyer to being involved with every aspect of preparing your company for the sale and the post-sale activities. Some brokers get you ready (like staging your home for an open house), and some just put a shine on what you already have. You will only know the difference by speaking with past clients. Check out past tombstones, look for names of companies that you may be familiar with, and do your homework. A quote from a happy seller on a website does not always tell the complete story.

There are many brokers available online by searching for "technology" M&A brokers. Each approaches the process differently and a few are geared more towards the "buy-side" but offer seller services as well. If you spend the time on due diligence, you will find the broker that best suits your transaction needs and you will be happier in the end.

A final thought on fees: Any broker who is willing to work only for a success fee should be viewed with caution. Their reward only comes when your company is acquired, and since they are not being paid to find you multiple buyers or offers, they will stop at the first offer that looks like it might work—probably not the best deal for you, the seller.

ROBERT INSIGHT:

After selling his consulting practice, Robert knew he was going to use an advisor this time around. The last experience, while positive, had been too stressful and he felt that he didn't receive the maximum value for his consulting division. Over the last six months, Robert had put some feelers out to some of the more obvious buyers, but he wasn't really getting the traction he expected. He also didn't want his competitors or employees to know he was considering a sale. He decided that using an M&A advisor would be best.

Robert had been scouting out a number of advisors and silently sitting in on webinars to understand more about how the process worked and who was selling companies in the IT industry that were similar in size to his. After talking to a few brokers, he realized there were multiple ways each firm approached the sales transaction process. And he was surprised by how much the fees varied by firm. All the firms he spoke to were prepared to present him multiple buyers, but some advisors wanted to determine their own value for his company while others said that was a waste of time and that the buyers would determine his value. Robert had a general idea of the value of his company, but he really wanted someone that was knowledgeable to validate it.

Robert had narrowed his selection down to two firms. Both seemed very capable, but they had very different approaches to selling his company.

Firm A was focused on a rapid process of getting him out in the market-place within four weeks. They would assist in the preparation of his blind profile and a PowerPoint but no company valuation. They would also run the sales process, finding buyers via websites and emailing the blind profile to their "extensive buyer list." Once the prospective buyers were vetted, the focus would then be on gathering due diligence documents. No virtual data room would be supplied. Their price was a $15K commitment fee to start the process, and a success fee of 6 percent for the first $2.5M, 3 percent for the next $2.5M, and 1.5 percent of the sales price thereafter. If Robert sold his firm for $5M, the total fees would be **(15,000+ 150,000+75,000) $240,000.**

Firm B was focused on lots of preparation up front, which meant uploading all generic due diligence documents to a secure data room in anticipation of buyer requests, performing a company valuation, and the preparation of the blind profile and PowerPoint deck with comparables and industry data for the prospective buyers. This "preparation" process would take about 90 days. Firm B would also run the sales process but would only contact *a small list (under 200) of very selective group of prescreened qualified buyers. Robert also felt that this firm really focused on IT businesses of his size. Their price was $5K per month with a success fee of a flat 4 percent with an expected valuation to come in at $5M. If he sold for more than 10 percent above that amount, his success fee would increase by 0.5 percent. He was told the process should take 9 months but no longer than 12. If he sold for $5M this would cost him* **(5,000 x 12) or $60,000 (12months max) + 200,000) $260,000.**

Robert didn't want to make a decision based upon price but more so on the value the firm could bring to him. He really wanted to get the process started so he could have his company sold by year end, but he saw the value of spending time in advance getting his company ready, and collecting and uploading all his contracts, customers, vendors, financials, assets, and IP to the secure data room. That way, when a LOI was presented he could immediately begin working with his attorney on the agreements and not be scrambling to gather all his documentation for the buyer's due diligence process. Good thing, too, because the list of items needed was long and exhaustive.

Robert liked that Firm B would prepare him with a supportable value for his company and help him strengthen areas of weaknesses that might be of concern to buyers. While this would take a few months to get ready, he knew it would make his company more valuable. Even though it might cost him a little more in the end in fees, he felt the increase in value that he could sell his company for by preparing with Firm B would outweigh the additional costs.

GOING IT ALONE, BECAUSE YOU CAN

Unlike what you will hear from a majority of brokers, I do believe you can successfully sell your company on your own. As we discussed earlier in this chapter, there are occasions where this makes total sense, like selling to your shareholders or to another company which you have partnered with on other projects. It depends on how knowledgeable you are about the valuation of your business and the level of your negotiating skills and your selling skills—in this case your ability to present why the buyer should buy your company. I want to be clear: While I have sold two of my companies without a broker, I would never sell a company without using the services of a good attorney and a CPA. So, for our discussion here, "going it alone" means selling without a *broker*. Going it alone is actually pretty common but should be categorized as either a *passive* or *active* approach. The passive approach is usually when some potential buyer contacts you, so let's start there.

A BUYER APPROACHES YOU FIRST

Most people count on the idea that someday, someone will come along and want to buy their company, or so they hope. And frankly, that is how most deals are transacted within a particular partner channel.

Typically, a company is targeted for acquisition by either someone they compete against or someone who wants to get into a vertical they serve. The buyer typically already knows who you are and the markets you serve and understands the value your organization would bring to the whole. Most technology providers are aware of who is doing well and who is acquiring the competition. The word gets around, as most tight partner channels are incestuous—meaning that salespeople, consultants, and developers hop from one to another.

If initially approached by a complementary, competitive provider, vendor or customer, you should at a minimum have the following ready:

1. NDA to be signed in advance by both parties. Nothing is exchanged until this is signed.
2. Three years of historical financials + current year to-date financials— include percent of recurring revenue and customer retention rate in footnotes.
3. Calculation of adjusted EBITDA.

4.   Current year projections.
5.   Current sales pipeline.
6.   Power point deck—see discussion later in chapter on marketing assets.
7.   Organization chart.
8.   List of revenue by customer—but mask the customer names.
9.   Completed assessment of company value, via the tools presented earlier or a formal valuation.
10.   Last three years of tax returns.

A more comprehensive list is reviewed later in this chapter under "marketing assets."

Do not present more information than this without a formal IOI or LOI to continue the process. Make sure to ask for proof of funds once an IOI is presented and before you sign an LOI. If your prospective buyer is struggling with an LOI, feel free to present your own. It is better to be upfront with what you are looking for than waste everyone's time and energy.

And be sure to set a timeline and deadlines. One of the biggest problems for sellers being unexpectedly approached by buyers, is that the buyer typically doesn't have a set timeline to finish the deal. Agree on this before you sign the LOI and create an opportunity to terminate if deadlines are not met.

Aside from all the important aspects like cultural fit, cohesion of the management team, and the cross-sell/upsell opportunity that the sale might bring, below are a few points to consider to help you evaluate if the offer makes sense.

Usually, the initial phone call by the buyer will give you some sense of their level of interest and sincerity; however, for the seller, many times the decision to move forward becomes one of gut instinct. Asking some of the questions listed below may help you decide if this is an opportunity worth pursuing.

Points to consider if approached by a complementary or competing partner:

1.   Are they at least 50 percent larger? A buyer will struggle acquiring a firm that is half their size. Ideally, the acquiring company should be at least 80 percent larger.

2.   Have they acquired other companies before? How quickly did the process go? Why was the acquisition beneficial to the business?

3.   How long ago was the last acquisition? Too many acquisitions in a short period of time is not a good recipe for success.

4.   If this is the first acquisition, do they have a timeline?

5.   Do they present an IOI first? Not everyone does, but it is a gauge of their interest.

6.   An LOI is not set in stone. If you don't like it, ask for changes until you are happy. The purchase agreement will be based on the LOI's major points.

7.   What does the noncompete look like? Are the main points in the LOI?

8.   How will they continue to grow their company while integrating your company? What are the synergies and cost savings they foresee? If they are willing to share this with you, this will be useful in calculating your EBITDA adjustments.

9.   Is the offer at least 50 to 60 percent cash? Offers less than that are below the industry standard and place too much emphasis on the earn-out or note payable.

10.   Do they have the cash to provide a 50 percent upfront payment? If not, how will it be funded?

11.   If funding is an outside bank or investment firm, ask for proof of funds for the acquisition.

12.   If the offer is too low, are you prepared to counter? Do you have statistics (now you do) of what other comparable companies are being offered to back-up your counter?

13.   Know and write down on paper your "walk away" number.

Find a coach, ideally someone with M&A and industry knowledge. Don't use a family member or rely on your attorney or accountant to do this.

While I caution against selling your company on your own, sometimes your size will dictate handling the transaction without a broker (see discussion above on when to use a business advisor), in which case I recommend that at a minimum you find a good M&A coach. If you decide to work with a coach, let the buyer know you have one. That way, if you need to revisit an issue or deal point, you can pin it on the guidance of your coach. Your coach can also have the more difficult or "tense" conversations, so words don't tarnish a working relationship that you will need to keep positive on a go-forward basis.

Remember that your coach can be your intermediary, the person who can remain emotionally detached, and who doesn't read more or less into the last email chain. Your coach can also be that "third party" who is advising on the transaction and making sure everyone is adhering to a timeline, as we laid out in Part I.

Many owners I have interviewed sold their companies independent of a broker. Most had an idea of what their company was worth, and if they didn't get their price, they would just decline the offer and wait for the next good offer. But that is actually easy to say and hard to do once you get into a "seller mindset"—unless you are really clear about your price and how you can support it.

For those less knowledgeable about the value of their company, I find instead that the owners get so emotionally wrapped up in the fact that an offer is forthcoming, that they cannot detach from the end result of *selling*. The seller becomes invested in a deal—any deal—and not necessarily the best deal. Emotions take over and it is hard for the seller to let go. A savvy buyer can usually see this and will drive down the price during the due diligence process. Unfortunately, this is the way many deals are consummated.

MARKETING YOUR OWN COMPANY

The larger your company and the more capable your management team, the higher the probability you can sell on your own. With the majority of brokers asking for at least 3 to 4 percent in fees, on a sale that nets over $20M, this could add up to over $750,000 in success fees—no small number. In smaller transactions, say less than $2M in net proceeds, a minimum success fee can be more than 4 percent of the total value of the deal. In either case, this may be more than an owner is willing to part with in fees.

While holding an auction is the likeliest way to get a better offer, it has the highest risk of exposing your company's plan to sell, which is not what most business owners want to do. Talking to a few buyers at once is ideal if you can make it happen. It allows you to keep them all on the same timeline, while playing one off the other in terms of timing and LOIs. This process of marketing to a large group of buyers at once is the methodology used by most brokers and it keeps the process moving quickly—but it requires a lot of energy. Most owners, however, speak to only one or a few buyers because they are not aware of all the possible buyers available. These buyers are mostly strategic buyers, as most people don't have access to the lists of financial buyers—contrary to a broker who specializes in this industry—but times have now changed.

For Sellers, Managing Risk

Method of Marketing	Pros	Cons	But...
Talk to one Buyer.	• Lowest risk of employees, customers and competitors finding out. • Probably quickest.	• Lowest likelihood of best deal.	*Doesn't mean it might not be a great deal.*
Talk to a few Buyers, serially.	• Second lowest risk. • Better chance of a better deal. • Third quickest.	• Second lowest likelihood of best deal.	*Doesn't mean it might not be a great deal.*
Talk to a few Buyers, all at once.	• Better leverage than two previous options. • Second quickest.	• Second highest risk. • Second most likely to get best deal.	*Doesn't mean it will produce a great deal.*
Hold an auction.	• Best leverage; likeliest to get a great deal. • Slowest.	• Materially higher risk that employees, customers and competitors will find out.	*Doesn't mean it will produce a great deal.*

Fig.3.1

Source: Service-Leadership, www.service-leadership.com.

One of the primary reasons many owners choose to use a broker is visibility to buyers outside their normal circle. But just as Zillow and Redfin allow home sellers to reach out to buyers, there are now good resources on the internet for lower middle market companies to find prospective acquirers as well. Here are a few online tools that can expand the visibility of your company while remaining anonymous during the process:

- **PitchBook**: https://pitchbook.com/. PitchBook is an online data depository of deals, buyers, and data. PitchBook tracks every aspect of the public and private equity markets, including venture capital, private equity, and M&A. When brokers mention they have access to 50,000+ buyers, it means they probably have a subscription to this service. At fees ranging from $15K – $18K per year (single user), you can get access to thousands of potential buyers. It is well worth the investment.

- **Axial**: https://www.axial.net/. Axial runs a private network that helps middle-market companies and advisors find the right buyers and investors. They connect the two via an online platform and offer intimate events, curated introductions, and the most sophisticated deal-oriented matching engine in the world. As soon as you upload your profile to the site, you immediately see a list of buyers who match the criteria. You can then begin a campaign toward announcing your company with these buyers. This is completely free for the seller. The buyer pays all fees to access the site and if a deal is transacted.

- **BankerBay**: https://www.bankerbay.com/. BankerBay is a deal origination platform that uses a complex algorithmic approach to match middle-market corporates seeking capital with the most relevant providers of capital anywhere in the world. Private equity funds and investment banks looking to invest in or lend to companies can access qualified deals from firms looking to raise capital or seeking investors in their business. Another free site for the seller.

In addition to buyers, PitchBook and Axial have a number of great articles and downloadable resources as well.

CREATING YOUR COMPANY OFFERING MATERIALS

In addition to the items mentioned in the chapters on The Deal Dynamics and Financial Fitness, you will need to prepare your company offering materials. This might be a good time to review the cost of a Quality of Earning Report, as many of these items and metrics will come from a well-prepared report. Again, if you are using an M&A advisor, these will be prepared by your advisor in advance of taking you to market; if not, they can all be prepared internally by your team. Here are the "must have" items to begin marketing your company:

- Teaser or Blind Profile
- Confidential Information Memorandum (CIM) – optional but recommended for larger, more complex companies
- PowerPoint Deck (instead of the CIM)
- Financials for the last three years + the current year, and projections for the current year
- NDA for prospective buyer to sign in advance of data (See Resources)

Most buyers don't have time to read a long-drawn-out document, especially if they are looking to complete a number of transactions in a given year. Buyers today want to see a quick snapshot of the company in the form of a two- to three-page infographic as a teaser or "blind profile." Larger companies still prepare a detailed Confidential Information Memorandum (CIM) to convey the most important information about their business, including its operations, financials (Balance Sheet, Income Statement, and Cash Flow), management team, industries served, geography and customer base, and other data relevant to a prospective buyer. However, the trend, as with most everything, is to present something visual and easy to digest, like the "blind profile." This will also come in handy for an upload to sites like BankerBay and Axial.

Below are the items that you should consider as part of your two- or three-page infographic. Programs like Adobe PDF, Adobe InDesign, Canva, or PowerPoint are programs that produce great results. Online web fronts like Fiverr.com, Freelancer.com, Upwork.com, and 99Designs.com are good resources to use, as they will create nice visuals for you while remaining outside of your group of peers and your team—for confidentiality purposes.

A typical Blind Profile or teaser infographic should contain the following elements:

- Brief description of the company—no more than 10 to 125 words

- Visual view of where in the country it is located (if more than one location list)
- Products and services (software sold, unique IP, customization services, cloud solutions, etc.)
- Number of employees, broken down by type (i.e., admin, sales and marketing, professional services, engineers, developers, etc.)
- Financial Information table that will include last three years of revenue and current year forecasted of: revenue, gross profit, sales and marketing, general and administrative expenses, and adjusted EBITDA
- Graph of revenue by service type and gross margin, if available
- Graph of percentage of recurring revenue or strong repeat revenue over last three years
- Five highlights spelling out why someone might be interested in your company (i.e., customer retention rate, vertical expertise, length of tenure of employees, highlights of either high YOY growth, EBITDA or recurring revenue)
- Logos of large vendors/awards/partners/certifications, if applicable
- List of vertical or sub-verticals you serve—use a pie chart format with vertical breakout
- Customer retention rate and locations of customers if dispersed
- Top customers by revenue—list top five customers (without names) and the percentage of overall revenue
- Whom to contact, email address, and link to NDA to review in advance

Once a prospective buyer becomes interested via your teaser profile, they will execute an NDA to gain access to more in-depth information including financials. This is where a PowerPoint Deck with 20 to 25 slides versus a lengthy word-rich document comes in handy. This PowerPoint deck is also going to be used to present to buyers, so make sure you can present the content while leaving time for questions within a 60-minute period. Some companies have even taken to creating videos of why they are a good acquisition target or have carefully scripted their PowerPoint presentation as a video that can be saved and sent to buyers as NDAs are executed. This saves time if multiple buyers are interested and it allows for a follow-up phone call to discuss any specifics.

Below is a list of items that you might consider in your PowerPoint deck, broken into specific areas. This of course will somewhat depend on your company and the products/services you sell:

1. Opportunity Overview:

    - The acquisition opportunity—no more than 8 to 10 points that describe the company
    - Unique value proposition—what makes you different
    - Your market potential and dominance
    - Competitive analysis—if appropriate
    - Industry trends and vertical trends

2. Company History and Awards/Certifications:

    - History of the company—keep to one or two slides
    - List industry awards and recognition
    - List product certifications or number of individual certifications in specific areas

3. Management Team:

    - Management team and brief biographies of each member—include an organization chart if not too complex or overwhelming

4. Intellectual Property:

    - List key and significant intellectual property by type (i.e., patents, trademarks, copywrites—and the status if not completed)

5. Sales and Marketing:

    - List key offerings of products/services—look at each significant revenue line item and explain each
    - Growth strategy—what is key to your continued growth
    - Sales pipeline and consulting backlog
    - Discuss any seasonality if applicable
    - List any key marketing assets—videos, books, conferences

6.   Customers:

- List names or logos of key large/significant customers
- Show graph of customer base by industry/vertical, size, or geography
- List or graph top 10 customers for the last three years
- Provide a general overview of customer contracts: terms, transferability, termination clauses
- If possible, show a graphic of customer retention rates for the last three years

7.   Partners/Vendors:

- List key vendors and suppliers with percentage of purchases from each
- List key partners—if selling through your own channel—show percentage of revenue by partner in a graph if possible

8.   Financials:

- Three-year historical financials: revenue, gross profit margin, sales and marketing, admin and EBITDA, add slide for current year by quarter, statement of Cash Flow
- Three-year recurring revenue trend (if positive and substantial)
- Three-year forecasted revenue, gross profit margin, sales and marketing, admin and EBITDA
- Any significant capital requirements or annual fees

9.   Other Items if applicable or relevant:

- List of internal applications used—accounting, CRM, ticketing, marketing automation, etc.
- Lease details—rent increases, lease terms, ability to assign
- List of employee benefits, insurance plans, cafeteria plans, incentives

10.   **Questions and Next Steps**

- Be sure to leave time at the end of your presentation for questions. Provide one last slide with your contact information and best times to reach you.

A simple two-page Non-Disclosure Agreement (NDA) that covers the confidential nature of the data being presented, along with the parties who will be reviewing the data, should be prepared in advance. A good example can be found in the resource section of this book. Keep the document short without undue legalese to keep people from spending time redlining your NDA. After all, you don't want to get hung up on legal documents this early in the process. With that said, be prepared for buyers to issue their own versions or make some modifications to yours.

Finally, make sure you use a file sharing site (virtual data room), and create a master folder that contains all of your data. You can copy all or part of this folder to interested parties as needed. Generally, I do not give out data unless it is specifically requested. I have listed a few data file sharing sites above, but PCmag.com has a great comparison if you are shopping for a service.[7]

Ideally, if you have a coach or other trusted business-savvy friend who can review this in advance and give you feedback—and is independent—it will certainly help with the final product. In Part II, Financial Finesse, there is a brief discussion on the documents that you should have available for the sale. Prepare these well in advance and keep them updated on a monthly basis. Using a secure public data room like Dropbox, Box.net, or Google Docs will allow you to give someone access to them at a moment's notice. Examples of NDAs, IOIs, and LOIs are available in the Resource section for guidance.

If you want to sell on your own without the use of a broker, I would suggest the more active approach because you can actually do this successfully with the tools available today.

PREPPING FOR THE BUYER CALL

Once an NDA has been signed, the buyer has been vetted, and your CIM or blind profile has been given to a buyer, the next step for an interested buyer is to schedule a call and have that all important "initial" conversation. Whether you decide to sell on your own or use a broker, there are common questions that you should be prepared to answer without hesitation. Conversely, there are general questions you should most definitely ask an interested buyer. You may want to supplement this list with your own as you uncover more information about the buyer and their past acquisitions, if any.

Knowing and practicing these questions in advance will help you sound polished and confident in this process. If you are using a broker or a coach, I would recommend role playing in advance for the typical questions you may be asked. Your advisor should be able to give you advice on what to say and how to say it, while keeping it sincere and honest. The experienced buyer can see through you quickly if you are "bullshitting," or as I like to call it, "tailoring" your answers to their needs. And certainly, if you don't know the answer, you're better off to tell them you will get back to them, rather than making something up on the fly that you may regret later. You can quickly lose credibility in the process if your responses (either in the discovery or the due diligence process) are flawed or just flat out incorrect.

This initial conversation is to get a feel if there is a fit, and it should not take more than 30 to 45 minutes. Anything longer, and it may appear you are too eager or don't have other buyers interested. These conversations are usually enjoyable and the most pleasant part of the process. Be consistent as to who from your company will have these conversations with the buyers. If speaking to multiple buyers, be sure to keep notes, as conversations start to blend after five or six. If you have multiple interested prospective buyers, don't pick your most favored to speak to first. You will hone your messaging after a few calls, so save the best conversations for last, after you have warmed up. Also, by then there shouldn't be any questions that are a surprise to you.

Questions asked by buyers:	*Why and what they are looking for:*
1. Why are you selling the company?	*Why? The buyer wants to know if you are burned out, need cash, want to move on to other things, have a reason (personally, medically, legally) why you are selling. This is probably the most single important question. It can possibly determine the type of offer you will receive. If the buyer can tell you need cash, expect a lower offer all up.*
2. What kind of offer are you looking for—cash, equity, note, earn-out?	*Why? To see what your expectations are, and how willing you are to extend the payment terms. Stating you want an all cash offer will turn many buyers off, so we don't suggest you do that unless there are extenuating circumstances.*
3. How and where do you see the future growth of the business?	*Why? A buyer wants to see if you are aligned with their strategy or if you have some insights to verticals or opportunities that they may not be aware of or see in your CIM.*
4. What are your company's greatest strengths?	*Why? Your strengths may shore up areas where they have a shortfall. This is a great conversation to make 1 + 1 = more than 2.*
5. Describe your company culture?	*Why? In part to see if it will mesh with their existing company(ies) or if you have some very out-there practices and policies they may not be able to continue.*

6. What is your role in the company?	*Why? What are you doing that no one else in the company knows how to do? This is a bit of a test to see if you work in or on the company, and how you would be replaced or need to be replaced if you decide not to continue post sale.*
7. Do you have a specific vertical you serve? Or what differentiates you from Company X down the street?	*Why? To see whether you can articulate your value proposition easily and succinctly. At this point, your revenue and EBITDA has created interest (meaning your historical past). Buyers are, however, more interested in your future potential and earning capability.*
8. Will you remain with the company post-transaction, and if so for how long?	*Why? First off, you need to be clear in your own mind what it is you want. If you want to leave soon afterwards, be clear about it. If you are willing to stay only for the earn-out period, be clear about that. If you really want to continue working in the company, then be clear about that as well. It is possible, but rare, that you find a buyer who wants you to leave shortly after the deal is consummated.*

9.	If not, who are the key people in the organization who will manage the business?	*Why? The buyer needs to know who will remain and can continue to serve the customers they have just purchased. If this is your goal, make sure all the key functions you perform are easily assumed by the remaining management team. If you are the main contact with your customers, the buyer will see this as a red flag and anticipate a drop in revenue if you leave.*
10.	Do you have other interested buyers?	*Why? Buyer wants to know if you are trying to create a bidding war or if they are the only offer, in which case you have less leverage over the price they offer you. You may want to defer this one to your advisor to answer.*
11.	Why did your [revenue, gross profit, EBITDA] increase or decline?	*Why? This is usually only asked if there is a drop in one of these metrics. If so, and there is a one-time reason, be sure to be able to explain it well. Also, if you anticipate a future change in margin structure offered by your key vendor, or you plan on changing your margins offered to your selling partners, now would be the time to expose this.*

12.	What percentage of your revenue is from your top five clients/customers?	*Why? Buyers want to make sure that, if there is any transition of customers due to the transaction, revenue won't be significantly affected. Having a customer who needs to renew their annual contract that represents more than 20 percent of your revenue will hold up a deal or potentially kill it completely if they are not under a binding contract.*
13.	Is there any customer you might lose if your company is acquired?	*Why? Are there customers, relatives, good friends, that will only work with you and will leave when you leave? Do your contracts allow for assignability without prior consent upon an acquisition?*
14.	If you had an injection of capital, what would you do with it?	*Why? This shows the buyers where you feel your future earnings or revenue shortfall may come from. Or areas where the company needs money to grow or build out additional products.*
15.	What growth markets do you see that you have not tapped into yet?	*Why? Similar to #14.*
16.	What do you plan to do after you sell?	*Why? This is a test question. The buyer doesn't want you to compete and so needs to hear loud and clear that you have a plan to do something else, whether that is to retire or do real estate investing or write a book about how to sell your company for millions. In any case, you need to communicate a plan that does not threaten a noncompete.*

Questions YOU should ask the buyers:	Why and what they are looking for:
1. What interests you about our company?	*Why? This will tell you what their future vision is for your company and whether you are a platform purchase or an add-on purchase to extend their reach. Knowing this answer will help you determine if your company can increase their accretive value—meaning: 1) will their earnings increase by acquiring you? and 2) are the products or services you provide easily sold into their existing customer base? If you know that you will be able to significantly increase their sales, this should also increase the multiple your company is worth to them.*
2. What are your top considerations when evaluating a company to acquire?	*Why? Are they looking for IP, a new vertical, geographical reach, human capital, or just additional customers?*
3. What are your long-term plans for the company?	*Why? This is a key question if part of your sales proceeds is transitioned into the new company as equity. If there is a plan to sell in the next five years (as is the case many times with PE firms), how likely is your value going to increase with the remaining equity in the New Co.?*

4. How do you plan to fund the acquisition?	*Why? Do they have enough cash? Will they need to pay with a note? This could indicate how much you will receive upfront as cash vs. being paid in installments. If the buyer needs to secure financing, this could be an issue, unless they already have a letter from their bank indicating their borrowing capability. You should request proof of funds or the ability to borrow BEFORE you sign an LOI.*
5. How do you typically structure your deals? (i.e. cash, note, earn-out, equity).	*Why? This will give you an idea of how an LOI might be structured. Most buyers keep with the same structure from deal to deal.*
6. If a PE Firm: Will this remain as a stand-alone company or be combined with another company?	*Why? This answer will help determine who you will be reporting to post acquisition. And this will potentially impact what happens to your existing employees. Further, if you are combined with another company, you will want to know what costs they would be able to eliminate in the new structure. Although it is premature to have a detailed discussion about this now, these costs should be considered to be added back into your adjusted EBITDA. It will also determine if you are part of a larger roll-up of additional purchases they plan to make.*

7. Do you plan on keeping the entire management team?	*Why? Do the economies of scale play into their strategy? Unless the buyer is very clear about eliminating some positions as part of the acquisition, you might need to take this response with a grain of salt. Too many owners have asked this question, to find out later the answer has changed. If you plan on staying, or if some of your key managers are needed for you to achieve your earn-out, you might consider negotiation of an employment contract for those executives as part of the transaction.*
8. If a PE Firm: How long do you keep your portfolio companies?	*Why? This will help you determine how long your investment in the New Co. can be monetized.*
9. If a PE Firm: What experience do you have in this industry?	*Why? Ideally, your buyer has experience in the industry you are focused on; if not, it could be a red flag as to your ability to achieve your earn-out and the future proceeds of your investment in the New Co. PE Firms are more likely to buy a company or buy into an industry where they don't truly understand all the nuances to be successful. The last thing you want is a failed acquisition that will inhibit your future earning potential.*

10.	If a PE Firm: Will I be a platform company or an add-on company to an existing portfolio?	*Why? Similar to #3 and #5. As the platform company, you will have more decision-making abilities. As the add-on company, you may be required to conform your policies and procedures to those already in use. This of course can be frustrating and restrictive, especially if your company has better processes and procedures. Be sure to understand this when it comes to calculation of the earn-out, as it is possible that your ability to manage the business operations and hence achieve the earn-out will be negatively impacted.*
11.	What is/are your future acquisition plans?	*Why: Similar to # 5, but this will give you an idea of how many acquisitions they have planned for the next couple of years. If there are numerous future acquisitions planned, will your company be combined with multiple others, and will that help or hinder your earn-out and future equity possibilities?*
12.	Have any of your previous acquisitions failed? And if so, why?	*Why? You probably won't hear about their failures as press releases on their website; hence, it is an important question to ask for obvious reasons. If there has been a failure, truly understand why and see if there is someone you can connect with who might be able to give you additional insights.*

13.	Who might you be reporting to in the future?	*Why? You have been the CEO for a while, so reporting to someone else who may not be as technical, as savvy, or as bright as you can turn out to be incredibly frustrating and cause for serious concern. And, it could limit your ability to achieve your earn-out. Or, it could be a tremendous learning opportunity. Ascertain this in advance to help you determine if your earn-out is possible or not, and whether you can enhance your professional skills by reporting to the right New Co. exec.*
14.	Who is involved in the acquisition decision process and who is the final approver?	*Why? The person who has made all the initial inquiries, and who has signed the NDA or IOI, may not be the ultimate decision maker. In most cases they are not. Knowing who the decision maker is, and getting a face-to-face meeting, will help eliminate any miscommunications or surprises later in the process. Your broker will typically have this figured out for you and will encourage those one-on-one conversations, but even then, at times, this final decision maker remains elusive until the end when the contract is signed.*

15. If there have been recent acquisitions, can you speak to the remaining management team?	*Why? While this person may be happy to speak to you, they may also be under contractual obligation not to disparage, discuss, or debate the process. If you do have an opportunity to speak to an owner that was acquired, I would pick one that was acquired at least 18 months prior. By this time, any honeymoon period has worn off and they are fully entrenched in the new business, and not mired in the post-acquisition integration (which can be a ton of work and very stressful).*
16. At what point will you be willing to share your financials? If not, then what were your revenue and profit margins this past year, and what are your year-over-year growth projections?	*Why? Obviously, you want to make sure that the company that is acquiring you is profitable. If your growth and profit margins are considerably greater than theirs, there might be cause for concern. If your buyer is a PE firm, this question might be altered somewhat. You might also want to find out how long this fund has been in existence. Are you early in their buying process, or later when they will plan on selling the entire lot of companies in the fund to liquidate and distribute profit to investors? This again will help you determine the time and likelihood of a return on your equity in New Co.*

17.	How long does your due diligence process take? And do you have a team that specifically focuses on this?	*Why? This will give you an idea if there is a team, either internally or externally, that will be responsible for this process. If you don't see a clear, organized answer to this question, then it may be a sign that the buyer hasn't done this before or may drag this process out.*
18.	Do you have a post-sale integration plan? How long does this typically take?	*Why? Life after the sale is key to the success of your earn-out. You want to see that the buyer has a plan for events, from writing the press release and making offers to your employees to communicating with your customers and ensuring the integration of websites and infrastructure into theirs; and what is the timing of these events? No plan? It means there will be a lot of scrambling going on after the sale and possible confusion with your employees and clients.*

ROBERT INSIGHT:

Robert was delighted to find that his broker had arranged several conversations with potential buyers. While he wanted his CFO to participate as well, Robert felt that it might be too distracting to have multiple owners on the call, so Robert took all the calls himself and debriefed with his CFO after each one. He arranged the list of buyers from most interesting to least interesting and started with his least interesting buyers. That way he could perfect his delivery and get more comfortable with the questions being asked. Almost every time, the first question, after all the niceties of location and weather had been discussed, was about why he was selling the company. Robert knew in his own mind that he wanted to exit within 12 to 18 months after the sale was completed. He felt this was a long enough transition but would be open to something sooner if the buyers felt that he was no longer needed. His flexibility was appreciated by each prospective buyer. He was also clear that his COO was content to stay with the company after the sale. This gave his prospective buyers comfort that key members of the management team would remain to retain consistency in operations.

THE BUYER OFFICE VISIT

All buyers eventually want a face to face visit, which typically happens after the LOI has been signed by the seller. If an IOI was issued initially, they may actually want the visit before the LOI is signed. This is a great opportunity to visit them at their location to get a sense of their operations and office dynamics. If their office is not ideal for confidentiality reasons, a mutually acceptable hotel or conference center will work fine. A mutual location where you are away from the distractions of an office allows you to focus on getting to know one another and determine if there is a good cultural and long-term fit. This is also a good time to "break bread" and get to know your potential buyer better. Food has a way of calming nerves and makes for a nice warm up as you are discussing menu options.

Once you have progressed further in the due diligence process, all buyers will eventually want an "office visit." This is obviously very important if you own your office space and the real estate is part of the transaction. Even if no real estate is part of the transaction, this visit is important if the buyer is going to continue to use your existing office location, furniture, and equipment. If the buyer is expected to take over the lease, they will want to make sure the facilities are on a par with their existing locations. If you maintain your own hardware offsite in a datacenter, you will need to add this to the visit.

Often these visits are to "look" at the culture and cohesiveness of the company. Culture can be found in subtleties such as the pictures on the wall, awards displayed on shelves, team photos, and how cubicles and desks are arranged. Common areas usually have message boards and posts or pictures of past events. White boards throughout the office can indicate group gathering areas and collaboration of teams. The number of open desks or workspaces may indicate remote workers or availability for growth within the space.

Treat an office visit like you would a special event at your home. Put everything in its place, get the carpets cleaned if they are stained, remove the stacks of piled up supplies, toss the dead plants, and just for good measure, have someone take an extra pass through the kitchen, especially the refrigerator. You never know who might look inside.

The timing of an office visit can be tricky. I always suggest it takes place *after* you are past the most difficult items of due diligence. It should be towards the end of the due diligence process. There is no point raising suspicion early in the sales process if you don't need to. If you plan to keep the sales process confidential, then suggest the prospective buyer visit after hours or take a tour on the weekend when no one else is around. They don't need to physically see butts in seats to know if an office or cubicle is being occupied. Strolling a buyer through an office, no matter how elusive you think you are, puts everyone on alert. Your closest and longest employees will sense this; don't underestimate their ability to perceive a change. If a buyer insists on seeing the office during regular business hours, in order to feel the energy, one way to introduce the visit to the employees is to refer to the visitor as a consultant, as the company is looking to expand and grow, which is actually the truth.

When to Disclose to Your Team

Deciding when to disclose to your management team that a sale is pending is different for every company and every deal. Disclosing too early exposes you to the possibility that your employees unintentionally leak this information to customers or suppliers. Disclosing too early will put your team on edge. Even if you assure them that their positions are secure, people will start to worry about job security, no matter how safe they have felt in the past. Before you realize it, performance starts to drift, revenue starts to slow down, future planning stalls.

For these reasons, many sellers interviewed for this book chose not to disclose their transaction to managers or employees until they were confident that the transaction would close, and that all major legal due diligence and legal issues had been resolved. Many times, that is not until the day before the close. Obviously, this decision is up to you, but most sellers chose to inform top management in advance of the close. Below are some reasons why sooner is sometimes better:

- Not disclosing the potential for a sale creates a tremendous burden on the owners. Gathering information needed to draft the CIM, accommodating due diligence requests, and providing the latest financial requests becomes overwhelming and stressful in a short amount of time.
- Owners become less "hands-on" and are no longer capable of extracting the information from their applications or may not know where to find it, and thus need to rely on key management to assist.
- Employees also become sensitive to office doors being closed more often than usual, unexpected travel, and unusually early or late days in the office, even while the owners think they are being coy.
- There are really only so many times you can ask your controller or accounting manager for lists of key vendors, revenue by customer, and historical income statements without someone eventually catching wind of a change, and then rumors begin. At some point, the requests for documents or data become too much to hide.
- The rumor of a sale will perpetuate the stress and uncertainty that people feel regarding whether they will have a job post-transaction, and that is the last thing a buyer will want. After all, your team is extremely valuable to your sale and to the buyer.

I counsel sellers to pick a core group of team members or management that will be key to keeping the due diligence process running. This will take a tremendous amount of pressure off the owners both mentally, physically, and emotionally, and demonstrate to the buyer that you have confidence in your management team, and that you trust them and need them as part of the new company.

If only your management team has been advised of the transaction to this point, I highly recommend that you announce this to your team before the new owners walk in the door—but preferably not on a Friday because you don't want people worried over the weekend with emails flying back and forth as everyone is trying to find out more information. You need time to explain why and how this change will benefit the company and also the professional careers of individuals moving forward. Walk them through the post-sale integration plans that have been established. Share with them your reasons for making this major decision. It is best that they hear it directly from you. Take time to reflect on the team's past accomplishments and the journey you have all taken together to this point. This is a major accomplishment. Congratulations!

The Female Factor

I had just finished hiking 500 miles of the Pacific Crest Trail when I decided to write this book. The trail had been a goal of mine since I had entered into the process of selling my last company. Unfortunately, my deal didn't close early enough in the year for me to hike the entire 2,650 miles, so I settled for just 500. I relished the thought of being entirely free to hike, camp, sleep, and eat anywhere along the trail and completely on my own timetable.

I had spent the last 16 years managing a company with a 24/7/365 service level agreement. Even though my team took care of those midnight requests, my phone was always by my side. It was the first thing I reached for in the morning and the last thing at night. Not having cellular connection as I made my way through the desolate passages and high altitudes of the Pacific Northwest Cascades was beyond liberating.

My gear for the weeks I would spend on the trail had been stuffed into a backpack. A tent, sleeping bag, one change of clothes, my stove, water bottle and some food, and my trusty trekking poles, were my basics. To stay under 30 pounds, I had to ditch all the nonessentials: Makeup, hair products, night cream, deodorant, and soap. Just my toothbrush, comb, toilet paper, bug spray, Chapstick, and some baby wipes were all I could fit into my pack. Okay, I did sneak in some eye cream.

Other than checking in with my husband when I had good cell connection, I was off the grid for days at a time. And to think that only 90 days earlier, I had dropped my office keys on my desk for the last time, leaving my post as CEO for good after having sold my company. I would begin this hike just as I had begun my company many years before—alone, afraid of what I didn't know and what I might encounter but with a plan.

I share this part of my journey because like many times before, I was one of a very small percentage of women hiking this distance and taking on the challenge alone. For example, a number of years before, when I owned my cloud technology company, I was invited to participate in two "Partner Advisory Councils" with Microsoft. One was comprised of U.S. owners specifically, and the second was an international group. While there were a few women in both groups, I was the only woman, in either group, who actually *owned* the company and was not in a support or representative capacity. This is no fault of Microsoft and by no means unique to their channel of partners. (I have found Microsoft to be more progressive than most channels regarding diversity.) Instead, it is truly indicative of the few women who own or are in the C level seat of a technology firm of substantive size. The plain fact is, there just aren't many women today who own and run technology companies, regardless of size, in any technology channel. And this needs to change.

Thankfully, organizations like *Women in Technology* and *Women in Cloud*, and awards like *Women of the Channel*, highlight those who have already made this journey and can provide support and guidance to those women who wish to pursue an incredibly exciting and rewarding career in technology.

I didn't want to end this book without one last chapter specifically dedicated to women who currently own, or aspire to own, a technology company, or who want to rise within management. Therefore, I would like to first share how I began this journey.

THE START: OMG, I AM PREGNANT!

I did not wake up one morning and decide I was going to start a company, let alone three. What really happened was I woke up one morning and found myself unexpectantly, but happily, pregnant. Four months later, I was both pregnant and now unemployed due to a bad economy. And then reality *really* hit...I was six months pregnant, no money in the bank, and no one wanted to hire me as I was due in three months and wanted an extended time off after giving birth. It was 1990, so that was asking for a lot! Just six months earlier my husband and I had purchased our first home. We raided whatever savings we had left after the forty-five hundred dollars we spent on our wedding! Yep, that's all we had to spend. We didn't want to go into debt.

Unfortunately, we purchased our home at the top of the real estate market which proceeded to crash within six months. We were completely underwater with a mortgage now much greater than the value of our home. We had virtually no furniture, not even a washer or dryer, and a baby on the way, but we were going to make this work! Thankfully, my husband had a well-paying job, but living in southern California required two incomes if we were going to pay the mortgage, buy some furniture, and put food on the table.

My degree was in accounting and taxation, so I began looking for contract work to get me through the next three months until I had our son. After a few months of maternity leave, I already knew I was not cut out to be a stay-at-home mom, even if we could squeak by on one income. It just wasn't who I was. Regardless, massive guilt followed. But, if I was going to work, I needed flexibility because my husband traveled, usually worked late, and sometimes worked weekends. I also wanted to be there for all those precious "firsts" of a new baby. So, I needed to start *my own* company. I just had no idea how.

Fortunately, and out of sheer will and necessity, I took what was a side hustle and turned it into a business. The part-time tax work morphed into accounting, which turned into a part-time controller gig, which turned into implementing a new accounting system. Over a few short years, the side hustle turned into a bonafide technology services company. In my mind, I was doing something I enjoyed while helping with the household finances. Never once did I think or plan for it to become anything more. And that's how it all started—no glorious business plan, no outside funding, just a need to pay bills, and be a good mom and wife.

INSERT MENTORS

The leaders at one of my clients who built large commercial buildings became my group of mentors. Every night after 5:00 p.m., the five male owners hit the restaurant bar in the first floor of their office building for a round of cocktails before heading home. Whenever possible, I would join them to learn how they worked deals and to hear how they grew their company. It was really a "boys only" group, but they accepted me as an equal because they knew I was good with numbers and could provide value from an accounting and tax perspective. Maybe they saw something in me that I didn't see in myself, but they willingly shared valuable advice on how to negotiate deals, protect myself legally, and grow my business.

Unfortunately, I later saw them run their company into the ground. The funding for commercial real estate dried up and in just a few short years, they declared bankruptcy. There were some valuable lessons there, too. Thankfully, one survived the ordeal and he remained a good friend and mentor pushing me constantly beyond my comfort zone. Each time I came up with a new idea or concept, he pushed me to pursue them, which ultimately led to the founding of two additional companies.

I was also blessed to have a wonderful husband who supported me to take the "calculated" risks. He was always my sounding board, even if he didn't understand the technology I was selling. He later became an integral and invaluable part of my business during its final few years.

I can truly say my mentors made a difference in my career and in my life. In short, they helped me think outside the box and stretch myself whenever possible.

THE FAQS OF A WOMAN IN TECH

If what I share next just encourages one or two women to climb higher, push harder, and face her fears, the entire book will have been worth it. This section is dedicated to answering the common questions that have been posed to me over the last 25 years as a woman founder, mother, wife, and technology business owner. Obviously, this is my view and other viewpoints are certainly valid, so take what makes sense for you.

1. Q: What aspect do you see most women struggle with when running a company?

    A: Hands down, knowing and understanding the numbers, regardless of the type of business. I had a leg up on most people in that I was a degreed accountant and tax specialist. Numbers, not words, spoke the truth to me. I found comfort in them, and I found it easy to make decisions if they worked in my favor. I find most women entrepreneurs need to get a stronger comfort level on their company financials, their investment portfolio, and a plan towards reaching their final number when it's time to call it quits.

    Cash, receivables, payables, and net profit as a percentage of revenue are all critical metrics and should always be reviewed. Creating annual financial budgets may seem tedious but this is key to your growth as it forces you to plan. However, with budgets, it is critical that you compare them to your actual results—so as to be able to adjust, fix, and modify as needed. You should be hands-on with this in the beginning and then you can pass it along, as long as you are presented daily with the numbers and metrics for your company. Lack of visibility creates problems quickly—always be in control of the numbers. If you feel overwhelmed by them, hire someone who is not and who can present them to you regularly. I have seen great visionaries, technically savvy entrepreneurs, and amazing sales driven companies fail because they didn't watch the numbers.

2.   Q: Do you need a technology degree or education to run a tech company?

A: Absolutely not. But here is the secret. You need to understand, conceptually, what you are selling so you can make your product or services better over time. Once you have your vision, then you need to surround yourself with bright people who understand the technology better than you do and whom you can trust. What is more important is your ability to ask questions and to listen to what your trusty team tells you. And if you don't understand the answer, ask again, another way. My last company was the most technical both in terms of the infrastructure and applications that we managed. I personally didn't know where the "on" button was for most of the hardware in our datacenter and I couldn't write a SQL script if my life depended on it—obviously pretty basic stuff but that didn't matter. I had a great team of people with whom I could envision, strategize, and debate, and that made all the difference.

If you find this hard to believe, then look no further than the new Tesla chairman, Robyn Denholm, who has been tapped to help Elon Musk run the electric car and energy company after a SEC settlement mandated Musk to give up the chairman title. She started her career in audit and accounting services at a large CPA firm; she has no technology degree.

3.   Q: Can you be a CEO, wife, and mom and do all three successfully?

A: Yes, but you have to overcome the "super-mom" syndrome. Okay, there are some super-mom's out there who can wash their family's clothes, clean their house every week, and pick up their child from one sports practice or extra-curricular activity to another. And make dinner every night too! They are rare, and I wasn't one of them; perhaps you are. But I think most women who try this will realize they are burning the candle at both ends and over time both work and home suffer. If a career is important to you then you need to be prepared to work the hours and handle the workload expected of your male counterparts and rely on capable help to do your housekeeping, cooking, errands and child-care.

If that sounds decadent and unrealistic, it was initially. We worked up to that over time. Just as I invested in my office team, I invested in a good "home" team. And because of that, I never missed a day at work when my child was home sick or missed an important "away" conference because my help was not available. I had my home team, backups, and all. And they definitely saved me and my sanity, especially for that brief time when I ran three companies all at one time. What *is* important, is that you show up for quality time with your family; have dates with your husband; hang out in the pool or at the beach with your kids; throw dinner parties for your friends and siblings; or be there for your aging parents. Whatever it is that brings you closer as a family. That is the stuff that really matters! I was more confident in my business life, and happier, because I knew I could leave my family for days attending a conference, or for as much as a month (when I took my sabbaticals every so often) and they would still be well taken care of. Yes, we had some mishaps, which can lead to the occasional mental meltdown (accompanied by lots of tears and expletives), but we thrived as a family none the less.

How do I know? I am still happily married after 29 years. I have a great relationship with my son. I was there caring for both my parents as they passed, and I still have time for ME. That's my proof that you don't have to be super-mom. We definitely need a great team in our office to accomplish our goals, and I feel that we need that same kind of support team at home. But this was *me* and what worked for *me*. You may not agree with my approach and that's okay, but find a way that works for you and helps you get over the "super-mom" syndrome. *She* is a fairytale; you are living in reality.

4.   Q: Do you ever feel disadvantaged as a female business owner?

A: I believe it is an incredible time to be a woman in technology and better yet, a woman business owner. Because I was always the CEO,

I never experienced the negative corporate experiences we often hear about. But, I would be lying if I didn't say that from time to time, I felt I had to work harder, longer, and smarter to prove my point to customers, vendors, and the occasional male colleague. I had some male clients over the years who felt they could make sexual advances at will or verbally abuse some of my female employees—a very precarious situation, especially when it is one of your largest clients. Obviously, situations like this cannot be ignored. Back then, social media didn't exist and there wasn't a #MeToo movement happening to raise awareness about the prevalence of harassment in the workplace. Culturally, we have definitely made *some* progress addressing this issue. But at the time, I had to learn how to handle situations like this very delicately, which usually meant a candid yet scary conversation with the client.

I find the younger you are, the more of a struggle this is. If you are too meek, you are often overlooked; if you are too assertive/aggressive, then you may be considered "hard to deal with"—all the typical stereotypes and disadvantages we have been faced with for years. I think if I had stayed in the corporate world, I would have felt this more, but as a CEO of my own company, I escaped much of it. As a CEO, I would say "no," I never truly felt disadvantaged as a female business owner, which is one reason why I encourage women to form their own companies.

Side note: As I worked my way through the process of selling my company, I did encounter some old-time male stereotypical behavior. For example, "You grew this company on your own? Should your husband be on this call? Are you sure you want to handle this negotiation point yourself? Why are you being so *difficult* with this contract language?" Honestly, it was almost hilarious at times. I am sure if I were a man, I would not have encountered most of this. Needless to say, M&A and private equity firms are also very male dominated fields. With more women entering into these areas, this too will change over time, and I hope to influence this change.

5.   Q: Does it hurt your feelings to be called a "B!T$#?"

A: First, I believe no man or women should ever use that word to describe a woman. In the early days, yes, something like this would have hurt my feelings for sure because, in part, I was not yet confident in my own abilities and how to run my company. As I got more competitive and more successful over the years, I can guarantee you I was called much worse "two-headed dragon" was my favorite. I also had an "outside" reputation of being difficult to work for, demanding, and aggressive—in other words, a true bitch. But, I truly believe that my team, and my customers and vendors who knew me well, viewed me as a generous and compassionate person. And frankly, as I got older, that is all I really cared about. Take great care of your team and your customers, and be fair with your vendors, and you will be greatly respected and rewarded over time. Don't worry what anyone else thinks of you because they just don't know YOU.

6.   Q: How important is a mentor(s)?

A: Super important! Ideally, you want both male and female mentors. People who have gone before you in what you are trying to accomplish. I am not a big fan of "paying" for mentors unless they are business advisors. A mentor is someone who is genuinely interested in your growth, which usually means you are not paying them, but most importantly, a mentor is someone who will give you honest and sometimes harsh feedback. Don't be fixated on just female mentors. Yes, of course, only women can share with you the challenges of rearing children, striving to be a great partner while simultaneously managing a household and career, or beginning menopause.

Men can be great mentors in other ways: Making big moves, being heard in a room, preventing you from over-nurturing a situation, etc. Not to say a female mentor cannot do that but sometimes you need to hear it from the opposite sex. I remember distinctly complaining about a situation to my male mentor. His response, "Suck it up and grow some balls. That's just how it is, so stop complaining and fix the problem!" While that sounds crass and maybe even politically incorrect, it snapped me out of my "this is not fair" funk and gave me a true dose of reality. I was being a wimp. He called me on it, plain and simple, and I am not sure that coming from a woman it would have had the same effect on me. If you haven't found a good mentor yet, then try to assemble a board of advisors and pay for their advice. They should not be your friends, as you are not looking for friend advice.

7. Q: How important is it to break out of your comfort zone?

A: I wish I had learned this earlier in life, as I believe I could have accomplished more. Here it is: Go do something completely "out there" on your own. Ideally, it challenges you both physically and mentally but it needs to be unrelated to your work. Parachute out of a plane if you have a fear of heights or falling. Learn to scuba dive if you are uncomfortable in the water. Spend two weeks building homes in a Third World country and learn how to use a power tool. Race 1000 miles in a sailboat, having never sailed a day in your life—just pick something!

I took three opportunities during my career to completely unplug and disengage from life, each for a one-month period and by myself. The first was traveling throughout Central America, the second was biking the South Island of New Zealand, and the most recent was backpacking through the wilds of the Pacific Northwest sleeping in a tent for weeks, and travelling alone with snakes, bears, and cougars lurking in the woods. On that journey, I found myself wading across swollen streams, picking my way across icy slopes, and clinging to my life as dirt fell out from underneath me while I was scrambling to reach a root and pull myself back on the trail. You don't need to be this extreme and take your life in your hands, but you do need to push the envelope and battle through it—fear, tears, and all. It is amazing what it does for your self-confidence all around, not just on a personal level but in your business life. Your aspirations become larger, richer, and more fulfilling. You discover your true inner strength. I am sure there are tamer ways to push yourself, but this is what totally worked for me. Find a challenge that will make you push yourself.

8.   Q: What are your biggest failures/regrets?

A: Not asking for help early enough or not asking because I didn't want someone to know what I didn't know. It's okay to say, "Help me understand [fill in the blank]" if you are not up to speed on a concept or thought. Again, advisors and mentors will help with this. As I got older, I always asked for help, mostly because I was confident in my abilities, but I simply didn't have the time to figure something out on my own.

Nevertheless, my biggest regret is not thinking "bigger." For example, early in my career I felt that an annual paycheck of $150,000 was a huge goal. But that number went up over time, slowly over the years to $200,000, then $250,000, then $500,000. I am pretty sure that if I had believed that $1M was a good annual paycheck, I would have gotten there. I use this as an example, but it can be applied to so many other areas. In hindsight, I didn't envision bigger fast enough, and it was really my own mindset that kept me back. My own personal glass ceiling. Think big, dream big, exit big!

There were, of course, many other failures and regrets, but I try never to look back. Learn from your mistakes—as there will be many—but always forge ahead!

9.   Q: Is bigger always better as it relates to company size?

A: No. I will be honest and say that I once had aspirations of opening up 12 consulting offices up and down the west coast to spread my reach. I projected my way to $100M in revenue, the number I knew I needed to take my company public. It took me a while to understand that this was my ego talking to me. After the third office, I realized I didn't want the life it took to visit each office and make sure my teams were all well run machines. I loved where I worked, my office was great, my house was great. I didn't want to work more than 40 to 45 hours per week. I didn't want to spend the time away from my family, traveling constantly. I also didn't want to oversee the management team I would need to put in place to operate this kind of organization. I would have needed to secure additional debt funding or to find outside investors and begin giving away part of my ownership. With the additional financing and debt, even if I sold the company, I might not be any better off than I was today, holistically. For me, "bigger" was ego driven and not necessarily better. Once I realized that, my views changed.

But, better was a goal I did want! So, instead I focused on increasing my revenue per employee and bottom line. I strategized on how to charge premium rates while delivering a better product. My goal was to increase my recurring revenue to over 95 percent, so I didn't have to worry about sales the next month. I no longer compared myself with my competitors or their latest press release announcing a big customer win. Bigger also doesn't always create more value. I encourage owners instead to think more strategically. I challenge anyone who thinks that a company with less than 20 people cannot sell for multiple millions. Look inside yourself and decide what you value and what makes you happy, and then make that decision about whether bigger is better or not.

10.   Q: Is gender diversity among the team important?

A: Diversity is extremely important for so many reasons, of which none are political. While "diversity" encompasses so much more than gender, I will contain my discussion to gender for this section. Men and women clearly approach problems and think differently; it is just how we are wired. In my very early years, we were 12 women working together—not good. Too much female presence wasn't healthy. In my later years, we were 15 men (and two women) working together, also not good. I looked long and hard to find female network engineers who I could include on my team. I finally found two, and oh, what a difference! The male dominance in the office quickly lessened, almost like they now needed to be on good behavior since there were

ladies present (don't you just love that!). The men became more compassionate with clients and each other, and the morale in the office
changed for the better. It was fun to watch. Where women at times
can be too nurturing, and men at times can be too harsh, bringing together the ideas of both makes for a healthy and happy medium. This
concept of diversity in the office also needs to extend to all board
seats, not just publicly traded companies. Companies should diversify
not because of some political mandate but because it just plain makes
for a better company overall. *

Diversity, of course, goes well beyond gender, age, ethnicity, physical
ability, political, religious beliefs, etc. But for women specifically, my
hope is that we don't just include women in meetings and on boards
because of a quota or mandate; we include women because they
deserve to be there, they have experience, and they have something
worthwhile to say. Let's hope we get there one day.

*In 2018, California passed a law requiring all publicly traded companies headquar-
tered in the state to include at least one woman on the board of directors by the
end of 2019 and between one and three female directors, based on the size of their
boards, by 2021.

Let me close this chapter with one final story: A few years ago, I was sitting
and chatting over a beer with a senior executive at a large annual technology
conference. We had met a number of years earlier at a reward celebration and
gotten along so well that we maintained a good friendship afterwards. Due to
our crazy schedules, we could only catch up personally at the conferences we
both attended and so this was one of those occasions.

Our company had just finished another fantastic year, and I had the
ability to bonus myself and my team handsomely. I then shared with him
that I had recently bought a second home and had spent a year remodeling
it, to perfection. He sat there listening intently and clearly happy for my good
fortune, and then proceeded to ask me what my husband did for a living.
There was a brief pause in the conversation...where I was hoping he would
recover and figured out the insertion of foot-into-mouth, but the pause went
on a moment too long. While I wasn't offended by the comment, I told

him with a gracious smile that my husband worked for me. Obviously, he made the assumption as many men still do, that the male is the predominant bread-winner in the family. The good news is that women in technology are shifting this paradigm.

Changing how men view successful women in technology may take longer than we hope or expect but this will change over time. In the meantime, let's encourage our young ladies not only to pursue a career in technology but also to remain strong, gracious, and unfettered in their pursuit to, one day, *get acquired for millions.*

100 Tips, Traps, and Tactics

This list of 100 tips is a compilation of responses from interviews with multiple technology service providers. In these tips you will find out what they learned and what they would have done differently in the sale of their company. This list works for every partner type and it is timeless.

The list is divided into four sections:

> 1) General Tips   Tips 1-23
>
> 2) Value Maximizer Tips   Tips 24-71
>
> 3) Tips Regarding Advisors Tips 72-87
>
> 4) Tips for Due Diligence   Tips 88-100

They are a combination of dos and don'ts but certainly weighing heavily on the don'ts. Sometimes the best lessons are learned from the challenges or mistakes others have faced...

General Tips

Tip 1: Run your company today as if you were to sell it tomorrow. Always be ready for a buyer as you never know when one will show up (i.e., the 50 percent+ unsolicited offers that come from other partners, vendors, and customers).

Tip 2: Stop working "in" the business and start working "on" the business. Buyers want to know that you are not the one doing all the sales, marketing, or lead development work.

Tip 3: Delay opening a new office in a foreign country (even if you are right next door) until you have at least $10M in sales in your home country. Establishing a new office and marketing to a new territory is a resource drain.

Tip 4: Don't let preconceived notions about prospective buyers ruin your deal process. Really get to know all potential buyers, regardless of their reputation. You never know.

Tip 5: If you're going to share that you're going through a transaction with your employees, keep people informed. Of course, it depends how open your organization is. However, if you try to keep it a secret, it adds another layer of complexity, and even when people sign NDAs, it always leaks. That's why, if you are keeping secrets, you need a contingency plan because it *will* leak. "Think about whether you want to be on the front-end telling people or the back-end reacting." – Kirk Dando, Dando Advisors

Tip 6: "Earn-outs for sellers who are going to exit are too often a disaster," says Scott Hakala, Principal at ValueScope, Inc. "The best earn-outs incentivize the people who run the business. Earn-outs for CEOs who are just standing back and collecting a paycheck often aren't good. Sellers always believe they're going to make the earn-out, then they are mad if they don't."

Tip 7: As the seller, never use your company email address, even if you feel your email is secure. Don't tie your personal email (forward) to your office email account. There's nothing worse than having a confidential email pop up at the bottom of your screen while you have others viewing your screen.

Tip 8: Don't compare your company with other similar companies that have sold recently. In other words, don't take a valuation for a considerably larger company (over $25M or more than 5x your revenue) and assume you should be worth the same. Larger companies fetch larger multiples.

Tip 9: Always understand and have included in writing in the LOI (in broad, but not too broad language) your noncompete terms, i.e. length and type of prohibited activity.

Tip 10: If you are compensating non-shareholders as part of the sale, be sure to investigate a termination/severance agreement. Also, be aware of the number of days you will you need to give your employees to review and sign such an agreement. State regulations vary, so avoid surprises by researching this now.

Tip 11: Do "take a pass" on buyers who are not at least 50 percent larger than you. Anything less may be insufficient for the acquiring company to success-fully digest and integrate your organization.

Tip 12: Do consider making an initial price suggestion if you are approached by an unsolicited buyer. Even though the normal process is to get the buyer to make an offer, and for them to explain to you how it was calculated, this sometimes anchors the offer at a much lower starting point. If you have a chance to "name your price," you should.

Tip 13: If approached by an interested party, determine if they are a strategic or a financial buyer and then present data that will be most compelling to them. While each group looks at financials, other data can be just as relevant, such as specific savings on cost, or the potential to upsell/cross-sell products.

Tip 14: The moment you sign an LOI, the deal becomes exclusive for a period of time, typically 60 days. Understand the deal structure completely before you sign. Otherwise, you may be locked in for a period of time and lose mo-mentum with other prospective buyers.

Tip 15: As the seller, you have more leverage in the negotiation prior to the LOI being signed. Once signed, the power shifts to the buyer. Know that now. You will immediately feel the shift.

Tip 16: Do understand your emotional involvement as well as the buyer's.

Whoever becomes emotionally involved in the deal loses power. Try to limit your emotional involvement. On the other hand, if the buyer becomes emotionally involved, it will be easier for you, the seller.

Tip 17: Never say "no" immediately to the prospective buyer, even if the ask is unreasonable. Instead, replace the "no" with "let me see what I can do." Then speak to your broker, accountant, attorney, or coach before generating a more nuanced response. This also gives your team time to strategize on a better solution than just a "no." And it makes the other side feel like they are being heard.

Tip 18: Be sure to fully understand what selling five years from today really means. Once you include a typical 24-month earn-out period, this could really mean seven or more years.

Tip 19: Don't allow a buyer to start down the path of extensive due diligence before offering up an LOI with the promise of a quick close at the end "because all the work will already have been done." This option limits your ability to negotiate because you won't have a starting number before the due diligence phase starts.

Tip 20: All businesses face risks. A common problem with many sellers is a tendency to avoid discussing risks in their business with the hopes that no one will find out about them until the deal is done. However, that is unrealistic, and furthermore, you will likely be required to represent in the purchase agreement that you have disclosed all material business issues. Disclose problems *early* so they can be addressed, rather than facing "deal killers" after you and the seller have invested your time.

Tip 21: Don't plan a vacation the week after the expected close date. Chances are your close may slip, and even if you do take the vacation, you will be working the entire time. Furthermore, the second you close, you will be needed to help with the transition plans.

Tip 22: Read the book *Finish Big: How Great Entrepreneurs Exit Their Companies on Top* by Bo Burlingham. If you are unsure about what you will do next (after the sale), this book will help you gain clarity.

Tip 23: TKAD – Time Kills All Deals. Need we say more? Bear this in mind and do what you can to keep things moving forward smoothly.

Value Maximizer Tips

Financial Fitness

Tip 24: Minimize intercompany expenses. It can hang up a deal or kill it entirely if you don't have the accounting straight.

Tip 25: If you don't have an ESOP now, don't start one. The complexity is simply not helpful. If you choose, you can compensate your key people or your entire organization at your own discretion once the deal is done. You don't need an ESOP to make it equitable for everyone.

Tip 26: Do not ever include personal nonbusiness expenses in your business accounting, no matter how creative (or legitimate) the reasons. Boats, racecars, family vacations, second homes and the expense associated with them should be kept off the balance sheet and P&L. Likewise, nannies as well as any other help not clearly related to the business should be removed from the payroll.

Tip 27: Now is not the time to minimize your profits to "save" on taxes. As much as you don't like to pay Uncle Sam your hard-earned profits, you also need to show as much going to the bottom line as possible if you plan on selling in the next three years.

Tip 28: Understand the difference between a stock sale and an asset sale early on. Both may result in taxable capital gains, but the long-term implications between the two can be very different.

Tip 29: Going overboard on EBITDA adjustments creates suspicion from buyers. Your adjustments must be concrete and auditable (i.e., don't remove your entire salary unless you have completely delegated all your responsibilities to others, then by all means remove it).

Tip 30: Never focus just on the price; the terms are important as well. Earn-outs, stock prices, employee retention, and disclosures and guarantees are all important to the final payout.

Tip 31: Understand, early in the process, how working capital will be calculated so you are not surprised at the end. Most buyers use the cash-free/debt-free method. Know in advance what items this will affect that may be hidden in your financials.

Tip 32: Be sure to understand how earn-outs are calculated. This can be an entire negotiation process of its own because many times they are not referenced in detail in the LOI.

Tip 33: Know early what amount is needed (if any) in an escrow account so you won't be surprised in the end.

Tip 34: If a note receivable is part of the transaction, understand how your broker will be paid on the note (in advance with a discounted value or paid as you receive payments).

Tip 35: While it may sound obvious, accounts receivable (A/R) greater than 120 days is suspect and will be discounted heavily in the working capital calculation. Collect all old A/R, even if you need to offer discounts or more favorable payment terms. A/R should be as clean as possible (including writing off small amounts).

Tip 36: Sell or distribute nonrevenue-producing assets or fully depreciated assets. They are just clutter or a reason to question items on the balance sheet. Fully depreciated hardware (desktops, laptops, monitors) sit on fixed asset schedules long past their actual use or may have walked out the door when employees were terminated.

Tip 37: If possible, try to time a close on the last day of a payroll. It makes the accounting much easier and the accruals much simpler.

Tip 38: Be sure to review your accrued vacation and sick time balances. In most cases, these will need to be paid out at the close, which can be an unexpected drain on cash as these balances often grow large over time.

Tip 39: Always have a strong understanding of your current monthly working capital before selling your company. Be proactive with this part of the negotiation and don't let the buyer decide on their own what it should be going forward.

Tip 40: Not all deferred income should be treated equally. Look closely to see if there are aspects of that number that can be removed from the working capital calculation.

Tip 41: Be realistic about the buyer's working capital requirements (unless you are eliminating a lot of payroll due to redundancy). Going forward, those needs will most likely be greater than your historical numbers. Rarely can you make a case for it to be less, especially if you are in a growth mode.

Tip 42: Try to have the last three years of capital expenditures and also current year capital expense projections handy. Capital expenditures don't show up in any EBITDA calculations, but the buyer's due diligence team will look for it.

Tip 43: Review your lease terms. How soon is your lease up? Is the lease assignable? If not, how will this affect the deal? Are you personally guaranteeing the lease? Knowing the answers to these issues and presenting that in advance to a prospective buyer strengthens your presentation and helps eliminate a "gotcha" that could hurt your negotiations.

Tip 44: Avoid hanging on to your company past its peak. This is very common. Obviously, the best time to sell your company is when your revenue is increasing, but if you cannot wait for a particular reason, you should work on increasing your gross profit margins and bottom line by reining in expenses. Top-line decline can be better tolerated with a bottom-line increase.

Revenue Readiness

Tip 45: Measure revenue (and COGS) by type. Some revenue (i.e., recurring revenue from subscriptions) is more valuable than others.

Tip 46: Understand your most profitable line of business (LOB) and focus completely on that. The more you focus, the faster you will grow.

Tip 47: Don't assume software/hardware annual enhancement or support renewals are recurring revenue; they are not. Unless you have a customer locked in for three years of payments, they can leave at any time and take their enhancement with them.

Tip 48: Identify key large-customer contract renewals as much in advance as possible, and work to accomplish those renewals at the earliest possible date. Don't let a deal close hang up on a large renewal.

Management Muscle

Tip 49: Shine. Make sure you or your organization are seen as thought leaders in your field of specialty and get it out there—on your website, at conferences, at trade association events. You just never know who is in the audience that might be a prospective buyer.

Tip 50: Create an advisory board—recruit people who have sold companies in the past so you can leverage their experience.

Tip 51: If you work more than 45 to 50 hours per week, that could be viewed as a negative by buyers, particularly if you plan to exit as part of the sale. Buyers will worry that you will need to be backfilled by more than one person.

Tip 52: Make yourself redundant—especially if you want to exit shortly after a sale is completed. A year before contemplating a sale, start to turn over key tasks to your management team.

Tip 53: If you have a strong management team, engage them in the due diligence process. This will give buyers a comfort level that management is on board with the sale.

Tip 54: Honestly evaluate your management team. Window dressing is only good for a while. If you know there are members of your team that are underperforming, make those changes now before you go out to the market.

Tip 55: While changing out a couple of managers may be necessary, stability is also key. Buyers look at employee turnover as much as they do customer turnover. If you need to make some significant changes, do it and then wait a couple of years before you go to market, if you can.

Tip 56: If you are looking to sell your company, don't go it alone unless you have a management team committed to helping with the process. Even then, seek out an advisor/coach to help identify viable buyers, keep them on pace, and smooth out the bumps along the way. The cost of a good advisor will more than pay for their fees in an increased offer price and in helping to engage multiple prospective buyers.

Value Proposition/Vertical

Tip 57: Got a value proposition? Can you recite it? If you cannot, then probably no one else in your company can, except for maybe the person that created it. Everyone should know the value proposition and be able to articulate it.

Tip 58: Did you give your vertical solution a name? Your packaged solution should be all over your website—hero image, inside pages, all your downloadable marketing materials.

Customer Satisfaction/Retention

Tip 59: Calculate monthly and annual churn (subscription-based services) on a regular basis. If more than 25 percent of your revenue is "as a service," the buyer will want to know what the churn rate is.

Tip 60: Review all your customer contracts well in advance of contemplating a sale. Is the contract assignable? If not, now would be a good time to create an addendum that will allow for this, as the probability of an asset sale is greater than a stock sale. This could be a deterrent in the end if not addressed well in advance.

Tip 61: Measure and promote customer satisfaction. When was the last time you calculated customer satisfaction? This is a key value driver. If you can boast of a number greater than 90 percent, be sure to issue a press release and put it on your website. Buyers will focus on this as an indicator of customer retention. Even if it isn't until August when you calculate this (for the prior year), still put it on your website somewhere.

Sustainable Success

Tip 62: How would a 5 or 10 percent decrease in margin from your largest supplier affect your bottom line? If the impact would be substantial, consider expanding your supplier base.

Tip 63: When was the last time you performed a "test" restore of critical systems? (i.e., CRM/ERP/ticketing systems). Buyers are now finally paying attention to the prevention of malware attacks, as well as the ability to recover from malware attacks or a host of other potential data catastrophes.

Tip 64: Avoid waiting until you are in due diligence with a buyer to get NDAs and confidentiality agreements signed by employees and external independent contractors. Don't let this be used as a leverage point by someone to get something.

Sales and Marketing

Tip 65: Shop your competition annually and assess your prices, strengths, and weaknesses, and then update your value proposition accordingly.

Tip 66: Know what your Customer Acquisition Cost (CAC) is. Exactly. A savvy buyer will want to know, and your answer should be clear and credible.

Tip 67: If you plan on selling in the next 12 to 18 months, don't burden your payroll with additional marketing staff. Unless you have a gaping hole that cannot be filled by outsourcing to a marketing firm, don't hire someone now.

Marketing teams are usually the first to go, therefore the time and cost to acquire additional employees is not worthwhile.

Tip 68: Limit investments. Need new tools and resources to launch projects? Use SaaS solutions that can be terminated with minimum notice.

Intellectual Property

Tip 69: Protect IP. If you are not authenticating through your active directory, you should regularly change passwords on protected sites that house your IP.

Tip 70: Clarify IP ownership. Review all agreements with outside contractors for development work. Make sure all IP is assigned to the company. Amend any agreements as needed in advance of the sale.

Tip 71: Avoid waiting until you are in the due diligence phase to gather your IP, i.e. copyrights, trademarks, trade secrets, and patents. It will be part of the due diligence process so have this organized in advance.

Advisor Tips

Tip 72: The attorney you have worked with to create your company and handle your day-to-day legal questions may not be great at critically reviewing your IOI, LOI, noncompete, and other deal documents. Find a transaction attorney who has experience in M&A deals.

Tip 73: Don't assume your tax accountant is the best person to go to for tax advice. He/she may not be versed in the nuances of an asset or stock sale. Find someone who has done large stock/asset sales and not just individual tax returns.

Tip 74: Avoid elephants and sharks when picking brokers. Elephants are companies that specialize in much larger transactions than your sale. Elephants will take on the business if there is a lack of deals in their pipeline. They may have a misguided notion of the valuation of your company (which they will realize sooner or later and lose interest). Avoid the elephants, as they will overcharge and underservice, and you will be trampled in their rush out the door. Sharks are harder to spot, but they have no technology industry specialization and they are motivated by the monthly retainer and valuation work they can sell you. Typically, they won't bring you more than one buyer. They may impress you with their deck and numerous tombstones of deals past, but typically those are not relevant to your size or industry.

Tip 75: Don't choose your broker based solely upon who gives you the highest valuation price for your company. While each broker will give you their best assessment based on what they "see" in the market today, they may give you an optimistic number or mirror the one you are looking for, but once the ink dries on the engagement contract, any valuation number they gave you becomes irrelevant. Check references!

Tip 76: Beware of brokers that use the "spray and pray" approach. Meaning, your broker should be very selective in who they send your CIM to. Just because your broker has a list of thousands of buyers doesn't mean they should be sending your profile to each one.

Tip 77: Have your Tax CPA "proforma" a sale in advance, either as an asset or stock sale, using your actual income and deductions to know what the tax consequences would be. If your CPA is struggling with this, find a different one.

Tip 78: If you decide not to use a broker, use an M&A coach. A good one is well worth the money and can handle the difficult conversations that you frankly don't want to have directly with the buyers. After all, you may be working together post sale and you don't want a heated conversation during the negotiations to ruin a good future working relationship.

Tip 79: Brokers will allow carve-outs (excluded potential buyers) for people who you are already in discussions with, or have agreed to discuss a sale with, in advance of signing an engagement letter. Be specific, open, and honest as to who might be interested in your company in advance and name them individually.

Tip 80: Understand how the minimum success fee is earned. Know if there is still a fee that has to be paid even if you identified the buyer in advance and the buyer is listed in your carve-out list.

Tip 81: Not all brokers calculate fees the same way. Don't assume that 4 percent of a deal is less than 5 percent. The step-downs or step-ups in the percentages of the success fees can make a difference, depending on how they are structured. Run though a sample deal first and understand how the fees work. Better yet, ask them to give you an example with a couple of term scenarios.

Tip 82: Know in advance how earn-outs will be handled with your broker. Are they paid up front or if and when you earn them? This can be negotiated. Again, it is best to walk through a sample transaction.

Tip 83: Understand if the commitment fee is applied against the final success fee or not. Don't assume; many contracts are silent on this point. This is also negotiable.

Tip 84: Many brokers charge monthly retainers. Will the monthly fee increase as your revenue increases or are you locked into a fee? If you are using a broker as part of preparing for a sale, this can be a different number from when you first engaged. Be sure to determine if the monthly retainer can be applied against the final success fee?

Tip 85: How an LOI is negotiated can have significant consequences to the seller. Get your attorney involved before you sign the LOI, not afterwards.

Tip 86: Make sure, also, that your legal counsel is not on vacation during the planned week of close.

Tip 87: Financial projections, if unrealistic, will create problems. It is better to dial them down or make them achievable, rather than unrealistic. Otherwise, it will hold up the deal if you don't achieve them. This can make your earn-out unachievable, and it can make a buyer question your financials in general.

Due Diligence Tips

Tip 88: Make sure all permits and licenses are up to date, even the "out of the ordinary" ones (i.e., filings with the Secretary of State, which include all the current officers and directors).

Tip 89: Never overlook chemistry/culture. While the deal numbers are important, chemistry between the founder/seller and the potential financial or strategic buyer may be the most crucial driver of a successful partnership. If you overlook this, the likelihood to achieve your full earn-out may be at risk.

Tip 90: Get a draft of the purchase agreement as soon as possible while in due diligence so you can see the level of detail in the agreement and what the disclosure schedules will be—so you can begin working on them.

Tip 91: If you see an error, miscalculation, or other misstatement of fact after the signing of an IOI or LOI, acknowledge the mistake and present new documents as soon as it is discovered. While the mistake may cost you some dollars in the end, if it is discovered instead by the buyer, it may compound any difficulties in the due diligence process.

Tip 92: Make sure all past shareholders have returned all stock certificates and have signed termination agreements with the company (regardless of a stock or asset sale).

Tip 93: NDAs and signed employment agreements should be accounted for in advance of a sale.

Tip 94: Always, always, no matter how large the buyer, ask for *proof of funds* for the sale transaction. Don't be shy about asking for financial statements both (balance sheet and profit and loss). If they are unwilling to supply financials, this is a red flag.

Tip 95: Eager sellers tend to disclose too much information too soon. If sending a customer list (especially to a strategic buyer), conceal customer names and contacts. Be selective in what is sent.

Tip 96: Don't necessarily assume that all buyers are looking for the same data. Just because one buyer asked for your churn rate, it doesn't mean the next one will. Approach this like an audit; don't volunteer information unless requested.

Tip 97: Due diligence is usually the most stressful phase of selling. Get as much help in preparing documents as you can. The more stressed you become, the more emotional you will probably become. Organize the documents you know will be requested for due diligence and do this in advance of when they will be needed. Start now with making sure you have e-copies of all the documents and update your e-files as new documents are created or older ones amended.

Tip 98: Disclosure schedules can be time consuming and are a key aspect of the definitive agreement. Make sure you list all *oral* agreements with employees, etc. For example, if someone can work from home certain days of the week, etc. While this might sound trivial, you want to let the buyer know *everything*. All nonwritten "side deals" should be disclosed.

Tip 99: All buyers eventually want an "office visit." Suggest they come after hours or take a tour on the weekend—when no one else is around. Strolling a buyer through an office puts everyone on alert that a potential change is about to happen, and you may not want that at this time.

Tip 100: Once an LOI has been signed, have a weekly call with the buyer to determine the progress that needs to be made each week.

Bonus Chapter
What are buyers thinking about?

Note: This chapter was contributed by
Revenue Rocket Consulting Group – Mike Harvath, CEO.

We are fascinated by mergers and acquisitions; each transaction, like each individual, is unique. The complexity of assessing, negotiating, mitigating, and accepting the inherent risks in each transaction, while navigating the personal and emotional landscape of the players and their advisors involved, puts M&A into a category all its own. There is little else like it in the business world today, and it is often the most frustrating and challenging event that an owner faces.

It is why our firm, Revenue Rocket, has focused on the IT Services, M&A space, for over 18 years—to creatively find a way to help our clients come together in the face of these challenges. Across that time, we have represented more buyers than sellers and the truth of the matter is: there are usually more reasons *not* to do a transaction than to *do* one.

The risks always appear larger than what really materializes. Legal, tax, and financial advisors are wired to find all the risks and all the reasons that a transaction shouldn't be done, under the theory that if you can live with the worst-case scenario, then you should do the acquisition. There are two problems with this: First, the worst-case scenario never happens, and second, the worst-case scenario will never get a deal done. What we hope to accomplish in this chapter is to distill out for you a handful of key lessons learned that will provide buyers as well as sellers with insights into *getting deals done successfully* both in the short run by getting a deal done, and in the long term by *both parties winning* because of the acquisition.

KNOW THE BUYER

A lot has already been said in this book about buyer profiles so we won't reiterate what is already written, but we want to make sure that you understand what kind of buyers there are and whether the one you are facing is an opportunistic buyer, a financial buyer, or a strategic buyer. Each of these types of buyers will have different expectations of value, rather different sets of objectives for an acquisition, and quite candidly, very different results in getting a transaction done.

Opportunistic buyers are...well, often shoppers not buyers. Let's be clear: There is a place for opportunistic transactions where you have been part of a peer group and you have similar core values and business interests that align sufficiently for a good transaction to occur; however, too often we run into companies who will buy if the "right" opportunity presents itself. Sometimes called tire kickers, they talk a good game, but when it comes down to writing the check, they don't because it "wasn't quite right." This is sometimes affectionately called the "Goldilocks Syndrome;" there is just something not quite right with each opportunity and this prevents them from getting it done. They are happy to spend the time digging through the seller's stuff and analyzing things many different ways, but usually the only transactions they can get done are with an ignorant or desperate seller who settles for a substantial discount to fair value.

We would qualify a good "opportunistic" transaction as one that is really at its core a strategic merger or acquisition. In the scenario where you have been a part of a peer group or alliance that has educated its members on value, operational, and financial performance, there are truly great opportunities for mergers and acquisitions to be done. That's because of the organizational maturity of both organizations, so the synergistic amalgamation of the two firms is really about the opportunity that the strategy and synergies bring. In other words, the reason for doing a deal like this is about one plus one being greater than three. It's not about getting a "buy."

THE FOUR PILLARS OF A SUCCESSFUL STRATEGIC ACQUISITION

Before launching into this section, we want to pause a moment and define success in this case. You can certainly argue that an acquisition for a corporate turnaround can be successful without following these principles or that a financial buyer can achieve their objectives without them. When we are addressing a successful strategic acquisition, we are referring to a win/win scenario where the convergence of the seller and buyer is creating a greater organization.

There are four core elements that must align to fully realize a successful strategic acquisition, and arguably all the horror stories that haunt buyers and sellers, often keeping them from even considering a transaction, is usually because one or more of these four elements were not aligned or thought through in advance. These elements also tend to follow a sequential order: cultural fit, strategic fit, and financial fit, followed by a fully executed post-merger integration strategy.

Simply put, if the cultures don't align, the transaction is almost certainly predestined to a rough and rocky road. Corporate cultural change is one of the most difficult things to implement in a business, as it involves the fundamental DNA of the organization. If the cultures align, you're off to a good start, and the next step is about the strategic fit and alignment. We must be able to map a path to a *"greater than three"* scenario to achieve success. If we can get strategic alignment, then usually we can find a path to a financial alignment that will get the seller to a number that will motivate them to sell, and the buyer to achieve a return on the investment that they can live with. The only way to get above a five times EBITDA (earnings before interest, tax, depreciation, amortization) as a transaction value is to have a greater than three strategy (more on this later).

Lastly, all the above is great, but it will not materialize unless there is a well-built and executed post-merger integration strategy that will guide the convergence process to realize the expectations of both companies. When there is alignment across all four aspects, we typically see *less than a 2 percent turnover* of customers and/or employees. Let's look at each of these elements in a little more detail.

"Great, so what do you mean by culture?" you might ask. This is a look at the DNA of an organization, and manifests itself in the core values, employee care, customer care, and operational care of the business. We are a big fan of *Traction: Get a Grip on Your Business* by Gino Wickman, and *Mastering the Rockefeller Habits* by Verne Harnish. Either of these are great guides to running a business, and aligning your day-to-day activity to your core values, purpose, and BHAG (big hairy audacious goal). If you don't currently embrace a strategic planning and business execution model, you should look at either of these. If you have already done so, it will radically accelerate the process of determining cultural fit.

Some buy-side clients will come out and say that if the seller doesn't embrace *Traction*, they don't want to buy them. These tools will force you to define all these cultural aspects as a part of the process. A good cultural test question for a buyer is to ask themselves of the seller, "Would I hire them to my team?" If you wouldn't want them on your team, then the company is probably not a good cultural match. This doesn't necessarily mean you will be keeping the leadership or the seller's CEO; it just means that the leadership will be the best barometer of the corporate culture.

Strategic fit may seem rather self-explanatory, but the main point we want to emphasize here is the need to qualify and quantify the strategic elements. Effectively, you need to build a model that identifies the strategic elements and also estimates a value for that alignment. When looking at the strategic fit, you will need to look at the cross selling, up selling, and down selling opportunities between the two organizations. You will want to also look at consolidation opportunities, redundancies, and/or operational efficiencies that exist. Most importantly, though, with all these elements, we must assign a financial value or value range that can be realized.

As for *financial fit*, we recommend that if you can realize an annualized rate of return greater than 20 percent, you should do the deal. That doesn't mean you can only pay a five times EBITDA multiple, it just means you must quantify the synergies well enough to pay for whatever the seller is willing to sell for. Remember also that a firm's actual value is achieved when you have a willing buyer and a willing seller agree to the price and terms. Also, it is important to understand that the *terms* of the transaction will have at least as much impact on the transaction value as the valuation will have.

The last pillar is having *a post-merger integration strategy*. The number one reason transactions fail is *poor integration*. The reason there is poor integration is that there was no real plan in the first place. A wish is not a plan. This may sound strange but for the integration to go smoothly, you must plan together to ensure success. Please never assume that it is simply going to work. And beginning to work on the plan once the deal is done is too late.

The integration strategy boils down to four main components.

First, create a detailed plan of what needs to happen—culturally, strategically, and operationally—for the buyer and for the seller, and with a timeline. Second, share the load; engage people across both organizations to map and oversee integration, creating teams to accomplish the work with an accountability for each action. Third, focus on early wins; the importance of this cannot be understated —you must highlight and applaud all the wins to show that you are making progress. People tend to fear the worst and focus on what isn't working, so the fourth point is communicate, communicate, communicate. Communicate what is going to happen (this will help to dispel fear of the unknown). Communicate what is happening (this builds confidence). Communicate what has happened (this will build trust).

THE VALUE PROPOSITION THAT A PREPARED BUYER CAN BRING TO THE TABLE

This book is particularly for sellers, preparing and helping them to maximize transaction value, but there are definite advantages for the prepared buyer that you should be aware of. This has a lot to do with the value proposition that a prepared buyer can bring to the table. As a seller, you can get all your ducks in a row and look great, but you will still have to find a suitor that not only is financially ready but also is strategically aligned to maximize transaction value.

On the other hand, if you are a prepared buyer, you could purchase either a well-prepared seller or an unprepared seller and, in many ways, bring a much greater value proposition to the unprepared seller than to the prepared seller. I am not advocating that buyers take advantage of unprepared sellers. We have worked long enough in this business and closed enough transactions to know that many sellers do not have the time, energy, resources, or experience to transform their business or to optimize the business for a transaction.

The point is that a best-in-class, prepared buyer can purchase an average or underperforming business and can breathe new life into it, bringing it to a level that the seller could not have achieved on his or her own.

A solid buyer can also provide a path for *everyone* to win. Be thoughtful about this: The goal of a successful transaction is not how cheaply a buyer can purchase a seller but whether they can accelerate both the growth and profitability of the parent company and the asset they are purchasing. Too often buyers negotiate with a win/lose style. Our competitive North American culture has created this rather erroneous idea that for every winner there must be a loser. However, mergers and acquisitions really fall into a category of either a win/win or a lose/lose scenario. We know of few transactions where one company really wins and the other really loses; they usually win or lose together.

In reality, it falls heavily on the buyer to make sure that everyone wins together. The big challenge here is that usually what is good for the seller is bad for the buyer and vice versa. It takes great thought and creativity to find ways to make sure that *both* parties have a clear path to success. This means careful consideration of the terms, deal structure, incentives, rewards, and penalties. In the end, the winning transaction is the one where the parties master the middle ground. And again, the buyer has the best opportunity to lead the way to the successful middle ground.

This is especially true of the final mile in negotiating the definitive agreements, where negotiating is most intense. Some of our most successful buy-side clients have realized that often the final points to be negotiated only impact the transaction a few percentage points. They have found that it is often best to concede on these points, not because they are weak, but rather because they see the bigger picture and fundamentally understand the significant amount of *relational good will* that can be built with the seller during the final stages of negotiation. This relational good will builds an immense amount of momentum going into post-merger integration activities, which are the most critical part of any transaction.

Good buyers are needed today to lead the TSP sector to a new level. The market is certainly consolidating and is filled with struggling companies. The baby boomer generation, which laid the foundations of the TSP industry, is retiring, thus adding to this movement. Sure, the strong companies will survive, but more important to us than the survival of the fittest is the survival of the best this industry has to offer. It is our desire to see great companies succeed, and great companies are the ones that have a strong culture and that understand what they bring to the marketplace. And they understand that they need to be ready, that they need to be strategic, and that they can create a path for others to succeed *with* them through their acquisitions. Every seller wants to know that what they poured their blood, sweat, and tears into as they built their business is now in an even better place when they move on and exit the business.

POST-MERGER INTEGRATION

In Part I of this book, the author discusses the six stages of a seller's transaction process. Stage VI is the post-merger integration and earn-out. Merger and integration literature is filled with relatively consistent data indicating that most mergers and acquisition, as many as 58 percent, "fail" relative to several measures, most notably relative to the specific financial and organizational goals established for each specific merger or acquisition. Therefore, it is necessary that we learn from those who have failed as well as from those who have succeeded. Below are seven rules of integration success and a checklist for post-merger success.

General rules for integration success

There are many schools of thought on the priorities in an integration process and general rules to follow for integration success. Here are seven rules that we have identified for success:

1. **Vision**. Do we have a sound, realistic, compelling vision for the long-term future of the new combined company?

2. **Leadership**. Do we quickly clarify leadership and roles, thereby reducing anxiety, confusion, misdirection, and critical loss of time?

3. **Growth**. Is our integration focused on *growth* development—finding the 1+1=3 plan, versus just the common "synergistic efficiencies" focus that looks mostly at cost and resource savings? Specifically, do we evaluate the *opportunities* possible in consideration of the merged company's customers, capabilities, competitors, costs, and culture?

4. **Early wins**. Do we plan for and accomplish "early wins" in order to rally resources, promote teamwork and community, inspire staff, encourage investors, and establish momentum?

5. **Culture**. Do we acknowledge that cultural differences exist, and do we specifically plan to benefit from the best of each company's culture? Do we develop a plan for cultural integration *before* the merger is executed? A failure in this area will erode our return rate on the deal after close, as staff will leave.

6. **Communication**. Do we have a specific detailed communication plan? Do we *prioritize* communication? Do we use the proper media given the nature of the message? Do we use the proper *people* as communicators?

7. **Risk management**. Do we view risk as a negative element to be avoided, or do we view it as the source from which gain is realized? Do we specifically and proactively plan for risk management, or do we address risk defensively and reactively?

Questions to ask a buyer to help determine post-merger success

Below is an excellent "checklist for post-merger success" which is based, *inversely*, on studies of *failed* mergers. As a seller, you should consider this list when assessing your prospective buyers:

- Does the buyer bring something unique to the deal so that competitive bids by other companies cannot push the purchase *price* too high?
- Is the merger or acquisition consistent with sound *strategy* with respect to diversification and other issues?
- Has the acquirer attempted to make accurate forecasts of the seller's business? For example, if appropriate, has the buyer assessed the seller's technology and customer contracts?
- Can the acquirer handle an acquisition of this size (the size of the seller)?
- Is there good *operating and market synergy* between the buyer and seller?
- Are there plans to boost combined *asset productivity*?
- Do the buyer and seller have reasonably compatible *cultures*?
- Do the buyer and seller share a clear *vision* of the newly combined company?
- Is this vision based in *reality*?
- Are the newly combined organizations able to achieve post-merger *alignment* of capabilities?
- Can senior managers subordinate their egos for the *common good* of the new organization?
- Do buyer and seller have an effective *communications program* in place to help the integration process?
- Will the acquirer strive for a *rapid pace of integration* in implementing the new company's vision?

Here is yet another "M&A planning checklist:"

- Are plans consistent with the intrinsic logic of the deal?

- Do the plans specify how the company will pay for the deal?
- Are there written plans to cover both the short term...and the long term...?
- Do the short-term and long-term plans mesh?
- Has the planning process involved both senior managers *and* employees most affected by the plans?
- Do the plans consider the operational and cultural realities of the two companies involved?
- Have senior managers and the board of directors reviewed the plan documents?
- Are senior managers and the board using the plans to make their decisions?
- Are the plans supported by the appropriate policies?
- Are the plans supported by adequate resources?
- Do the plans specify the measures and milestones of progress?
- Who will be held accountable for achieving the plans?
- Have the plans been distributed to all appropriate parties?
- Is there a program for communicating the plans internally?
- Is there a program for communicating the plans externally?

These checklists provide you with high level guidelines for thinking about integration. It is always a good idea to get outside competent and experienced advisors for M&A, legal and accounting motions associated with any deal. Please visit our website at https://www.revenuerocket.com/checklists to download a copy of these checklists and for other M&A tips and guidelines.

Resources

The following resources can be downloaded from my website https://rosebiz-inc.com/book-resource:

Part I
- Sample Indication of Interest (IOI) – sample shown below
- Letter of Intent (LOI) - sample shown below
- Due Diligence Checklist – sample shown below

Part II
- Adjusted EBITDA Excel worksheet – sample shown below
- Revenue by Industry and Opportunity Score Worksheet

Part III
- M&A Advisor Checklist
- Preparing for the Buyer Call
- Sample Non-Disclosure Agreement
- 100 Tips, Traps and Tactics

All images in color are downloadable from the link above.

ASSESSMENTS:

- Value Maximizer Assessment™ - https://rosebizinc.com/ValueMax.
- PREScore™ Questionnaire – https://rosebizinc.com/PersonalScore.

SAMPLE INDICATION OF INTEREST (IOI)

Dear Seller:

We are pleased to submit this Indication of Interest ("IOI") which sets forth terms under which ABC Buyer Enterprises Inc. (or an affiliate) would conduct due diligence and propose a transaction (Described below) with XYZ Seller.com, Inc. ("XYZ Seller"). We are prepared to submit a Letter of Intent ("LOI") within 10 days of meeting with management, and we target 60 days to definitive Agreement and closing from acceptance of the LOI.

1. **Transaction:** ABC Buyer (or one of its affiliates1) anticipates that it would acquire 100% of XYZ Seller's assets free and clear of any options, liens, or other claims, including the settlement of all in-the-money options. ("Transaction").

2. **Acquisition Consideration:** Contingent on further diligence, ABC Buyer is prepared to offer a purchase price of $XXXXXXX ± 15% ("Purchase Price") paid in cash at closing.

    This price is an "enterprise value" (cash-free and debt-free) and assumes a normalized level of tangible working capital.

3. **Financing:** The Purchase Price will be funded from cash currently available to ABC Buyer and would not be subject to any financing contingency.

4. **Transaction fees:** Each party will pay its own fees and expenses incurred during the Transaction (including but not limited to broker, legal fees, etc.). For clarity, ABC Buyer will pay its transaction fees and XYZ Seller's fees will be paid by XYZ Seller equity holders or from excess cash.

5. **Due Diligence:** The indicated valuation range and specific consideration amount is subject to further customary due diligence. We expect that you will allow us further access to XYZ Seller's books, records, products, customers, and management. Our primary focus

will be to validate the financial, customer, and contract representations that have been made. Specifically:

a) Management meeting and discussion (in person)
b) Analysis and review of detailed TTM financials, by customer and engagement. TTM as of 4Q20XX shows approximate revenue of $XXM, gross margin of $XXM, and adjusted EBITDA of $XXXM
c) Analysis and review of churn/renewal rates and follow on revenue from existing customers
d) Analysis and review of in-force client contracts, including diligence of maintenance and support obligations
e) Review and diligence of facilities, operations, staff composition, and capability
f) Determination of post-close transition plan for employees, related party agreements, and required certifications

6. **Contingencies:** We currently anticipate that the closing of the Transaction would be contingent upon the following, with no post-closing contingencies:

a) We shall have conducted our due diligence investigation and be satisfied with the findings thereof.
b) Any transaction would be subject to the negotiation and execution of definitive agreements. The agreement would contain representations, warranties, covenants, and conditions customary in similar transactions, including all necessary third party consents.
c) XYZ Seller has had no material adverse change in its assets, business, or financial condition.

7. **Corporate Authorization:** Final agreement is subject to approval by our Board of Directors. ABC Buyer is a privately held company with a close relationship with its Board and is able to move quickly through the approval process.

8. **Timetable:** We expect a definitive agreement could be executed within (usually 60 days) from the acceptance of an LOI, with closing as soon as practical after that. Due diligence will be conducted simultaneously with the negotiation of the required agreements.

This IOI is nonbinding and subject to further discussions to address the terms of any agreement we may ultimately reach. This letter is not a commitment to enter into a definitive final agreement.

We have signed a mutual nondisclosure agreement and are able to begin our diligence process at your convenience. We look forward to your response.

ABC Buyer

SAMPLE LETTER OF INTENT (LOI) - ASSET PURCHASE

Dear Seller

We are pleased to submit this Letter of Intent which sets forth the terms and conditions pursuant to which ABC Buyer Enterprises, Inc. ("ABC Buyer," "we," "us," "our") would proceed with the transaction described below with XYZ Seller.com, Inc. ("XYZ Seller," "you," "your").

1. **Transaction:** ABC Buyer anticipates that it would acquire 100% of XYZ Seller's assets clear of any options, liens, or other claims. ("Transaction"). This Transaction would be structured as an asset purchase.

2. **Acquisition Consideration:** We are prepared to offer a purchase price of $XXXX ("Purchase Price"), paid in cash at closing. This price is an "enterprise value" and other than as specified in ¶3, assumes no cash, accounts receivable, debt, or liabilities. We currently do not anticipate requiring any holdback or escrow.

3. **Working Capital and Cash:**

   a) The indicated Purchase Price includes acquisition of sufficient cash to offset balance sheet security deposit liabilities. You may withdraw any excess cash before closing.

   b) The indicated Purchase Price does not include the purchase of any accounts receivable ("Seller Retained AR") or current liabilities (including, without limitation, accounts payable or any accrued payroll).

4. **Financing:** The Purchase Price will be funded from cash currently available to ABC Buyer and would not be subject to any financing contingency.

5. **Transaction fees:** Each party will pay its own fees and expenses incurred during the Transaction (including but not limited to broker, legal fees, etc.). For clarity, XYZ Seller's transaction fees will be paid by XYZ Seller equity holders or from excess cash.

6. **Due Diligence:** Closing of the Transaction is subject to further customary due diligence. You will allow us further access to your books, records, products, customers, and management. Of specific importance will be:

   a) Confirmation of TTM financials. As of December 31, 20XX, XYZ Seller had approximate revenue of $XXM, gross margin of $XXM, and adjusted EBITDA of $XXM.

   b) Analysis and review of churn/renewal rates and follow on revenue from existing customers

   c) Analysis and review of in-force client contracts, including confirmation of billing history and diligence of in-force obligations

   d) Review and diligence of hosting facility, operations, staff composition, and capability

7. **Contingencies:** We currently anticipate that the closing of the Transaction would be contingent upon the following, with no post-closing contingencies:

   a) We shall have conducted our due diligence investigation and be satisfied with the findings thereof.

   b) Any transaction would be subject to the negotiation and execution of definitive agreements with mutually agreeable terms. The agreement would contain representations, warranties, covenants, and conditions customary in similar transactions, including the obtaining of all necessary third-party consents.

   c) There shall be no material adverse change in the assets, business, or financial condition of XYZ Seller prior to the closing.

   d) Determination of post-close transition plan for employees, related party agreements, and required certifications/entitlements.

8. **Transition and Non-Compete**: We anticipate that Owners will:

   a) Provide xx months of post-close transition services under a transition services agreement that compensates owner with $XXX.

   b) For a period of 3 years from the closing of the Transaction, agree to (i) not engage in business that is competitive with the current business of XYZ Seller and (ii) not sell any products or services to current customers of XYZ Seller, including companies that had been customers of XYZ Seller at any time during the 12-month period preceding the closing of the Transaction, and (iii) not solicit any employee of XYZ Seller.

9.   **Integration:** XYZ Seller will provide ABC Buyer access to such source code as the parties may agree and a development resource to assist in understanding, building, and testing such code. Such information shall be shared subject to our Mutual NDA.

10. **Corporate Authorization:** Final agreement is subject to approval by ABC Buyer's Board of Directors and its parent company.

11. **Timetable:** We will provide best efforts to complete a definitive agreement in XX days from the acceptance of this proposal, with closing immediately following. Due diligence will be conducted simultaneously with the negotiation of a merger agreement.

12. **Exclusivity:** For a [XX] (usually 60-days) period commencing upon acceptance of this proposal, XYZ Seller will negotiate exclusively with ABC Buyer and will refrain from negotiating or entering into any agreement with other parties that contemplate the sale of its capital stock or assets.

13. **Proposal Timing:** This proposal is effective until [Date] at 5pm CT.

14. **No Binding Obligation:** Although it is the parties' understanding that the parties intend to negotiate in good faith, this letter agreement is merely a Letter of Intent and does not constitute a binding obligation on any of the parties to this letter, except for the provisions of ¶12 (Exclusivity).

This proposal is subject to further discussions with you to address the terms of any agreement we may ultimately reach. We look forward to your response.

ABC BUYER ENTERPRISES, INC.   **XYZ SELLER, INC.**

DUE DILIGENCE SAMPLE CHECKLIST – CONDENSED VERSION

Summary Due Diligence Checklist

A.   Financial

1.   Balance Sheets for prior three years and current year to date

   a)   Any off-balance sheet debt, obligations

   b)   Any nonoperating assets

   c)   Significant account policies including how revenue is recognized, how is fixed bid recognized

   d)   Depreciation and Amortization Schedules

   e)   List of hardware/software used by business

   f)   List of assets to be included in sale

   g)   List of assets to be excluded from the sale

   h)   Inventory list and inventory aging report

2.   Income Statements for prior three years and current year to date

   a)   Bad debt write-offs for prior two years and current—customer name, amount, and reason

   b)   List all normalizations, Add backs, and Excess Executive Comp

3.   Tax Returns

   a)   Corporate Tax Returns last three years

   b)   Sales Tax Returns last three years

   c)   Property Tax Returns for Personal Property

4.   Accounts Receivable aging at EOY for prior two years and current YTD

5.   Accounts Payable aging at EOY for prior two years and current YTD

6.   Revenue/GM breakouts

   a)   Master list of customers who have purchased last two years, revenue generated, and preferred vendor status

    b)   Revenue by month of top 10 customers each year, last three years, and YTD

    c)   Revenue by vendor (last three years and YTD)

    d)   Revenue and GM Projections for current year by month/explain forecasting methodology

    e)   The 2019 Proforma cashflow report

    f)   Revenue and Gross Margin by practice/division last three years and YTD (by month)

    g)   Revenue and Gross Margins on maintenance contracts and time and material projects last three years and YTD (by month)

7.   Payroll records

    a)   Payroll records for prior three years and current QTD

    b)   Payroll tax returns for prior three years and current QTD

    c)   Worker Comp reports for prior three years and current QTD

8.   Corporate bank statements for prior two years and current year, plus bank reconciliation statements for the current year

9.   Operational Reports

    a)   Work-in-Progress Report—explanation of all the work in progress, its status, total revenue booked, and amounts still to be invoiced

    b)   Bill rates (prior and current year)—employee and subcontractors

    c)   Delivery team percent utilization rate

    d)   Billed hours and/or hours worked in maintenance contracts for prior three years and current year

    e)   Reimbursement policy for travel expenses—customer reimbursed, how, when etc.

    f)   Credit/collections policy and procedures

B.   Company Operations

1.   Corporate Records

    a)   Articles of Incorporation and Corporate Bylaws

    b)   Corporate Record Book of minutes and resolutions

    c) State Certificate of good standing

    d) Capitalization Table

    e) Buy/Sell agreements

    f) Operating agreements

    g) Member control/shareholder agreements

2.   Management and Employees

    a) Org Chart

    b) Resume of key employees (or LinkedIn links)

    c) Schedule describing following

        i)   Exec compensation agreements

        ii) Resume of key executives

        iii) Indemnity agreements with D&Os

        iv) Family relationships among D&Os

    d) Summary plan description of Employee Benefits

        i)   Claims data

        ii) Loss ratio for last three years

        iii) Hard claims data and/or experienced accounting summary

        iv) Description of fringe benefits, holidays, vacations, tuition, COBRA, etc.

    e) Description of pay cycle and pay day policy (holidays, PTO, etc.)

        i)   Employee manuals current and past

        ii) Description of employee training and annual budget

        iii) Payroll cycles and pay dates

    f) List all company/employee certifications

        i)   Total number of certifications

        ii) Current level, highest level possible

        iii) Cost to get to adequate level

    g) Summary of Employees including salaries/commissions and employee status

    h) Historical and current year turnover for consultants/employees

       i) Employee issues that have been reported to any member of management that could result in future claims (sexual harassment, wrongful termination, etc.)

       j) Training—list any training commitments that have been made to particulate employees and estimated costs and time involved with each commitment

3. Marketing and Sales

    a) Samples of marketing and other matters
    b) 30-60-90-day sales pipeline
    c) Business plan/Leadership Management tools
    d) List of any membership
    e) Press releases, articles within the past three years
    f) Standard forms for Master Services Agreement and SOW
    g) List of Industry/market events that are attended

4. Standard delivery methodology and change order process

    a) Customer engagement management process
    b) Project/Service Delivery process or methodology
    c) Change order process
    d) Resource allocation process and tools
    e) Performance metrics (data and description)

5. Financial Operations

    a) Invoicing policy
    b) Collections policy
    c) Revenue Recognition
    d) Inventory Management policies

6. Results of any past audits from state/federal agency

    a) Litigation—schedule of suits/actions pending or threatening
    b) Past litigation with customers
    c) Current claims/complaints that may result in litigation

C.   Contracts and Commitments

1.   Employee Agreements—noncompete and nondisclosure agreements, offer letters, job descriptions, and copy of current standard documents used

2.   Independent contractor—noncompete and nondisclosure agreements, job descriptions, and copy of current standard documents used

3.   All customer/client contracts

4.   All license agreements and reseller agreements

5.   Any other NDA, mutual confidentiality agreements, or other legally binding agreements

6.   All docs evidencing borrowing guarantees including:
   a)   Bank Loans
   b)   Lines of Credit
   c)   Financing installments (computers, auto, etc.)
   d)   Other

7.   Insurance
   a)   E&O Insurance
   b)   Workers compensation
   c)   D&O Insurance

8.   Leases
   a)   Real estate property leases/mortgages
   b)   Equipment leases of personal property used in business
   c)   Equipment leases of business
   d)   Cell phone program, commitment, term

9.   Description of any verbal or unwritten understanding or commitments including any implied warranties or guarantees

10.   Copies of licenses, permits, and or government consents

a) Any reports filed/correspondence with any state/federal or foreign government agency within the past three years

b) Any order/rule of state/fed/foreign governmental agency affecting the business

11. Schedule and copies of all Joint Venture and Partnership agreements

12. Intellectual property (schedule and copies)

a) Intellectual property owned and licensed

b) Software, patents, trademarks, service marks, copyrights, licenses, etc.

D.   Final Due Diligence & Closing Items

(This phase includes the final checklist of items necessary to be accomplished to affect a closing of the merger or acquisition.)

1. Disclosure documents for Definitive Agreement

2. Financial

a) Accrued vacation detail

b) Updated financials

c) UCC Lien Releases if applicable

d) Any updates on customer contracts, revenues, lost sales, etc.

e) Proforma Balance Sheet

3. Company Operations

a) Any changes to contracts and commitments

b) All other agreements, commitments involving services, products with value of more than 10K

c) WIP (Work in Progress) detail

(Source: IT Valuations - https://www.itvaluations.com/.)

Notes

(1) https://feld.com/archives/2015/02/rule-40-healthy-saas-company.html

(2) Per RoseBiz survey of M&A advisors selling technology service providers under $100M, conducted in 2019. (Outlier numbers were removed.)

(3) https://www.mckinsey.com/industries/high-tech/our-insights/subscription-myth-busters

(4) https://www.divestopedia.com/definition/835/free-cash-flow-fcf

(5) http://www.channelfutures.com/msp-501/top-msp501-companies-report-vertical-market-focus

(6) (https://hbr.org/2010/07/stop-trying-to-delight-your-customers

(7) https://www.pcmag.com/roundup/306323/the-best-cloud-storage-providers-and-file-syncing-services

(8) https://www.divestopedia.com/definition/755/working-capital-adjustment

(9) https://www.axial.net/forum/what-expect-indication-interest/

(10) https://searchitchannel.techtarget.com/definition/cloud-service-provider-cloud-provider

(11) https://www.techtarget.com/search/query?q=Paas&type=definition&pageNo=1&sortField

(12) https://www.divestopedia.com/14/9581/ma-fee-guide-2018

(13) https://www.bloomberg.com/news/articles/2017-09-01/
why-private-equity-has-963-billion-in-dry-powder-quicktake-q-a

(14) https://www.microsoft.com/en-us/Investor/acquisition-history.aspx

(15) https://en.wikipedia.org/wiki/
List_of_mergers_and_acquisitions_by_Apple

(16) https://en.wikipedia.org/wiki/Salesforce.com#Acquisitions

(17) 2019 Technology Marketing Benchmarks and Trends Report – The
Partner Marketing Group

(18) https://www.zacks.com/stock/news/285695/
accenture-hits-52week-high-on-acquisitions-amp-partnerships

(19) https://www.youtube.com/watch?v=VBtrZIQlARQ&feature=youtu.
be&list=PLhv7PB4dZMyRmfYrc46qfwG0oUVrIQy7e

(20) https://www.channelfutures.com/msp-501/
channel-futures-reveals-2019-msp-501

ACKNOWLEDGMENTS

This book could not have been written without the help of so many people sharing their knowledge and stories with me ~ so many, that I am concerned I will inadvertently leave someone out. Please forgive me and let me know so that I can make amends another way or in a future version.

The overwhelming reason for writing this book is literally to give back to the community that I have been a part of and learned from for 25+ years. While I have always run my own company, I have always felt connected to a much larger community via various channels; Citrix, Sage, ASI, SAP and Microsoft, to name a few. The companies and the people connected to them have shaped in many ways my values and how I grew as a business owner. Some of my most memorable experiences have taken place in exotic parts of the world due to my channel and company experiences; Bali, New Zealand, Hawaii, Banff, Austria, British Columbia, Croatia, Costa Rica, and Tahiti. I will cherish those times forever in my heart.

The book idea was born on the Pacific Crest Trail, as a get-a-way from my own company sale, with my newly found hiking partner Vladimir Hanak. After sharing our life stories over hundreds of Oregon miles, he encouraged me to write this book and to share my knowledge. For this Vladimir, I thank you. The journey ~ for me ~ could so easily have ended there.

Once the idea was hatched, it then took a team of colleagues to help me through the tough part of writing this and the emotional rollercoaster that comes with believing one moment you have something worthwhile to share, and the next not. For this, I relied heavily on my past colleagues, channel partners and advocates; Karlton Prillerman, Bob Cohen, Steve Chapman, Anya Ciecieski, Elena Baeva and Mike Gillis. Who knew writing a book and picking a cover could be so difficult? You all gave me inspiration in so many ways you probably don't know. Christy Spokely, thank you for being there during my most difficult writing months and being that political sounding board one needs from time-to-time. A special thanks to my traveled friend Mark Stuyt who always believes in me – for everything.

Life lessons are shared in stories. To all the partners I confidentially interviewed for this book (both buyers and sellers); thank you for being genuine in your advice regarding both successes and challenges, as well as sharing deal multiples, contract specifics, and your personal stories. Your guidance is shared individually and collectively throughout the book via *Robert* and the *100 Tips*.

A special thanks to Dana Willmer of CloudSpeed. I owe much of the research and benchmark data to him. He has always been my go-to person for truth in my numbers and theories. He is key to the chapter on Intellectual Property and his work around the *IP Staircase*. More importantly he has been a constant friend helping me through some of those doubtful and uncertain times as a budding author. Thank you for being that tireless sounding board and helping me ferret out the future.

To the women in technology who have helped me over the years and who work tirelessly to achieve more and to see that women enter, learn and grow in this industry, I am especially grateful; Theresa Brown, Pam Johnson, Lindsay Zwart, Kati Hvidtfeldt, Cecilia Flombaum, Kristi Hofer, Chaitra Vedullapalli, Gretchen O'Hara and Gavriella Schuster. A special thanks to Mishel Justesen for her insights on technology marketing and transitional leadership.

Kudos to the authors that gave me sage advice and helped me through a few mental blocks, Mark S. A. Smith (*From MSP to BSP*) and JJ DiGeronimo (*Accelerate your Impact*) and likewise to the team at Book Launchers; Julie, Jacqueline, Sarah, and all those who worked tirelessly on this book – given my "out of order" crazy schedule requests. Likewise, my independent technology editor Alan R. Earls, who helped make sure everything made sense and could be that independent sounding board who understood my audience so well. Thank you as well for editing and word-smithing the Value Maximizer Assessment™. The Value Maximizer Assessment which started as a vision in

Excel turned into a real product, thanks to the development efforts of Rick Tuttle from Papasoft and Eslam Samy for his graphics.

Throughout the writing of this book I received a tremendous amount of support from brokers and business advisors, who shared content, advice, numbers, strategies, contacts, and much, much more; Rick Murphy (Cogent Mergers), Tom Wilson (Decision Point), Mike Middleton (Q1 Capital), John Austin (Austin Dale Group), Diane Horton (Tequity), the Corum Group and the team at Equiteq. A special thanks to Paul Dippell (Service-Leadership) for contributing content, and Mike Harvath (Revenue Rocket) for taking the time to contribute the "Buy-side" bonus chapter. Finally, a special thanks to Reed Warren (IT Valuations) and Diana Christopherson (IT Mergers) for believing in me and sharing valuable insights and contacts.

Maintaining a well-run network is key to the success of a company, whether you are a large organization or a budding author like myself. My deepest thanks to Doug White, for our years together and for continuing to look after me and answer my distress calls at all hours as I wrote this book.

The life experiences to write this book can be in part attributed to two ladies who helped shape my personal and business success and who soared with me during the good times and supported me endlessly through the challenging times; Rebecca Bunas and Melissa Sanders. I could not be here to share this content without the support you both provided me over a span of 22 years. I will cherish our business relationship and friendship forever.

Finally, I am sure no one is happier that I have completed this book than my husband and business partner Glen Medwid, who has put his own retirement partially on hold, while I have asked him to review copy, check calculations, validate algorithms, file DBAs and copyrights. He has once again held down the fort and more while I venture out into something new. But, more importantly, he encouraged me to continue when I wasn't sure I could and challenged me to write the best book possible. To my son Matt, you have seen first-hand with me and in your own life; companies, come and go! A book, however, remains as a legacy. Thank you for being part of that journey with me.

www.ingramcontent.com/pod-product-compliance
Lightning Source LLC
Chambersburg PA
CBHW071322210326
41597CB00015B/1313